CAMBRIDGE CLASSICAL STUDIES

General Editors

W. K. C. GUTHRIE   A. H. M. JONES   D. L. PAGE

LIBERTAS
AS A POLITICAL IDEA AT ROME
DURING THE LATE REPUBLIC
AND EARLY PRINCIPATE

LIBERTAS
AS A POLITICAL IDEA AT ROME
DURING THE LATE REPUBLIC
AND
EARLY PRINCIPATE

BY

Ch. WIRSZUBSKI, M.A., Ph.D.

CAMBRIDGE
AT THE UNIVERSITY PRESS
1968

PUBLISHED BY
THE SYNDICS OF THE CAMBRIDGE UNIVERSITY PRESS
Bentley House, 200 Euston Road, London, N.W.1
American Branch: 32 East 57th Street, New York, N.Y.10022

Standard Book Number: 521　06848　7

First printed　1950
Reprinted　1960
1968

First printed in Great Britain at the University Press, Cambridge
Reprinted in Great Britain by William Lewis (Printers) Ltd, Cardiff

UXORI SACRUM

PREFACE

This study is a revised version of a dissertation for the Degree of Doctor of Philosophy submitted to the University of Cambridge in the year 1946. In the present version, besides some slight additions here and there, the section "What Libertas meant to Tacitus" has been added to chapter 5.

In its original form, this study was written at Cambridge under the supervision of Professor F. E. Adcock. Needless to say, I alone am to blame for all its shortcomings as well as for the opinions I venture to express in it. But the shortcomings would have been more serious, and the opinions more obscurely expressed, were it not for Professor Adcock's stimulating criticism and invaluable advice. Nor should I have been able to write in a borrowed language without his encouraging guidance. For all this I would offer him my sincere thanks.

I would also thank the British Council for scholarships which made my studies at Cambridge possible.

Cн. W.

Jerusalem
April, 1947

CONTENTS

PROLEGOMENA

CHAPTER 1

GENERAL CHARACTERISTICS OF LIBERTAS

CHAPTER 2

CIVIL DISCORD: OPTIMATES AND POPULARES

Chapter 3

THE DECLINE OF THE TRADITIONAL FORM OF GOVERNMENT

Chapter 4

THE AUGUSTAN PRINCIPATE IN RELATION TO LIBERTAS

CHAPTER 5

PRINCIPATUS ET LIBERTAS RES OLIM DISSOCIABILES

PROLEGOMENA

1. LIBERTAS—A CIVIC RIGHT

Freedom, comprising as it does two different concepts, namely "freedom from" and "freedom to", neither of which admits of any but general definitions, is a somewhat vague notion. This is also true of the Latin "libertas". Libertas primarily denotes the status of a "liber", i.e. a person who is not a slave,[1] and comprises both the negation of the limitations imposed by slavery and the assertion of the advantages deriving from freedom. In view of its twofold meaning, liberty can perhaps more easily be explained if slavery, its direct opposite, is explained first.

Without entering into detailed discussion, the salient characteristics of slavery in Roman law can be described as follows:[2] slavery at Rome is a legal institution whereby one person is subjected to the mastery (dominium) of another person:[3] slaves are almost entirely rightless and can neither be entitled to possess or do anything, nor to contract liabilities:[4] a slave is always "in potestate" and "alieni iuris".[5] Broadly speaking, therefore, slavery consists in rightlessness and subjection to dominion.

It appears from these characteristics of slavery that the term "persona sui iuris", which signifies the status of complete personal freedom, implies that to be free means to be capable of possessing rights of one's own, and this is possible only if one is not subjected to someone else's dominium (or patria potestas). Libertas therefore consists in the capacity for the possession of rights, and the absence of subjection. Obviously, the positive and negative aspects of libertas, though notionally distinct, are essentially interdependent and complementary.[6]

[1] See Th. Mommsen, *Römisches Staatsrecht*, III, p. 62.

[2] For a full discussion of this subject see W. W. Buckland, *The Roman Law of Slavery* (1908) (=*Slavery*), pp. 1 ff.; Id. *A Text-Book of Roman Law* (1921) (=*Text-Book*), pp. 62 ff.

[3] *Gai Inst.* I, 52; *Inst.* I, 3, 2; *Dig.* I, 5, 4, 1.

[4] Servile caput nullum ius habet, Paulus, *Dig.* IV, 5, 3, 1. Cf. *Inst.* I, 16, 4; *Dig.* L, 17, 22 pr.; XXVIII, 8, 1 pr. See also Buckland, *Slavery*, p. 3.

[5] *Gai Inst.* I, 48–52 = *Inst.* I, 8 pr. sq. = *Dig.* I, 6, 1 pr. sq.

[6] Subjection to dominium causes ipso facto the extinction of all the rights and liabilities of a freeman, and, on the other hand, release from dominium (i.e. manumission) causes ipso facto a slave to acquire rights and to contract liabilities.

The negative aspect of *libertas*, as any other negative concept, is self-defined (although, of course, it is of necessity ill-defined). On the other hand, the definition of the positive aspect presents some problems. For if, positively, freedom means the capacity to enjoy certain rights of one's own, two questions arise: First, whence does that capacity spring? Is it innate or acquired? Secondly, what is the character and extent of the rights in which freedom consists? To answer these questions we must inquire into the nature and foundation of *libertas*, and may well start with the definition of freedom in the *Digest*.

"Libertas est naturalis facultas eius quod cuique facere libet, nisi si quid vi aut iure prohibetur. Servitus est constitutio iuris gentium qua quis dominio alieno contra naturam subicitur."[1] If, as this definition lays down, freedom is a natural faculty, everyone is originally free; and, since the positive institution of slavery is contrary to nature, it follows that freedom is a natural right innate in every human being.[2] But noble though it is, this concept of freedom was foreign to Roman law under the Republic and the Early Principate.[3] The theory concerning freedom and slavery prevalent in that period may be gathered from the legal practice, most clearly perhaps from the peculiar institution whereby Roman citizenship, and not freedom only, was bestowed on slaves manumitted in due form.[4] This institution did not arise from generosity

[1] *Dig.* I, 5, 4 pr. Cf. also *Dig.* I, 1, 4 and XII, 6, 64. Since the word "naturalis" is possibly interpolated, the definition as it now reads in the *Digest* may be of later date than its original author, Florentinus, a jurist of the late second or early third century A.D. Cf. F. Schulz, *Prinzipien des römischen Rechts*, Munich, 1924, p. 95 n. 2.

[2] Buckland, *Text-Book*, p. 62, explains this definition as meaning that liberty is dependent upon the subject's internal freedom from the restrictions of his lower nature. But if that were the case it would be difficult to see why subjection to dominium should be "contra naturam", i.e. contrary to Nature.

[3] Ius naturale from which this conception of freedom derives is, with the exception of Cicero, a product of the Imperial period. See Buckland, *Text-Book*, pp. VI and 52 f. It is noteworthy that Gaius (second century A.D.), *Inst.* I, 52, regards a master's potestas over his slave as an institution of Ius Gentium but not as being contrary to nature.

[4] See Cic. *Pro Balbo*, 24; Ulp. *Reg.* I, 6; *Dig.* XXXVIII, 2, 1 pr. Bestowal of Roman citizenship on slaves manumitted in due form was unrestricted under the Republic, see Buckland, *Slavery*, pp. 444 f. Restriction in this matter was introduced by the Lex Aelia Sentia of A.D. 4. Informally manumitted slaves

on the part of the Romans; had manumission effected merely release from dominica potestas, the slave would have become a res nullius, not a free man, because to be free means to be a member of a civic body.[1] A Roman citizen who by being made a slave is excluded from any polity suffers extinction of all his rights, personal and political,[2] whereas a slave admitted to Roman citizenship by manumission "vindicta aut censu aut testamento" acquires full freedom.

The essentially civic character of libertas can also be seen from the status of foreigners at Rome. The Roman State recognized and protected the freedom of those foreigners alone who were citizens of States which concluded a treaty with Rome. All other foreigners, although not necessarily treated as actual slaves, were, while in Roman territory, in the legal position of a servus sine domino, which meant that they were considered rightless and the Roman State would not protect them if they were deprived of their freedom.[3]

It is therefore clear that the Romans conceived libertas as an acquired civic right, and not as an innate right of man.

2. LIBERTAS AND CIVITAS

We must now consider the extent of libertas. At Rome and with regard to Romans full libertas is coterminous with civitas. A Roman's libertas and his civitas both denote the same thing, only that each does it from a different point of view and with emphasis on a different aspect: libertas signifies in the first place the status of an individual as such, whereas civitas denotes primarily the status of

enjoyed de facto freedom while considered as de iure slaves; see Tac. *Ann.* XIII, 27, 4: quos vindicta patronus non liberaverit velut vinculo servitutis attineri. Cf. also Buckland, *Slavery*, p. 445. The compromise resulting in the creation of the so-called Latini Iuniani was an innovation of the Early Empire. For the date of the Lex Iunia see Buckland, *Slavery*, pp. 534 f. and *C.A.H.* vol. x, p. 888 ff. For a recent discussion of manumission see D. Daube, Two Early Patterns of Manumission, *J.R.S.* xxxvi (1946), pp. 57 ff.

[1] See Buckland, *Slavery*, p. 136 n. 4, p. 439; *Text-Book*, p. 73. Cf. Daube, *op. cit.* p. 62.

[2] This is the so-called Capitis Deminutio Maxima.

[3] See Th. Mommsen, Bürgerlicher und peregrinischer Freiheitsschutz im römischen Staat, *Juristische Abhandlungen, Festgabe fuer Georg Beseler* (1885), pp. 255, 263; id. *Staatsrecht* III, pp. 590 f., 596, 598 f.; and also E. Schönbauer, *Z. Sav. St. Rom. Abt.* XLIX (1929), p. 371.

an individual in relation to the community.[1] Only a Roman citizen enjoys all the rights, personal and political, that constitute libertas.

The so-called Capitis Deminutio Media whereby a Roman loses citizenship while retaining freedom[2] does not contradict this conclusion. For Capitis Deminutio Media means loss of Roman citizenship as a consequence of the acquisition of a different citizenship.[3] And, besides, the freedom which one retained after the loss of Roman citizenship was qualitatively different from that which one had enjoyed before, for libertas ex iure Quiritium is freedom in respect of private and public law alike, whereas the libertas of a person who was not a Roman citizen (Quiris) was freedom in respect of private law only.

If then the libertas of a Roman is conditioned by his civitas, the amount of freedom a Roman citizen possesses depends upon the entire political structure of the Roman State. In Rome—as elsewhere—freedom of the citizen and internal freedom of the State are in fact only different aspects of the same thing. Therefore libertas civis Romani or libertas ex iure Quiritium must be defined in terms of libertas populi Romani Quiritium.

3. LIBERTAS POPULI ROMANI

With regard to peoples or States libertas is used in either of the following two senses:

(a) Sovereign independence and autonomy,[4] the prominent feature of which is "suae leges",[5] a term equivalent to the Greek *autonomia*. The opposite of a populus liber is populus stipendiarius or subjectus.[6] This aspect of libertas need not be

---

[1] See Mommsen, *Freiheitsschutz*, p. 255.

[2] *Gai Inst.* I, 161; *Inst.* I, 16, 2; Ulp. *Reg.* 11, 12.

[3] Festus, *s.v.* deminutus (p. 61, ed. Lindsay): Deminutus capite appellatur qui civitate mutatus est. Mommsen, *Staatsrecht* III, 42 f., pointed out that loss of citizenship was as a rule a consequence of mutatio soli.

[4] On the practical interpretation of freedom and autonomy in Roman foreign policy in the East, see A. H. M. Jones, Civitates Liberae et Immunes in the East, *Anatolian Studies presented to W. H. Buckler*, Manchester, 1939, pp. 103 ff. See also M. Grant, *From* Imperium *to* Auctoritas, Cambridge, 1946, pp. 338 ff., 346 ff., 401 ff.

[5] Carthago libera cum suis legibus est, Livy XXXVII, 54, 26; Liberos, immunes, suis legibus esse iubent Corinthios, XXXIII, 32, 5.

[6] See Jones, *loc. cit.*

dealt with in the present study, since during the period with which it is concerned Rome's own independence was too secure to be a problem at all.

(b) Republican form of Government. In this respect the opposite of libertas is regnum which, if used in its proper sense, invariably implies absolute monarchy.[1] The relation between king and people is considered to be analogous to the relation between master and slaves. Consequently monarchy is called dominatio; and subjection to monarchy servitus. Freedom enjoyed by a State negatively means absence of dominatio, just as freedom enjoyed by an individual negatively means absence of dominium. But in respect of States, just as in respect of individuals, the negative aspect of freedom does not alone constitute complete liberty. Tacitus voiced a deep-seated conviction of the Romans when he said that the Armenians, who had expelled their queen, were "incerti solutique et magis sine domino quam in libertate";[2] for mere removal of dominatio may eventually result in anarchy, whereas libertas consists in rights which rest on positive institutions.

The Romans dated their own freedom from the abolition of monarchy and identified it with the republican constitution of the commonwealth.[3] The res publica populi Romani Quiritium[4] is the practical embodiment of libertas populi Romani, just as civitas Romana is the embodiment of libertas civis Romani. Ultimately, therefore, the nature and extent of libertas are determined by the nature and form of the Roman constitution.

[1] When Porsenna sent an embassy to Rome urging the restoration of Tarquin (cum ille peteret quod contra libertatem populi Romani esset) the Romans replied: Non in regno populum Romanum sed in libertate esse. ita induxisse in animum, hostibus portas potius quam regibus patefacere; ea esse vota omnium ut qui libertati erit in illa urbe finis, idem urbi sit (Livy II, 15, 3). This passage is typical of the republican attitude towards monarchy. For regnum as a somewhat loose term of political invective implying domination rather than monarchy, see below, pp. 62 ff.

[2] Ann. II, 4, 3.

[3] See Ad Herenn. IV, 66; Sallust, Cat. 7, 2–3; Cic. Pro Flacco, 25; Livy I, 17, 3; 60, 3; II, 1, 1–2; VIII, 34, 3; Pliny, Paneg. 44; 57; Tac. Ann. I, 1, 1; Hist. I, 16. For a detailed examination of the notion res publica see Rudolf Stark, Res Publica, Göttingen Diss. 1937.

[4] This is the description used on formal occasions; see Varro, De Ling. Lat. (ed. Goetz–Schoell) VI, 86; Livy VIII, 9, 8.

4. The Object of this Study

But the Roman constitution is not itself a constant. The Romans were well aware that their republican constitution was the result of long and gradual development.[1] And libertas, while identified with the republican constitution during the Republican period, continued to be a popular slogan and a constitutional principle under the Principate. The question therefore arises, whether the political content of Roman libertas changed according as the Roman constitution was transformed.

It is proposed in this study to describe the meaning of libertas as a political idea at Rome during the two hundred odd years between the Gracchi and Trajan, a period in which the Republican constitution gradually gave way and was finally superseded by the Principate which, in its own turn, considerably changed during the first century A.D.

In the period at which this study begins, Roman republicanism had already reached its highest stage of development. In the long course of that constitutional development certain general principles were laid down, and certain practices established. Those principles form the constitutional background of the political struggle which resulted in profound constitutional changes. In order to avoid the confusion that may arise from mistaking political programmes for constitutional principles, or vice versa, it is desirable in the first of the subsequent chapters to determine and isolate those general principles which from a theoretical point of view constitute Roman republicanism and Roman political liberty.

[1] See Cato the Elder's remark in Cic. *De Rep.* II, 1, 1–2. See also Polyb. VI, 11, 2 f.

CHAPTER I

GENERAL CHARACTERISTICS
OF LIBERTAS

1. LIBERTAS—LEGES

As has been seen, libertas at Rome and with regard to Romans is not an innate faculty or right of man, but the sum of civic rights granted by the laws of Rome; it consequently rests on those positive laws which determine its scope. This fundamental idea implies that libertas contains the notion of restraint which is inherent in every law.[1] In fact, it is the notion of restraint and moderation[2] that distinguishes libertas from licentia, whose salient feature is arbitrariness; and libertas untempered by moderation degenerates into licentia.[3] True libertas, therefore, is by no means the unqualified power to do whatever one likes; such power—whether conceded or assumed—is licentia, not libertas. The necessary prerequisite of libertas is the renouncement of self-willed actions; consequently, genuine libertas can be enjoyed under the law only.

There is profound truth in Cicero's saying, "legum idcirco omnes servi sumus ut liberi esse possimus".[4] For were it not for the restrictions imposed by law, everyone would be free to do always as he liked, and that would result—to use Hobbes' phrase— in a "bellum omnium contra omnes", that is to say, it would result, not in the enjoyment of complete freedom, but in its self-

---

[1] Quint. *Inst.* VII, 5, 5: Lex omnis aut tribuit aut adimit aut punit aut iubet aut vetat aut permittit. Cicero in *De Leg.* III, 10 uses "iussa vetita" in the sense of "leges".

[2] Livy XXIV, 25, 8: Ea natura multitudinis est: aut servit humiliter aut superbe dominatur; libertatem, quae media est, nec struere modice nec habere sciunt. Cic. *Pro Planc.* 94: Libertatem...non in pertinacia, sed in quadam moderatione positam putabo. Cf. Tac. *Dial.* 23 *ad fin.*

[3] Cic. *Pro Flacco*, 16: Illa vetus (Graecia)...hoc uno malo concidit, libertate immoderata ac licentia contionum. Livy XXIII, 2, 1: Licentia plebis sine modo libertatem exercentis; XXXIV, 49, 8: Libertate modice utantur: temperatam eam salubrem et singulis et civitatibus esse, nimiam et aliis gravem et ipsis qui habeant effrenatam et praecipitem esse.

[4] *Pro Cluent.* 146. Cf. 147.

B

destruction through excess. Fools, observed Tacitus, identified licentia with libertas.[1]

The element of restraint inherent in libertas is not necessarily, nor primarily, self-restraint; it is not, nor expected to be, solely the result of *sophrosyne* which voluntarily follows the maxim "nothing to excess". "Modus" and "moderatio" may be imposed on libertas from outside without destroying it. Libertas is quite consistent with the dictates of the disciplina Romana, mos maiorum, and instituta patrum,[2] because it is conceived of as a right and faculty, not of an isolated individual, but of the citizen in the organized community of the Roman State. As will be seen later, libertas at Rome was not the watchword of the individual who tried to assert his own personality against the overriding authority of society.

It would be very misleading indeed if a definition like "Quid est enim libertas? Potestas vivendi ut velis", or "(Libertas) cuius proprium est sic vivere ut velis",[3] were taken without qualification to represent the Roman concept of freedom. This Stoic definition of abstract freedom stresses only the subjective free will of the agent, whereas with the Romans libertas was in the first place the objective right to act.[4] The Romans conceived of libertas, not in terms of the autonomy of the will, but in terms of social relations, as a duty no less than a right: a right to claim what is due to oneself, and a duty to respect what is due to others, the latter being exactly what acceptance of the law amounts to, for to be law-abiding ultimately means to respect rights other than one's own. Libertas postulates that everyone should be mindful of other people's freedom no less than of his own.[5]

---

[1] *Dial.* 40: Licentia quam stulti libertatem vocabant. Some editors emend: vocant.

[2] Livy v, 6, 17, puts into the mouth of Appius Claudius Crassus, tr. mil. cos. pot., the following ironical remark: Ea demum Romae libertas est, non senatum, non magistratus, non leges, non mores maiorum, non instituta patrum, non disciplinam vereri militiae. Cf. H. Kloesel, *Libertas*, Breslau Diss. 1935, p. 34.

[3] Cic. *Parad.* 34 and *De Off.* I, 70. Cf. Epict. *Diatrib.* II, 1, 23 and IV, 1, 1. Dio Chrys. *Or.* XIV, 3 ff., examines and refutes this definition of freedom.

[4] See R. von Ihering, *Geist des römischen Rechts*[3], II, 1, pp. 219 f.

[5] Livy XXIII, 12, 9, puts into the mouth of a Carthaginian the remark: Si reticeam, aut superbus aut obnoxius videar: quorum alterum est hominis alienae libertatis obliti, alterum, suae. VII, 33, 3: Haud minus libertatis alienae quam dignitatis suae memor. Cf. also II, 10, 8; Cic. *De Off.* I, 124.

Nor must Livy's remark that libertas "suis stat viribus, non ex alieno arbitrio pendet"[1] be misunderstood. What Livy had in mind was probably not the autonomy of the will, but the idea that freedom was enjoyed of right, not on sufferance, and that freedom meant self-reliance.

Livy singled out "imperia legum potentiora quam hominum"[2] as the essential feature of the free Commonwealth, and Sallust made Aemilius Lepidus say that the essence of Roman freedom was, among other things, to obey none but the law.[3] Both writers pointed to the same idea which Cicero expressed in his dictum "legum servi sumus ut liberi esse possimus", namely, that freedom can exist only under the rule of law.

2. Aequa Libertas

Before we examine the particular rights that in the Roman view constituted freedom, and the manner in which the Romans sought to secure the rule of law, another essential point may be profitably discussed here.

Does libertas imply democratic equality (*isonomia*), and, if so, to what extent?

One of the interlocutors in Cicero's *De Re Publica* (I, 47) is credited with the following view:

Itaque nulla alia in civitate, nisi in qua populi potestas summa est, ullum domicilium libertas habet; qua quidem certe nihil potest esse dulcius, et quae, si aequa non est, ne libertas quidem est. Qui autem aequa potest esse, omitto dicere in regno, ubi ne obscura quidem est aut dubia servitus, sed in istis civitatibus in quibus verbo sunt liberi omnes? Ferunt enim suffragia, mandant imperia, magistratus, ambiuntur, rogantur, sed ea dant, quae, etiamsi nolint, danda sint, et quae ipsi non habent, unde alii petunt; sunt enim expertes imperii, consilii publici, iudicii delectorum iudicum, quae familiarum vetustatibus aut pecuniis ponderantur. In libero autem populo, ut Rhodii sunt, ut Athenienses, nemo est civium, qui...

Two principal points emerge from this plea for democratic egalitarianism, one explicit and the other implicit: (*a*) The rights in

---

[1] XXXV, 32, 11.   [2] II, 1, 1.

[3] *Hist.* I, 55, 4 M: Nam quid a Pyrrho Hannibale Philippoque et Antiocho defensum est aliud quam libertas et suae cuique sedes neu cui nisi legibus pareremus? Cf. [?] Sallust, *Ad Caes. senem* II, 5, 3: Nullius potentia super leges erat.

which libertas consists must be virtually equal for all; (*b*) Libertas is the *upper* limit of political rights. In conjunction these two points imply that libertas ought to amount to complete egalitarianism and true government by the people. Thus aequa libertas would coincide with the Greek ἐλευθερία καὶ ἰσονομία.

In comparison with this exposition of democratic equality—obviously Greek in origin, and probably purely literary in purpose—the other testimonies concerning aequa libertas are of a different character; and the difference between them arises, as will presently be seen, from a different concept both of aequitas and, particularly, of libertas.

Copious and very instructive evidence concerning aequa libertas is to be found in Livy's account of the Early Republic, in which this phrase occurs in contexts that clearly show that a political meaning attaches to it. The views expressed in that portion of Livy's narrative, being either his own or those of his annalistic sources, represent to some extent the opinions current in the Late Republican period.

Livy summarizes the claims of the plebs which led to the setting up of the Decemvirate (III, 31, 7): "Si plebeiae leges displicerent,[1] at illi communiter legum latores et ex plebe et ex patribus, qui utrisque utilia ferrent quaeque *aequandae libertatis* essent, sinerent creari".

About their achievement in drafting the original ten Tables the Decemvirs are made to say: "Se…omnibus, summis infimisque, *iura aequasse*" (III, 34, 3).

Appius Claudius the Decemvir, when impeached after he had laid down his power, "commemorabat suum infelix erga plebem Romanam studium, quo *aequandarum legum* causa cum maxima offensione patrum consulatu abisset".[2]

The struggle for the right of conubium and the plebeian consulship is represented in similar terms (IV, 5, 1 ff.):

Regibus exactis utrum vobis (sc. patriciis) dominatio an omnibus *aequa libertas* parta est.

And,

Itaque ad bella ista…, consules, parata vobis plebes est, si conubiis redditis unam hanc civitatem tandem facitis, si coalescere, si iungi miscerique vobis privatis necessitudinibus possunt, si spes, si aditus ad

---

[1] See Livy III, 9, 2 ff.   [2] *Ib.* 56, 9. Cf. III, 61, 6; 67, 9.

honores viris strenuis et fortibus datur, si in consortio, si in societate rei publicae esse, si, quod *aequae libertatis* est, in vicem annuis magistratibus parere atque imperitare licet.[1] Si haec impediet aliquis...nemo dimicaturus pro superbis dominis, cum quibus nec in re publica honorum nec privata conubii societas est.

Non posse *aequo iure* agi ubi imperium penes illos (patres) penes se (plebem) auxilium tantum sit; nisi imperio communicato nunquam plebem in parte pari rei publicae fore (VI, 37, 4).

It appears from the above instances that "aequa libertas", "aequum ius" and "aequae leges" mean the same thing, namely a law equally binding on patricians and plebeians, and the equality of the fundamental political rights which alone would ensure the Plebs an equal share in the common weal (consortium and societas rei publicae; in parte pari rei publicae esse). It will be observed that aequa libertas is used in these passages with regard to the Plebs as a whole, and not with regard to any individual.[2]

Since, as has been seen, libertas is a sum of rights, it is very significant that it should be identified with aequum ius, for the essence of aequum ius is that it is equally binding on all.[3] Livy declares that when Scipio Africanus was impeached in 187 B.C.,[4]

[1] The same idea occurs in the senatorial criticism of the Decemvirs, "qui comitia, qui annuos magistratus, qui vicissitudinem imperitandi, quod unum exaequandae sit libertatis, sustulerint", III, 39, 8. It is interesting that the last clause is reminiscent of Aristotle's ἐλευθερίας δὲ ἐν μὲν τὸ ἐν μέρει ἄρχεσθαι καὶ ἄρχειν, *Polit*. VI, 2, p. 1317b, 2. It is not impossible that Livy adopted this view from his sources, which projected back into the early days of Rome the propaganda of the homines novi of the Late Republic. A smattering of Greek ideas in the post-Gracchan period is not surprising.

[2] The *Thesaurus Linguae Latinae* records only two instances of aequa libertas used with regard to personal rights: Terence, *Adelphoe*, 181 ff. (the original is by Menander): *Aeschinus*. Nam si molestus pergis esse, iam intro abripiere atque ibi Usque ad necem operiere loris. *Sannio*. Loris liber? *Ae*. Sic erit. *Sa*. O hominem impurum! Hicin libertatem aiunt esse aequam omnibus? —and Quintil. *Declam*. 301, p. 185, 15 f. (Ritter): Si alio accusante dicerem causam, sciebam et expertus proxime eram esse nobis aequam etiam adversus divites libertatem; sed me quamquam indignissime petar, non tam lex, quam ratio prohibet a conviciis.

[3] Seneca, *Ep*. 107, 6: Aequum autem ius est non quo omnes usi sunt, sed quod omnibus latum est. Cf. *Ep*. 123, 16: Mors malum non est. Quid quaeris? Sola ius aequum generis humani.

[4] XXXVIII, 50, 4 ff. It is to be observed that Livy mentions Valerius Antias as his authority.

some regarded the impeachment as disgraceful ingratitude to a man who served his country so well, whereas others observed that:

Neminem unum tantum eminere civem debere ut legibus interrogari non possit; nihil tam aequandae libertatis esse quam potentissimum quem-que posse dicere causam. Quid autem tuto cuiquam, nedum summam rem publicam, permitti, si ratio non sit reddenda? Qui ius aequum pati non possit, in eum vim haud iniustam esse.

It appears that equality before the law was considered the most essential characteristic of aequa libertas.[1]

Cicero's view of aequa libertas is in the highest degree illuminating. Cicero declared in his *De Re Publica* (1, 69) that the ideal form of government which he described offered "aequabilitatem quandam magnam qua carere diutius vix possunt liberi"; elsewhere he mentioned aequitas iuris as synonymous with libertas,[2] and stressed its importance;[3] he thought monarchy was unacceptable because it deprived the citizens of commune ius;[4] and, finally, he eloquently spoke about communis libertas.[5] Nevertheless, he strongly dis-owned the idea of complete equalitarianism (aequabilitas) for the reason that it disregarded dignitas.

Nam aequabilitas quidem iuris, quam amplexantur liberi populi (i.e. democratic equality), neque servari potest...eaque, quae appellatur aequabilitas, iniquissima est. Cum enim par habetur honos summis et infimis, qui sint in omni populo necesse est, ipsa aequitas iniquissima est (*De Rep.* 1, 53).

And similarly,

Et cum omnia per populum geruntur quamvis iustum atque moderatum, tamen ipsa aequabilitas est iniqua, cum habet nullos gradus dignitatis (*Ib.* 1, 43).

It is to be observed that dignitas is a pre-eminence which does not rest on laws, nor on privileges; it is the esteem a worthy personality

---

[1] See also Quintil. *Declam.* 301 quoted above, p. 11 n. 2; Cic. *De Off.* II, 85: Iuris et iudiciorum aequitate suum quisque teneat. Cf. Ascon. 84, 2 Clark.

[2] *Pro Planc.* 33: Ubi illa aequitas iuris, ubi illa antiqua libertas.

[3] *De Off.* I, 124: Privatum autem oportet aequo et pari cum civibus iure vivere, neque submissum et abiectum, neque se efferentem.

[4] *De Rep.* I, 43: Sed in regnis nimis expertes sunt ceteri communis iuris et consilii. Cf. *De Off.* I, 53; Livy III, 56, 10.

[5] *II in Verr.* v, 169 f.; ap. Dio Cass. XLIV, 33, 2: τῆς κοινῆς καὶ ἐλευθερίας καὶ ὁμονοίας. Cf. Brutus and Cassius in *Ad Fam.* XI, 2, 2; Val. Max. VI, 3, 2.

commands, "alicuius honesta et cultu et honore et verecundia digna auctoritas".[1]

Cicero's criticism of equalitarianism reveals a cardinal difference between the Athenian *eleutheria* and the Roman libertas. In fifth- and fourth-century Athens *eleutheria* was tantamount to democracy, which meant government by the people founded on complete equality of political rights (*isonomia* and *isegoria*);[2] obviously the democratic principle of complete equality was incompatible with regard for ἀξία.[3] On the other hand, at Rome the consummation of libertas was the Res publica which might, but need not, be a democracy. In fact, the Roman republic never was, nor, on the whole,[4] was meant to be, a democracy of the Athenian type; and *eleutheria* with *isonomia* and *parrhesia* as its chief expressions appeared to the Romans as being nearer licentia than libertas.[5]

Notionally, too, aequum ius is entirely different from the Athenian *isonomia*, and this difference throws much light on the meaning of the Roman concept. Uppermost in ἰσότης is the notion of parity, whereas in aequitas it is fairness, justice, equity.[6] *Isonomia*[7] is equality of rights and parity of standing interpreted in terms of extreme democracy, whereas aequum ius or aequae leges means above all equality before the law,[8] but not equality of political rights enjoyed by all the citizens. There is nothing to suggest that

[1] Cic. *De Invent.* II, 166. Needless to say free men only can have dignitas: Species ipsa tam gratiosi liberti aut servi dignitatem habere nullam potest, Cic. *Ad Q. Fr.* I, 2, 3.

[2] For the Greek concept of equality see Rudolf Hirzel, *Themis, Dike und Verwandtes, ein Beitrag zur Geschichte der Rechtsidee bei den Griechen*, Leipzig, 1907, pp. 228–320 and especially pp. 240 ff.

[3] See Arist. *Polit.* VI, 2, p. 1317a, 40–b, 4.

[4] The few possible exceptions will be discussed in the next chapter.

[5] Cic. *De Rep.* III, 23: Si vero populus plurimum potest omniaque eius arbitrio reguntur, dicitur illa libertas, est vero licentia. See also Cicero's criticism of the Greek Assemblies of the People, *Pro Flacco*, 15 ff.; and Phaedrus, I, 2, 1 f.: Athenae cum florerent aequis legibus Procax libertas civitatem miscuit Frenumque solvit pristinum licentia.

[6] See Cic. *Partit. Orat.* 130.

[7] Derived from ἴσα νέμειν rather than ἴσος νόμος, see Hirzel, *op. cit.* pp. 242 ff. Cicero probably had ἰσονομία in mind when he wrote "cum enim par habetur honos summis et infimis,... ipsa aequitas iniquissima est", *De Rep.* I, 53.

[8] Cic. *Topica*, 9; *De Off.* II, 41 ff.; *Pro Cluent.* 146.

the Romans had ever regarded the pecuniary circumstances required for the tenure of public offices as inconsistent with aequum ius or aequae leges. The plebeians knew from experience that one could be free and yet discriminated against, and therefore they attached great importance to equality before the law and to the fundamental rights of citizenship. But the right to govern was not considered a universal civic right. The Athenians sought to establish equality in respect of the right to govern, whereas the Romans sought to safeguard their rights against the power of the government. It is an interesting fact that whereas Cicero declared that the composition of the government determined the character of the constitution, Aristotle deduced the various types of constitutions from the various possible bases and extents of equality.[1]

The notion of res publica postulates for every citizen a fair share in the common weal; it postulates the participation of the people in State affairs; it postulates that the government should be for the people;[2] but it does not necessarily imply the principle of government by the people. Libertas primarily consists in those rights which (a) affect the status of the individual citizen, and (b) ensure that the State is a real res publica; the nominal right to govern is included among them, but its actual exercise is subject to the possession of auctoritas and dignitas—two qualities that played a remarkable part in Roman life, both private and public.[3] Libertas and dignitas are not essentially incompatible—as are, in Aristotle's view, eleutheria and axia—because libertas, with regard to an individual, is merely the *lower* limit of political rights.[4]

Therefore aequa libertas, with regard to Rome, does not imply the democratic isonomia of Periclean Athens. It implies equality, but on a different plane: at Rome aequa libertas indicates the repudiation of legal discrimination between citizens, such as the former discrimination against the Plebs. Privilegia, i.e. laws of personal exception,

---

[1] Cic. De Leg. III, 12. Arist. Polit. IV, 8, pp. 1294a, 19 f.; Eth. Nic. v, 3, pp. 1131a, 20 f.; Polit. III, 9, pp. 1280a, 7 f.

[2] Cic. De Rep. I, 39; 43; III, 43 f.; Ad Att. VIII, 11, 1–2.

[3] See R. Heinze, Auctoritas, in Hermes LX (1925); and H. Wegehaupt, Die Bedeutung und Anwendung von dignitas in den Schriften der republikanischen Zeit, Breslau Diss. 1932.

[4] Tac. Ann. XIII, 27, 3: Non frustra maiores, cum dignitatem ordinum dividerent, libertatem in communi posuisse.

were opposed; and, similarly, the law whereby front seats in the
theatre were reserved for senators only is said to have been resented
on the ground that it was inconsistent with aequa libertas.[1]

It appears, therefore, that aequa libertas means equality before the
law, equality of all personal rights, and equality of the fundamental
political rights; but it does not preclude differentiation beyond this
sphere.

3. LIBERTAS AND DIGNITAS

If libertas is merely the minimum of political rights which in
principle admit of various degrees of dignitas,[2] the right balance
between libertas and dignitas is a matter of great importance. Cato
the Elder said, "Iure, lege, libertate, re publica communiter uti
oportet; gloria atque honore,[3] quomodo sibi quisque struxit".[4]
A generation later, M. Antonius the orator wished "libertate esse
parem cum ceteris, principem dignitate".[5] Such a position is attainable, if at all, only by means of moderation and consideration which
alone can establish the balance between dignitas and libertas. He
who claims dignitas for himself ought to be "haud minus libertatis
alienae quam dignitatis suae memor", to use Livy's famous phrase.[6]
This however reveals the real crux; libertas and dignitas do not
exclude each other provided dignitas is toned down so as not to
exceed the limit set by aequa libertas; but it is a grave problem
whether untempered dignitas can be upheld without colliding with
and trying to override aequa libertas. Is it at all possible to be—as
Antonius wished—libertate par cum ceteris and princeps dignitate
at the same time? Can one excel "praestantia dignitatis" without
"transire aequabilitatem iuris"?[7] And, on the other hand, will not

[1] Livy XXXIV, 54, 5: Omnia discrimina talia, quibus ordines discernerentur,
et concordiae et libertatis aequae minuendae esse. Cf. Mommsen, Staatsrecht
III, pp. 519 ff.

[2] See above, p. 14 n. 4.

[3] Gloria and honos are the chief constituents of dignitas. Honos, in the
sense of public office, engenders auctoritas.

[4] Malcovati, Orat. Rom. Frag. I, p. 218, no. 249.

[5] Cic. Phil. I, 34.

[6] Livy VII, 33, 3.

[7] Cic. De Orat. II, 209: Superioribus invidetur...si...aequabilitatem iuris
praestantia dignitatis aut fortunae transeunt. See also Livy XLV, 32, 5; and the
instructive anecdote in Diod. Sic. XXXVII, 10, 2.

the fortification of libertas be regarded as a challenge to dignitas?[1]
There seems to be an inevitable tension between libertas and dignitas
which may be mitigated if a proper balance is kept between them.
But such a balance is neither simply nor easily achieved.

Adeo moderatio tuendae libertatis, dum aequari velle simulando ita se
quisque extollit ut deprimat alium, in difficili est, cavendoque ne metuant,
homines metuendos ultro se efficiunt, et iniuriam ab nobis repulsam,
tamquam aut facere aut pati necesse sit, iniungimus aliis (Livy III, 65, 11).

There is another thing that made the harmonious coexistence of
libertas and dignitas difficult. Socially and economically the Roman
society was not homogeneous, and there was nothing to prevent the
nobles from identifying dignitas with the distinctions and preserves
of their own class. The result was that the nobles, irrespective of
their own achievements, began to consider dignitas as something
naturally due to them for the reason that it was well earned by their
ancestors. Such a development could only nurse the seeds of discord,
which rapidly developed into open strife accompanied with all the
bitterness of social antagonism. And just as dignitas became
a watchword of "vested interests" so could libertas be used as
a battle-cry—sincere or feigned—of social reform.

The conflict between libertas and dignitas, "contentio libertatis
dignitatisque", as Livy (IV, 6, 11) put it, was a salient feature of
Roman domestic politics during the Republican period. This conflict was forced by certain individuals or groups whose exorbitant
claims, based on dignitas and directed to dignitas, became incompatible either with the freedom of their fellow citizens, or the
freedom of the State as a whole. It is well to bear this fact in mind so
that the struggle for liberty at Rome may not be represented in
terms of the issue "individual versus State" in which the practical
problem is, in Mill's phrase, "how to make the fitting adjustment
between individual independence and social control".[2] The Roman

---

[1] Livy III, 67, 9: Sub titulo aequandarum legum nostra iura oppressa
tulimus et ferimus.

[2] J. S. Mill, On Liberty (Everyman's Library), pp. 68 f. Mill (op. cit. p. 131)
asks "What, then, is the rightful limit to the sovereignty of the individual over
himself? Where does the authority of society begin? How much of human life
should be assigned to individuality, and how much to society?" Such questions
were not asked at Rome; and it seems that the third question only could have
had a meaning there.

citizen sought to assert and safeguard his rights, not against the overriding authority of the State, or the tyranny of the majority, as it is sometimes called, but against other citizens who were stronger than himself, or against the officers of the State who, in the pursuit of their own private interests, might encroach upon his rights, abusing the power that had been entrusted to them. The crucial problem of libertas at Rome was how to make the fitting adjustment between the equality of the fundamental rights of all and the supremacy of some. This problem, as will be seen later, became very acute under the Late Republic, and the failure to solve it brought with it many dangers.

4. THE BALANCE OF POWERS[1]

As has been said, the very existence of libertas depended on the rule of law. At Rome the law commanded wide respect independent to some extent of the sanctions which enforced it (witness, for example, the observance of the so-called imperfectae leges); nevertheless, since laws do not themselves rule in the literal sense, the rule of law could only be established if provision was made for (a) a power strong enough to enforce the law where necessary, and (b) means of preventing, if necessary, those who wield that power from abusing it. The vital dependence of libertas on the proper solution of these problems is too obvious to need stressing.

Three main organs made up the republican constitution at Rome: populus, magistratus, senatus. Separation of Powers was unknown, but there was at Rome a remarkable balance of Powers designed to prevent any of them from overriding the authority of the others and seizing complete control of the State. Although the concurrence of all the Powers was necessary for the smooth running of State affairs, it is characteristic of the Roman constitution that the power of the senior magistracies (imperium) was the pivot of the whole constitutional system.

The sovereignty of the People[2] was a cardinal principle of the

[1] Mommsen's *Römisches Staatsrecht* has been consulted throughout. References are given in cases of particular importance only.

[2] For the purpose of the present study, which is concerned with the later period of the Republic, the difference between Populus and Plebs may on the whole be disregarded, as the Lex Hortensia put plebiscita and leges on equal footing.

Roman republican constitution. The acceptance of this principle, however, did not produce the same results at Rome as, for example, at Athens, because the competence of the sovereign People and the manner in which the People exercised its sovereign rights were different from what was practised in the Athenian democracy.

The Populus Romanus was the ultimate source of power, the supreme legislature, and the final court of appeal. The Assembly of the People (comitia) elected the magistrates, enacted or repealed laws (leges), and, in the capacity of iudicium populi, confirmed or annulled sentences of death or flogging passed on Roman citizens in the courts of criminal justice.

These prerogatives were subject to certain indirect limitations: any Assembly to be lawful had to be convened and presided over by a competent magistrate, i.e. a magistrate who possessed the ius agendi cum populo, or, in the case of plebeian assemblies, cum plebe.

Further, the Assembly could not on its own initiative propose candidates for public offices, nor introduce bills and motions, nor put before the magistrate any questions. The People had to listen to what they were told, and to cast their votes according to the motion (rogatio) introduced by the magistrate. Private persons of distinction were on occasions called on by the presiding magistrate to address the Assembly,[1] but as a rule magistrates only spoke in the comitia and contiones. The citizen had a vote, but he had no right to make his voice heard: freedom of speech, in the sense that any citizen had the right to speak, did not exist in the Roman Assemblies.[2]

[1] Cf. Mommsen, *Staatsrecht* I³, pp. 200 f.; III, pp. 300 f., pp. 394 f.

[2] Tenney Frank (Naevius and Free Speech, *Amer. Journ. Phil.* XLVIII (1927), pp. 105–10) and his pupil Laura Robinson (*Freedom of Speech in the Roman Republic*, Johns Hopkins University Diss. Baltimore, 1940) contend that the Romans under the Republic enjoyed freedom of speech and of criticism of the government. In the last resort, their thesis is based on the assumption that the Twelve Tables did not provide for action against slander, the provision "si quis occentavisset" (Cic. *De Rep.* IV, 12) being in their view a measure against casting spells, not slander. The thesis, however, in the form it was put forward by Prof. Frank and by Dr Robinson, seems to be unacceptable, mainly for the following reasons. First, the Twelve Tables distinguished between "malum carmen incantare", which means to cast a spell, and "occentare", which according to Festus *s.v.* (p. 191, ed. Lindsay) means "convicium facere". See Ed. Fraenkel, *Gnomon* I, pp. 187 ff.; Ch. Brecht, *s.v.* Occentatio in PW, XVII, cols. 1752 ff. and especially cols. 1754 f.; and A. Momigliano (reviewing L. Robinson's dissertation) in *J.R.S.* XXXII (1942), p. 121.

Another point of great consequence is intercessio.[1] As has been said, the Assembly could vote only on motions introduced by a competent magistrate. Until the actual voting took place the motion remained essentially an act of the magistrate, and as such was open to veto by par maiorve potestas. In theory intercessio overrode the authority of the magistrate only, not of the Assembly; but in practice it prevented the Assembly from exercising its sovereign rights.

Until the second half of the fourth century B.C. any law passed by the People, as well as the results of the popular elections, had to be ratified by a subsequent patrum auctoritas.[2] This limitation of the People's sovereignty was virtually removed by the Lex Publilia (of 339 B.C.) and Lex Maenia,[3] which provided that the patrum auctoritas should be given before the voting took place.

Secondly, Dr Robinson, *op. cit.* p. 4, argues that it would be amazing to find the Romans punishing verbal insult before the beginnings of conscious literature. She therefore concludes a priori that the repression of occentatio referred to magic, for the belief in magic belongs to a primitive stage of culture. This argument, however, misses among other things the vital point that slander need not be "conscious literature" nor any literature at all. Thirdly, even if it were true that the Twelve Tables did not provide for action against slander, there would still remain the question whether the absence of a libel law alone amounts to freedom of speech and criticism. For there is an essential difference between the right of free speech and the possibility of slandering with impunity. The line of demarcation is not always strict, yet it undoubtedly exists. Cf. Momigliano, *op. cit.* p. 123.

The plain fact, from a political point of view, is that the Roman People went to the Assemblies to listen and to vote, not to speak. Magistrates, leading senators and barristers enjoyed freedom of speech and made the most of it; but they cannot be identified with the Roman People. The People could show their approval or dissatisfaction in many ways (see, e.g., Cic. *Pro Sest.* 106 ff.), but they could make no constructive criticism.

[1] For the intercessio of rogationes see Mommsen, *op. cit.* I³, pp. 283 ff. It is not necessary here to discuss obnuntiatio, since it was its abuse, rather than its proper use, that played a conspicuous part in obstructing the procedure of the Assemblies under the Late Republic. For obnuntiatio see T. Frank, *C.A.H.* VIII, p. 367; St. Weinstock, in PW, XVII, cols. 1726 ff.; Mommsen, *op. cit.* I³, pp. 110 ff.

[2] It is not necessary here to discuss the question whether by patres all the senators or the patrician senators only were meant, cf. Mommsen, *op. cit.* III, pp. 1037 ff. Similarly, it is of little consequence for the present purpose whether judicial verdicts of the People had also to be ratified by patrum auctoritas or not, cf. *op. cit.* III, p. 1039.

[3] Of unknown date but probably not much later than 290 B.C. Cf. Mommsen, *op. cit.* III, p. 1042, and E. Weiss, PW, XII, col. 2396, *s.v.* Lex Maenia.

Suffrage was general at Rome, but it was not until the second half of the second century B.C. that it was freed from a kind of control. Originally voting was oral, and voters from the lower classes, if they were clients of some noble, were expected to vote in conformity with the auctoritas of their patron. The method of oral voting exposed the client to eventual victimization, if he did not pay due heed to the auctoritas of his patron. So long as this method prevailed, the franchise was denied its full effect, because it lacked freedom. This state of affairs was changed by the four Leges Tabellariae which provided for the secret ballot: the Lex Gabinia of 139 B.C., concerned with the election of magistrates; the Lex Cassia of 137 B.C., concerned with trials on appeal before the People; the Lex Papiria of 131 B.C., concerned with the enactment of laws; and, finally, the Lex Coelia of 107 B.C., which applied the ballot to trials for treason (perduellio).[1] The Lex Cassia is known to have encountered long-drawn opposition, and all the Ballot Laws were very much resented by staunch Optimates.[2] The Leges Tabellariae were regarded as a great achievement of the commons, and the ballot was called "the guardian of liberty".[3]

Whatever may have been the advantages gained by the Ballot Laws, they did not increase the competence of the Assemblies. Save for the judicial powers of the Assembly, the People possessed neither the right nor the means of controlling the Executive; the controls through the election of magistrates and through legislation were indirect and, in fact, slight. The People were given information concerning State affairs (contiones), but they had no say in outlining the policies (apart from the declaration of war) which the Executive pursued within the limits of its own competence.

The Senate also could be convened and presided over only by a competent magistrate, i.e. one who possessed the ius agendi cum senatu, as a rule one of the consuls. The senators were called on by the presiding consul in order of rank to state their opinion on the matter which he put before the House. Those who were thus called on were allowed to speak any length of time on any subject they

---

[1] See Cic. *De Leg.* III, 35 ff.

[2] See Cic. *Brut.* 97; *Pro Sest.* 103; *De Leg.* III, 34 and 36; *De Amic.* 41.

[3] Cic. *Pro Sest.* 103; *De Leg.* III, 34 and 39; *De Leg. Agr.* II, 4; *Pro Planc.* 16; *Pro Cornel.* ap. Ascon. 78, 1 C.

considered of importance with regard to public affairs.[1] It would, however, be an overstatement to consider freedom of speech a general principle of Roman parliamentarianism. As a rule a senator could not demand to speak, and the presiding consul was neither obliged nor expected ever to call on the "back-benchers" (pedarii) whose only opportunity of stating their views was a division of the House (pedibus in sententiam ire). There was freedom of speech in the Senate, but in fact not for all the senators.[2]

From a constitutional point of view the Senate was the advisory council of the Executive. It was, by convention, the duty of the senior magistrates—except commanders in the field—to consult the Senate before undertaking any action that under the existing laws and within the competence of the magistrate in question affected the community.[3] The counsel of the Senate was given in the form of a Senatus Consultum.

In theory the Senatus Consulta were merely recommendations to be followed by the magistrates, "if they deem it proper to do so" (si eis videatur). But a resolution of the Senate carried all the weight of auctoritas the senators possessed between them, and therefore no magistrate would without serious reasons leave it unheeded. Thus the Senate got control of the policies pursued by the Executive.

However great and decisive may have been the influence of the Senate on the Executive, it rested ultimately on auctoritas and custom rather than on statutory powers. So long as the Senate's authority was unchallenged its pre-eminence in Roman affairs was assured; but in principle it was challengeable, and when at last it was challenged, auctoritas senatus became the subject of a long controversy.

The striking feature of the Executive in the Roman Republic was the vast extent of its power and prerogatives. There is much truth in Cicero's and Livy's dicta that the power of the consuls was regal in character.[4] The mandate of the consuls was irrevocable before

[1] See Mommsen, op. cit. III, pp. 939 ff.
[2] Ib. p. 962.
[3] Ib. I[3], p. 310. Such actions of the Executive as affected individuals only did not have to be referred to the Senate.
[4] Cic. De Rep. II, 56: Uti consules potestatem haberent tempore dumtaxat annuam, genere ipso ac iure regiam. Cf. De Leg. III, 8. Livy II, 1, 7: Libertatis

expiry; they were unimpeachable during their term of office; they commanded unconditional obedience, and possessed judicial and coercive powers. Such an Executive, if untempered and unchecked, might easily become dangerous for the liberties of its people.[1]

To provide against the contingency of the government becoming too strong for the freedom either of individual citizens or of the whole State, the Romans resorted, not to curtailment of the Executive's powers, but to a system of constitutional checks imposed on the duration and exercise of those powers.

Imperium and potestas were invariably granted "ad tempus", as a rule for one year, after which period, unless prorogatio imperii took place, they automatically expired.

With the exception of the dictator,[2] interrex, and praefectus urbi —all of them being emergency magistrates—all magistracies consisted of two or more colleagues of equal standing (par potestas), each colleague being empowered both to act alone and to oppose any action undertaken by his equals or juniors (intercessio by par maiorve potestas).[3]

Intercessio is in fact the most effective check imposed on the Executive during the tenure of office, for, as has been seen, neither the People nor the Senate could stop a magistrate from doing what

autem originem inde magis quia annuum imperium consulare factum est quam quod deminutum quicqam sit ex regia potestate numeres. Cf. IV, 3, 9; VIII, 32, 3. See also *Dig.* I, 2, 2, 16; Dion. Hal. VI, 65, 1; Polyb. VI, 11, 12. Several more instances are cited by Mommsen, *op. cit.* II[3], p. 93.

[1] Perhaps it is not inappropriate here to quote Abraham Lincoln's dictum, "It has long been a grave question whether any government not too strong for the liberties of its people, can be strong enough to maintain its existence in great emergencies" (10 Nov. 1864; *Select Speeches*, Everyman's Library, p. 221).

[2] Kloesel, *Libertas*, p. 31, asserts that dictator and magister equitum "eigentlich dasselbe ist wie zwei Konsuln; nur ist der Diktator letztlich ungebunden". This statement ignores the fact that the Master of the Horse had only praetorian rank, see Mommsen, *op. cit.* II[3], p. 176.

[3] For intercessio cf. Mommsen, *op. cit.* I[3], pp. 266 ff. Intercessio of par potestas was based on the principle "in re pari potiorem causam esse prohibentis" (*Dig.* X, 3, 28). Cf. the references cited in Mommsen, *op. cit.* I[3], p. 268 n. 2. Since the introduction of Bills and motions for senatus consulta were in the first place acts of a magistrate, they could be vetoed by par maiorve potestas, see Id. *op. cit.* I[3], p. 280 ff. For the purpose of this study it is of little consequence whether intercessio was prohibitive only or annulling as well, see Id. *op. cit.* I[3], p. 266 n. 4.

was in his competence to do. Intercessio was especially powerful in the hands of the tribunes, who for all practical purposes acted as if possessing maior potestas with regard to all magistrates, except the dictator.[1] The tribunate as a sacrosanct and overriding authority is the chief means of holding in check the vast imperium of the consuls.[2] Since its exercise depended mainly on the discretion of the intercessor, that right could easily be abused with the grave result of paralysing the work of government. The evil potentialities of the tribunician veto were nowhere more clearly recognized than in the Lex Sempronia de provinciis consularibus, carried by C. Gracchus, which exempted from tribunician intercession the assignment of consular governors to provinces. On the other hand, the tribunician intercession was, as will presently be seen, a most effective protection of personal rights.

As has been said, potestas ad tempus and par potestas, i.e. the limited tenure and collegiality of office, provided against the possibility of the Executive becoming permanently uncontrollable; and it is these two that were spoken of by the Romans as the beginning and the safeguards of political liberty.[3] The continuation of office beyond the statutory limits was denounced as regnum, the most invidious term of political invective in republican Rome.[4] And, as will be seen later, the resistance to extraordinary powers purported to champion the cause of freedom against its real or alleged suppressors.

It appears from what has been said that the working of the Roman constitution depended on the cooperation of the People, the Senate, and the Magistrates, especially the consuls and the tribunes. But a harmonious cooperation between them was not attainable without a large amount of goodwill. The limits of the particular powers were not always clearly defined, which was a potential source of friction. With the ascendancy of the Senate over the consuls, which took place during the Middle Republic,[5] the question could arise whether the Senate or the People was the supreme power in the State. What made this question a grave one was not only its

[1] See Mommsen, op. cit. I[3], p. 26 n. 1.
[2] See Cic. De Rep. II, 58; De Leg. III, 16; Appian, Bell. Civ. I, 1. Cf. Livy II, 33, 1; 54, 5; IV, 26, 10.
[3] Livy II, 1, 7; IV, 24, 4; Sallust, Cat. 6, 7. Cf. Livy III, 21, 2; IV, 5, 5.
[4] See, e.g., Livy VI, 41, 3; IX, 34, 16.
[5] Cf. T. Frank, C.A.H. VII, p. 818.

C

constitutional implications, but, and perhaps mainly, its social background; for however the issue may have been stated it was not at bottom a purely constitutional issue, nor was it fought out for purely constitutional ends.

5. The Rights of the Individual

All the institutions discussed in the previous section provided mainly against the possibility of the Executive becoming too strong for the freedom of the State, but, with the exception of the iudicium populi, did not provide direct protection for the liberties of the individual citizen. Such protection was essential in view of the fact that the Roman Executive possessed both judicial and coercive powers. It is characteristic of the Roman idea of freedom that some of the most effective checks imposed on the imperium and potestas derived from the desire to protect the rights of the individual citizen. In this connexion it may be well to consider separately the liberties of the private citizen.

Nego potuisse iure publico, legibus iis quibus haec civitas utitur, quemquam civem ulla eiusmodi calamitate affici sine iudicio; hoc iuris in hac civitate etiam tum, cum reges essent, dico fuisse; hoc nobis esse a maioribus traditum; hoc esse denique liberae civitatis ut nihil de capite civis aut de bonis sine iudicio senatus, aut populi, aut eorum qui de quaqua re constituti iudices sint, detrahi posse (Cic. *De Dom.* 33).

Punishment without formal trial and conviction is a violation of freedom.[1] This principle of "nulla poena sine iudicio" lends particular importance to the independence of law-courts.[2]

(Consules) ne per omnia regiam potestatem sibi vindicarent, lege lata factum est ut ab eis provocatio esset neve possent in caput civis Romani animadvertere iniussu populi; solum relictum est ut coercere possent et in vincula publica duci iuberent.[3]

Provocatio, which in civilian life protected the life and person of a Roman citizen, was regarded as the mainstay of freedom: "arx

[1] See Cic. *De Dom.* 43; 47; 77; *De Leg.* I, 42; Ascon. 41, 13 f. c; Livy III, 13, 4; 56, 10–13.

[2] Cic. *II in Verr.* II, 33 and v, 175.

[3] Pompon. *Dig.* I, 2, 2, 16. See also Cic. *De Rep.* II, 53; *De Leg.* III, 6; Livy II, 29, 10; IV, 13, 11. For the limits of provocatio see Mommsen, *op. cit.* III, pp. 352 ff.

tuendae libertatis" (Livy III, 45, 8); "unicum praesidium libertatis" (Id. III, 55, 4; cf. III, 53, 4–6); "vindex libertatis" (Id. III, 56, 6); "vindiciae libertatis" (Cic. *De Rep.* III, 44); "patrona civitatis ac vindex libertatis" (Id. *De Orat.* II, 199).

The right of appeal to the People was in fact an aspect of the right of formal trial, because the Assembly, acting as a iudicium populi, was a supreme court of appeal which revised the verdict of the magistrate,[1] and not merely a sovereign authority entitled to pardon the crime, or commute the sentence, without hearing the case.

Just as provocatio was regarded as a guardian of freedom so a civilian magistracy "sine provocatione" was regarded as tyranny, and the Plebiscitum Duillianum imposed the death penalty on anyone who left the Plebs without tribunes, or set up a magistracy not subject to provocatio.[2]

The Lex Valeria de provocatione was a so-called lex imperfecta, and a sanction was added to it by the Lex Porcia which exempted citizens from flogging "iniussu populi".[3] Hence the Lex Porcia is sometimes praised as a guardian of freedom: "Porcia lex virgas ab omnium civium Romanorum corpore amovit...Porcia lex libertatem civium lictori eripuit."[4]

Provocatio protected a citizen's life and person, but it did not apply to other personal rights. These could be protected against the arbitrary injustice of magistrates by (the tribunician) auxilium.

The object of the tribunate was the protection of the citizen— plebeian and patrician alike—who was wronged by the civil authorities in the city of Rome.[5] The tribune was entitled to succour (auxilium ferre) any citizen who appealed to him for that purpose (appellare tribunos), intervening on his behalf as maior potestas. As a matter of fact, auxilium is the intercessio of par maiorve

---

[1] See Mommsen, *op. cit.* III, p. 351.   [2] Livy III, 55, 14.

[3] Cic. *De Rep.* II, 54; Livy X, 9, 4 ff.

[4] Cic. *Pro Rab. perd. reo*, 12; cf. ap. Ascon. 78, 1 c (lex Porcia): principium iustissimae libertatis. *II in Verr.* v, 163: O nomen dulce libertatis, o ius eximium nostrae civitatis, o lex Porcia legesque Semproniae (cf. *Pro Rab.* 12). See also Sallust, *Cat.* 51, 22; Ps.-Sallust, *In Cic.* 5.

[5] Cf. Ed. Meyer, Der Ursprung des Tribunats und die Gemeinde der vier Tribus, *Kl. Schr.* I², pp. 335–61 (=*Hermes* XXX, 1895, pp. 1 ff.); Mommsen, *op. cit.* II³, pp. 291 ff.; I³, p. 278; I³, p. 66; G. W. Botsford, *The Roman Assemblies* (1909), p. 263.

potestas lodged against a magisterial order in consequence of an appeal to the said potestas by the complainant,[1] and therefore any par maiorve potestas could be approached for this purpose.[2] The tribunes were the authority par excellence in that matter because the tribunate was set up for the purpose of auxilium,[3] and because the tribunes enjoyed for this purpose the standing of maior potestas even against the consuls.[4] The tribunate was therefore regarded as the protection of freedom,[5] and auxilium and provocatio were called "duae arces libertatis tuendae".[6]

Although provocatio and auxilium were often mentioned in the same breath, there is a great difference between them. Provocatio was the citizen's right. A sentence of death or flogging passed in the first instance could not without violation of the law be executed before the Assembly confirmed the verdict. The case is different with auxilium. Strictly speaking the citizen had no right to auxilium; he had only the right of appellatio, i.e. if he thought he was wronged by an order of a magistrate, he was entitled to seek the help of a tribune, or any par maiorve potestas, for the purpose of opposing that order.[7] The approach to the tribune ought not to be denied, as witness the laws prescribing that tribunes should not be absent from the city a whole day, nor lock their house doors at night.[8] Appellatio is absolutely necessary if auxilium is to take place at all; but it did not invariably result in auxilium. The reasons for that are, first, that auxilium could not be given in the case of decrees against which there was no appeal;[9] and, secondly, that the decision whether or not to intercede as requested by the appellant rested entirely with the tribune, who might well refuse to intercede, if he did not deem

---

[1] See Mommsen, op. cit. 1³, p. 274 and p. 278.

[2] See, e.g., Caesar, Bell. Civ. III, 20.

[3] Cic. De Leg. III, 9: Plebs quos pro se contra vim auxilii ergo decem creavit, ei tribuni eius sunto. See also Livy III, 9, 11, and above, p. 25 n. 5.

[4] See above, p. 23 nn. 1 and 2.

[5] Sallust, Hist. III, 48, 12 M: Vis tribunicia telum a maioribus libertati paratum. Cic. De Leg. Agr. II, 15: Tr. pl. quem maiores praesidem libertatis custodemque esse voluerunt. Livy III, 37, 5: Tribuniciam potestatem munimentum libertati. Diod. Sic. XII, 25, 2: (Δήμαρχοι) φύλακες τῆς τῶν πολιτῶν ἐλευθερίας.   [6] Livy III, 45, 8. Cf. III, 53, 4.

[7] Cf. Mommsen, op. cit. 1³, p. 274.

[8] See Id. op. cit. II³, p. 291 n. 2, and Botsford, loc. cit.

[9] See Mommsen, op. cit. 1³, pp. 278 ff.

it right to do so.[1] It is true that a tribune was expected to aid a wronged citizen—that was what tribunes were for—and it may be assumed that, as a rule, auxilium was given where it could and ought to have been given; but it was given as a result of the tribune's right to grant it, and not of the citizen's right to demand it. Auxilium was an institution of which the citizen could avail himself, but it was by no means his indefeasible right as was provocatio. The citizen's right was appellatio, whereas auxilium was the tribune's right.

We come now to the question how far the authority of the State extended over the private affairs of the citizens. As has been said, the Romans did not conceive of their freedom in terms of the issue Individual versus Society; it is not therefore surprising to find that the censorial cura morum, which extended over all the branches of public and private life,[2] and the Leges Sumptuariae were not on the whole considered to be an encroachment on personal liberty. The high regard for antiqui mores and the realization that the welfare of the community depended on the behaviour of its members probably went a long way towards reconciling the Romans to the censorial cura morum. There is no evidence of protests against this as such, but as to the Leges Sumptuariae there is some evidence of occasional misgivings. Thus the Lex Oppia of 215 B.C., which at the time of Hannibal's invasion imposed austerity standards on female attire and ornaments, and forbade women the use of carriages in the City and towns, caused an outburst of protests by the discontented women, and was repealed in 195 B.C. If Livy's account of the event (XXXIV, 1 ff.) is indicative of what the Romans thought on the subject of the Leges Sumptuariae, it would appear that their advocates believed that such laws arrested the differentiation in standards of living, and by preserving an outward uniformity strengthened the inner unity of society; their opponents, on the other hand, did not question the principle on which these laws rested, they only questioned the desirability of austerity in certain circumstances.

There is, however, some evidence which, if genuine, would go to prove that on occasions the very principle underlying the Leges

[1] For examples of denied auxilium see Livy III, 56, 5; Val. Max. IV, 1, 8; Pliny, N.H. XXI, 3, (6), 8 f. See also Livy IX, 34, 26.
[2] Cf. Mommsen, op. cit. II³, pp. 375 ff.

Sumptuariae was challenged in the name of libertas. According to Valerius Maximus:

M. Antonius et L. Flaccus censores (97 b.c.)[1] Duronium senatu moverunt, quod legem de coercendis conviviorum sumptibus latam[2] tribunus plebis abrogaverat. . . : "Freni sunt iniecti vobis, Quirites, nullo modo perpetiendi. Alligati et constricti estis amaro vinculo servitutis: lex enim lata est quae vos esse frugi iubet. Abrogemus igitur istud horridae vetustatis rubigine obsitum imperium. Etenim quid opus libertate, si volentibus luxu perire non licet?"[3]

It would be hard to tell whether this protest, even if historical, was typical.

It is typical of the Roman's concern for personal freedom that the prohibition of the second tenure of an office was first applied to the censorship, and one case only is known of a man having been censor twice.[4]

By means of the censorship and the Leges Sumptuariae a very considerable control could—at least in theory—be exercised over the private life of the citizen. And if under the Republic the Romans did not have to endure too much hardship of regimentation, it was in part due to the discrepancy between the nominal rights and the actual means of control their government possessed, and in part to the character of the people who governed them.

As has been seen, the Romans had no freedom of public meetings: any gathering of the People had to be convened and presided over by a competent magistrate.[5] On the other hand, under the Republic they enjoyed wide freedom of association for religious, professional,

---

[1] See Münzer in PW, v, col. 1862 *s.v.* Duronius (3).

[2] Münzer, *loc. cit.*, supposes that the Lex Licinia of 103 b.c. is referred to.

[3] Val. Max. II, 9, 5. I owe this reference to Kloesel, *Libertas*, p. 13. Kloesel's comment seems to imply that the speech of Duronius, as it stands, was directed against the censorship ("gegen diese von starkem Ethos getragene Magistratur"). Unless one is inclined to think that the word "imperium" refers to the censorship, there is no other support for Kloesel's assumption. Imperium, however, refers to imperium legis not to imperium censoris, the latter expression being impossible as the censors possessed potestas only, not imperium. Duronius, as Valerius Maximus clearly says, proposed to repeal the law, not to depose the censors.

[4] See Mommsen, *op. cit.* I[3], p. 520, especially n. 2.

[5] See above, p. 18, and Livy XXXIX, 15, 11.

and political purposes. The right of association was granted to all, but it could be curtailed and suppressed by administrative procedure.[1]

Religious freedom in the modern sense was hardly known at Rome. The Roman religion was a State religion, and every citizen was expected to observe it as a matter of course. That religion, however, while it imposed on the citizen the observance of a certain form of worship, did not impose a creed. The observance of the State religion did not exclude the simultaneous observance of any other religions or cults, provided their rites were not repugnant to the accepted morality, or their tenets subversive in the eyes of established law. The ban on the Bacchic Orgies in 186 B.C. arose from moral, not theological, considerations.[2] It must also be remembered that till the times of Domitian there was no equivalent to the *graphe asebeias* at Rome, and that the maxim "deorum iniuriae dis curae" testifies to a sense of religious tolerance no less than of religious indifference. It would therefore seem that, although in theory religious freedom was not recognized, in practice the Romans enjoyed wide freedom in matters of religion. Needless to say, all this applies to Roman citizens only, aliens resident at Rome being in a different position.

The Romans, although they admitted the authority of the censors over the intimate affairs of their private homes,[3] had a clear concept of the sanctity of the home.[4] "Quid est sanctius", says Cicero (*De Dom.* 109), "quid omni religione munitius, quam domus unius cuiusque civium? Hic arae sunt, hic foci, hic dii penates; hic sacra, religiones, caerimoniae continentur; hoc perfugium est ita sanctum omnibus, ut inde abripi neminem fas sit." Cicero's view, which occurs again in his *In Vatinium*, 22, is confirmed by two eminent jurists of the Imperial period: "Gaius libro primo ad xii tab.: Plerique putaverunt nullum de domo sua in ius vocari licere, quia domus tutissimum cuique refugium atque receptaculum sit, eumque qui inde in ius vocaret, vim inferre videri" (*Dig.* 11, 4, 18). And, similarly, "Paulus libro primo ad Edictum: Sed etsi is qui domi est

---

[1] Cf. Mommsen, *De Collegiis et Sodaliciis Romanorum*, Kiel, 1843, pp. 32–35; and *Staatsrecht* III, p. 1180.

[2] Cf. Livy xxxix, 8 ff., and the S.C. de Bacchanalibus, Dessau, *I.L.S.* 18.

[3] Dion. Hal. xx, 13, 3. Cf. Mommsen, *op. cit.* 11[3], p. 376.

[4] Cf. F. Schulz, *Prinzipien des römischen Rechts*, p. 109; R. v. Ihering, *Geist des römischen Rechts*[3], 11, 1, pp. 158 f.

interdum vocari in ius potest, tamen de domo sua nemo extrahi debet" (*Dig.* II, 4, 21).

It cannot be said that a Roman's home was entirely immune from encroachment, yet it provided a considerable measure of security and inviolability.

Cicero in his *Pro Caecina* (96 ff.) and *De Domo Sua* (77 ff.) declared that the freedom and citizenship of a Roman were indefeasible rights: "Maiores nostri...de civitate et libertate ea iura sanxerunt, quae nec vis temporum, nec potentia magistratuum, nec res iudicata, nec denique universi populi Romani potestas, quae ceteris in rebus est maxima, labefactare possit" (*De Dom.* 80). It may well be doubted whether this sweeping statement, and the arguments supporting it, is an expression of Cicero's considered opinion on the subject; rather it seems to be merely an expedient view advanced for the sake of the case in hand.[1] As a general rule this view is untenable, and Cicero himself elsewhere records several instances that disprove it.[2] From a purely legal point of view there was nothing to prevent even the enslavement of a citizen.[3] But, with regard to the Middle and Late Republic and for all practical purposes in ordinary circumstances, there is much truth in Cicero's saying. For after nexum had been abolished and banishment had fallen into disuse, and, on the other hand, before Sulla provided for voluntary exile in anticipation of condemnation, civitas and libertas were practically inviolable so long as the citizen remained at Rome.[4] And this meant that a Roman's "life, liberty, and property" were reasonably secure.

It appears from what has been said in the preceding pages that libertas, while it falls short of democracy and egalitarianism, means freedom from absolutism, and the enjoyment of personal liberties under the rule of law.

The following two chapters will trace the meaning and effectiveness of libertas in Roman politics during the crisis of Roman republicanism.

---

[1] Cf. Mommsen, *op. cit.* III, p. 43 n. 2 and p. 361 n. 1.
[2] See *De Orat.* I, 181.
[3] Mommsen, *op. cit.* III, p. 361 n. 1.   [4] *Ib.* pp. 42 ff.

CHAPTER 2

CIVIL DISCORD: OPTIMATES AND POPULARES

1. THE BACKGROUND OF THE STRUGGLE

A salient feature of Roman domestic politics during the century or so preceding the final collapse of republicanism was the fierce antagonism between the so-called Optimates and Populares.[1] They opposed and sometimes fought each other, and often claimed—each side after its own fashion—to be the champions of libertas. It would therefore be worth while seeing whether the rival contentions of the Optimates and Populares affected the conception of political freedom during Rome's transition from the Republican form of government to the Principate. For this purpose the true character of the Roman constitution, and the manner in which it actually worked—as distinct from its underlying principles and inherent potentialities—needs to be considered.

The form of government between the Second Punic War and the Gracchi, which Polybius and Cicero described as a mixed constitution, was in fact an aristocratic republic in everything but name.[2] This fact was apparent to contemporaries, and even frankly

---

[1] These terms, after some aberrations of modern interpretation, have come into their own in recent times. See, above all, H. Strasburger, PW, XVIII, cols. 773 ff., *s.v.* Optimates, and M. Gelzer, *Die römische Gesellschaft zur Zeit Ciceros*, *N.Jhb.f.kl.Alt.* XLV (1920), p. 1 ff. For this and the subsequent sections the following were of great use throughout: H. Last, *C.A.H.* IX, chapters I–IV; R. Syme, *The Roman Revolution*, Oxford, 1939; M. Gelzer, *Die Nobilität der römischen Republik*, Leipzig, 1912; F. Münzer, *Römische Adelsparteien und Adelsfamilien*, Stuttgart, 1920; H. Strasburger, PW, XVII, cols. 785 ff. *s.v.* Nobiles; Id. *Concordia Ordinum, eine Untersuchung zur Politik Ciceros*, Frankfurt Diss. 1931; W. Kroll, *Die Kultur der ciceronischen Zeit*, Leipzig, 1933, vol. I, pp. 10 ff.

[2] Polyb. VI, 11 ff.; Cic. *De Rep.* It was apparently with reference to the theory of the mixed constitution that Tacitus remarked: "Cunctas nationes et urbes populus aut primores aut singuli regunt; delecta ex iis et consociata rei publicae forma laudari facilius quam evenire, vel si evenit, haud diuturna esse potest" (*Ann.* IV, 33, 1). So far as Rome is concerned there is no gainsaying this remark.

admitted by the very supporters of that régime.[1] It ought, however, to be added that the ascendancy of the nobility must have been established without straining the constitution, for observers so divergent in standpoint and opinion as Cicero and Sallust agree that the Middle Republic was, in the main, a period of concord and model government.[2]

Although all Roman citizens had the vote and, in theory at least, could vote as they would, there was not complete sovereignty of the People; for, as has been seen, it was only People and Magistrate together that constituted the sovereign electorate and legislative power. Furthermore, a great many plebeians were the clients of the nobles, and as such were expected to follow at the polls the auctoritas of their patrons, who, until the secret ballot was introduced, were in a position to exercise some pressure on the voting of their clients.[3] On the other hand, it seems that the power of the People became diminished by acquiescence no less than by usurpation. During the late third and early second centuries B.C. Rome had chiefly to face problems of warfare and foreign policy which, as a matter of established constitutional practice, had to be dealt with by the Senate and the senior magistrates; and, if these were properly handled, there was little or no need at all to refer such problems to an Assembly of the People. It is true the People had reserved to it the right of declaring war, but the history of the beginning of the Second Macedonian War shows how the People could be induced to follow senatorial policy.[4] The Senate passed its resolutions which the People did not always find it necessary to ratify, so that, by acquiescence, the decrees of the Senate obtained the force of law.[5]

Another factor that greatly contributed to the increase of the Senate's power was the transformation of the tribunate. When the Struggle of the Orders was over, the tribunes ceased to be the champions of the under-privileged, and became the allies of the

[1] Cic. De Rep. II, 56. Cf. Polyb. VI, 13, 8.

[2] Cic. De Rep. I, 34; 70; De Leg. II, 23; III, 12; Pro Sest. 137; Sallust, Cat. 9; Jug. 41; Hist. I, 11 M.

[3] Cf. above, p. 20.

[4] See Livy XXXI, 6 ff. Cf. M. Holleaux in C.A.H. VIII, pp. 164 f.

[5] Sallust, Hist. III, 48, 16 M: Magna illa consulum imperia et patrum decreta vos exequendo rata efficitis, Quirites, ultroque licentiam in vos auctum atque adiutum properatis. Cf. ib. I, 72 M. See also T. Frank in C.A.H. VIII, p. 359.

ruling class, to which indeed many tribunes belonged.[1] The tribunician veto served the Senate well as an effective check both on the Assembly and on the Executive, and, it must be added, it was the only really effective check the Roman constitution of the Middle Republic possessed.[2] From a constitutional point of view, the alliance between the Senate and the tribunate was perhaps the most solid foundation for the senatorial supremacy in the State. In view of the fact that plebiscita and leges were equally binding, it was of prime importance that bills introduced to the Concilium Plebis by the tribunes were previously discussed and approved by the Senate.[3] Thus the centre of power was gradually shifted to the advantage of the Senate. It is noteworthy that during the century between the tribunate of C. Flaminius in 232 B.C., who, without consulting the Senate and against its opposition, carried a plebiscitum which provided for the distribution of the Ager Gallicus to Roman citizens,[4] and the tribunate of Ti. Gracchus, there do not seem to have been attempts to challenge the authority of the Senate.[5] Hannibal's invasion and the wars in the East probably arrested the development of Rome towards democracy.

In so far as institutions are concerned, it was the Senate that ruled Rome at that time; but the counsels of the Senate itself were swayed by a comparatively small group of the nobiles, the aristocracy of office, prominent among whom were the consulars to whom the procedure of the Senate gave practical advantages.

The nobility of the Late Republic is sometimes described by modern scholars as "the privileged class".[6] This description is true

[1] See the interesting passage in Livy x, 37, 9 ff.

[2] See Cic. *De Leg.* III, 23; Livy IV, 48, 6. Cf. above, pp. 22 f.

[3] Cf. T. Frank, *C.A.H.* VIII, p. 367.

[4] See Polyb. II, 21, 7 f. Cf. T. Frank, *C.A.H.* VII, p. 806; and F. Münzer, PW, VI, col. 2496, *s.v.* Flaminius (2). See also Livy XXI, 63, 2 f.

[5] But there were in the second century B.C. attempts to challenge the position of the nobility, as for example by Cato the Elder (consul in 195, died in 149 B.C.) or C. Cassius Longinus (consul in 171 B.C.; for whom see Münzer, *Röm. Adelsparteien*, pp. 219 ff.). The Gabinian and Cassian Ballot Laws (of 139 and 137 B.C.) were also a blow to the aristocracy, see above, p. 20, and below, p. 50.

[6] See, e.g., W. Schur, Homo novus, *Bonner Jahrbücher*, CXXXIV (1929), pp. 54–5; H. Strasburger in PW, XVII, col. 1226, *s.v.* Novus homo. Mommsen's views are too well known to need particular references.

only in so far as "privilege" means advantage. If, however, "privilege" means superior legal status, the nobiles enjoyed no privileges, except such distinctions as the ius imaginum and the toga praetexta, which all the curule magistrates enjoyed,[1] and the front seats in the theatre, which were reserved for the senatorial and equestrian orders.[2] Unlike the nobility of some other countries who enjoyed privileges with little or no power, the Roman nobiles possessed power without privileges. The privileges that the old patriciate enjoyed were almost entirely swept away, only to make way for the formation of the new nobilitas, whose political and social supremacy was in many respects similar to the supremacy of the patriciate, largely because its social structure and habits of thought and conduct remained essentially the same.

The supremacy of the noble families rested in part on their wealth, their large followings (clientelae), and the alliances with their peers,[3] and in part on other less material but, at Rome, none the less tangible factors, namely, auctoritas, dignitas, and nobilitas.

As has been said in the previous chapter, libertas comprised the right to enact laws and elect magistrates, but, for all that is known, the Romans did not, as a rule, interpret this as the right actually to govern themselves.[4] It was a deep-rooted habit of thought and behaviour with the Romans to consult competent advisers before undertaking anything of importance, whether in private or in public

---

[1] For the ius imaginum see Mommsen, *Staatsrecht* I[3], pp. 442 ff.; for the toga praetexta see I[3], pp. 418 ff.

[2] See *op. cit.* III, pp. 519 ff.

[3] Cf. R. Syme, *op. cit.* p. 10 ff.; F. Münzer, *op. cit.* pp. 225 ff.; M. Gelzer, *Nobilität*, pp. 43 ff. and *N. Jhb. kl. Alt.* XLV (1920), pp. 1 ff. *Rhet. ad Herenn.* I, 8, deserves notice in that it seems to contain the propaganda of the Populares in a nutshell. See also E. Wistrand, Gratus, grates, gratia, gratiosus, *Eranos* XXXIX (1941), pp. 22 ff.; and K. Hanell, Bemerkungen zu der politischen Terminologie des Sallustius, *Eranos* XLIII (1945), pp. 263–76.

[4] The innovations of the Gracchi and some other people will be discussed later. Livy III, 39, 8 (vicissitudo imperitandi quod unum exaequandae sit libertatis), and IV, 5, 5 (aequae libertatis est in vicem annuis magistratibus parere atque imperitare), do not contradict the above statement: the first passage stresses the idea of annual, as opposed to permanent, imperium; the second refers to the right of the plebs, as a body, to a share in the government; neither implies that every citizen has a right to govern. Cf. above, p. 11 n. 1.

life.[1] Libertas is not so much the right to act on one's own initiative as the freedom to choose an "auctor" whose "auctoritas" is freely accepted.[2] The Roman, quite rightly, recognized as a matter of course that some people were better qualified than others to become auctores, that is to say that they were worthy and able to suggest to others what they ought to do,[3] and, so long as the acceptance of auctoritas was not exacted, he also did not consider it incompatible with his freedom to follow their lead. Such a frame of mind, combined as it was with the fact that a political career of any significance demanded the possession of considerable wealth, made the existence of a ruling oligarchy (in the original sense and without any odious connotation) inescapable. In his *De Re Publica* (1, 47) Cicero put into the mouth of an interlocutor a description of States in which everyone is nominally free (istae civitates in quibus verbo sunt liberi omnes): "The People cast votes, elect commanders and magistrates, are canvassed for votes, and have Bills proposed to them; but they grant only what they would have to grant even if they were unwilling to do so, and they do not themselves possess what others seek to obtain from them. For they have no share in the Executive, in deliberation on public affairs, and in the courts of selected judges, all of which are given on the basis of ancestral

---

[1] On one occasion the censors struck the name of a senator off the Senate roll because he divorced his wife without first taking advice, see Val. Max. II, 9, 2. The prerogative of the Senate derived from the duty of every magistrate to take advice before doing anything new. The resolutions of the Senate were styled "consulta" even when they became decrees, and a vetoed resolution was nevertheless an "auctoritas".

[2] On auctoritas see R. Heinze, Auctoritas, *Hermes* LX (1925), pp. 348–66, and *Von den Ursachen der Grösse Roms* (1921), pp. 32 ff. I have not been able to procure the dissertation of Fritz Fürst, *Die Bedeutung der auctoritas im privaten und öffentlichen Leben der römischen Republik*, Marburg, 1934.

[3] Val. Max. III, 7, 3: Nasica contrariam orationem ordiri coepit. Obstrepente deinde plebe, tacete, quaeso, Quirites, inquit, plus ego enim quam vos quid rei publicae expediat intellego. Qua voce audita omnes pleno venerationis silentio maiorem auctoritatis eius quam suorum alimentorum respectum egerunt. Indicative of the importance of auctoritas in public life is also the episode related by Ascon. 22, 5 ff. c: when M. Scaurus was accused of having caused the revolt of the Allies, he went to the Forum and declared "Q. Varius Hispanus M. Scaurum principem senatus socios in arma ait convocasse; M. Scaurus princeps senatus negat; testis nemo est: utri vos, Quirites, convenit credere?" Qua voce—adds Asconius—ita omnium commutavit animos ut ab ipso etiam tribuno dimitteretur.

birth and wealth." This description fits the Roman Republic very well. The common citizen could not hold public offices (honores), unless the Romans had followed democratic Athens in attaching salaries to them. The real question was, not whether few only should govern, but who should be those few. And, in deciding this, dignitas and nobilitas were of prime importance.

Dignitas,[1] in a political sense, signifies either a particular office, or the prestige a Roman acquires through the tenure of an office.[2] It contains the notion of worthiness on the part of the person who possesses dignitas,[3] and of the respect inspired by merit on the part of the people.[4] But unlike honos, which is limited in time, and gloria, which is transient, dignitas attaches to a man permanently, and devolves upon his descendants.[5] And it is dignitas above all other things that endows a Roman with auctoritas.[6]

In the Late Republic (which is the earliest period from which literary evidence for the meaning of dignitas is extant) dignitas often denotes not only the respect freely inspired by a person's merit, but also—and in the first place—a title[7] to be given, through office, the allegedly deserved opportunity of exercising one's auctoritas in the State.[8] Dignitas assumes the meaning of an

---

[1] See especially Helmut Wegehaupt, *Die Bedeutung und Anwendung von dignitas in den Schriften der republikanischen Zeit*, Breslau Diss. 1932. Although on some points this dissertation seems to adopt too purely literary an approach to historical problems, it is a very valuable study. For different views see R. Reitzenstein, Die Idee des Prinzipats bei Cicero und Augustus, *Gött. Nach.* 1917, pp. 432 ff.; V. Ehrenberg, Monumentum Antiochenum, *Klio* XIX (1925), pp. 200–7; E. Remy, Dignitas cum otio, *Musée Belge* XXXII (1928), pp. 113 ff.

[2] Wegehaupt, *op. cit.* pp. 22 ff.

[3] *Ib.* pp. 9 ff. and p. 19.

[4] *Ib.* pp. 17 ff.

[5] *Ib.* pp. 12 ff.; Heinze, *Ursachen*, p. 30; Cic. *Pro Sest.* 21; *Pro Mur.* 15 ff.

[6] Cic. *De Inv.* II, 166: Dignitas, alicuius honesta et cultu et honore et verecundia digna auctoritas. See also Wegehaupt, *op. cit.* p. 12.

[7] Sallust, *Jug.* 85, 37: Nobilitas...omnes honores non ex merito sed quasi debitos a vobis repetit. Pliny, *Paneg.* 69: Iuvenibus clarissimae gentis debitum generi honorem...offerres.

[8] See Caes. *Bell. Civ.* I, 7, 7; 9, 2; III, 91, 2; Cic. *Ad Att.* VII, 11, 1; *Pro Lig.* 18. Very illuminating is also Sallust, *Cat.* 35, 3–4. Cf. Reitzenstein, *op. cit.* p. 434. For a somewhat different view see Wegehaupt, *op. cit.* p. 37.

influential position; it epitomizes the achievement of a person, or a person's ancestors, and, at the same time, forms the basis for further aspirations.[1]

Being inheritable, dignitas is closely allied with nobilitas. In fact, nobilitas originally was nothing but the respect for a person's ancestral dignitas.[2] Nobilitas meant renown gained through the display of virtus,[3] and, obviously, one who was "well-known" (nobilis) on account of his own, or his ancestors', virtus was considered to possess the worthiness (dignitas) to conduct public affairs. Since nobilitas and dignitas were considered inheritable, birth and name, even apart from wealth and relations, were important factors in politics. Under the Empire a satirist might ask, Stemmata quid faciunt,[4] and a philosopher might aver that genealogical trees made people known rather than noble.[5] Not so under the Republic. Names and pedigrees counted for much. A famous name might sway an election,[6] and one's ancestral "images" might, as it were, stand surety for one's worthiness.[7] Even Cicero's mastery of words fell short of disguising the fact that he was ill at ease before the dignitas of Appius Claudius.[8] And was it just extravagance on his part when the quaestor Caesar—as he then was—reminded the Romans that his family (at the moment in partial eclipse), being descended from Venus, partook of the reverence due to the gods?[9] Caesar must have known the sentiments of his fellow citizens.[10]

The supremacy and pre-eminence of the nobility was traditional, and, as such, might have been acceptable to the rest of the people, were it not for the fact that at Rome prestige meant power, and the

---

[1] Wegehaupt, op. cit. pp. 37, 41, 45 f.

[2] Cic. Pro Sest. 21; Heinze, Ursachen, p. 30.

[3] Cic. Ep. ad Hirt. frag. 3 (Purser): Cum enim nobilitas nihil aliud sit quam cognita virtus. See also Sallust, Jug. 85, 17.

[4] Juvenal, VIII, 1.   [5] Seneca, De Benef. III, 28, 2.

[6] Cic. In Pis. 2; II in Verr. V, 180.

[7] Sallust, Jug. 85, 29. Cf. Cic. De Leg. Agr. II, 100.

[8] See the very illuminating Ad Fam. III, 7, 4–5.   [9] Suet. Div. Jul. 6, 1.

[10] It is also noteworthy that C. Gracchus—qui unus maxime popularis fuit, Cic. De Dom. 24—said in the Assembly (Schol. Bob. 81, 20 St. = Malcovati, Orat. Rom. Frag. II, p. 139, no. 44): Si vellem aput vos verba facere et a vobis postulare, cum genere summo ortus essem... nec quisquam de P. Africani et Tiberi Gracchi familia nisi ego et puer restaremus, ut pateremini hoc tempore me quiescere ne a stirpe genus nostrum interiret, etc.

ambitious desire to enhance one's prestige gradually destroyed the harmony between the dignitas of some and the libertas of all.

All the nobiles had in common a strong impulse towards the assertion of their own dignitas. And since dignitas rested in the last resort on the tenure of public offices, the latter became the goal of that ambition, and the nobiles came to look upon the whole structure of the State from the standpoint of the honores. Cato the Elder, a self-made man, maintained that "Iure, lege, libertate, re publica communiter uti oportet; gloria atque honore, quomodo sibi quisque struxit".[1] The frame of mind of the younger Africanus, Cato's rival, must have been totally different, for he said: "Ex innocentia nascitur dignitas, ex dignitate honor, ex honore imperium, ex imperio libertas."[2] This libertas is not the libertas communis founded on aequae leges, but a sectional and exclusive libertas belonging to a Scipio and his like, to whom the attainment of honores and imperia was freedom, their own freedom, of course. And if that is how the nobles conceived of the relation between dignitas and libertas, the question arises whether in the long run the dignitas of the nobles could remain compatible with the communis libertas and aequae leges of the Roman People. For power was increasingly concentrated in the hands of the nobles, and "all power tends to corrupt".

During the second century the nobles held the chief magistracies, the military commands, the provinces, the treasury, the law-courts.[3] They enriched themselves by hook or by crook, evicted small holders from their land, and mismanaged public affairs. Although nobilitas originally meant distinction through service and merit, not blue blood, and as such its ranks could not in theory be closed, it hardened into an exclusive, arrogant, and complacent clique, jealous of its possessions, and determined to retain its power and to perpetuate its rule. Their dignitas came to mean reckless and unjust domination.[4]

Opposed to the rule of such an oligarchy were many of the dispossessed, who longed for economic security; many of the plain

[1] Malcovati, I, p. 218, no. 249.
[2] Ib. p. 241, no. 22. Cf. Cic. De Off. I, 13.
[3] See, e.g., Sallust, Jug. 31, 20; 41, 7; Cat. 39, 1 f.
[4] See C. Gracchus frag. 27, 45, 46 (Malcovati, II, pp. 133, 140); Sallust, Jug. 31; 41; 85; Cat. 11 ff.; Plut. Ti. Gracchus 8; Cic. II in Verr. v, 175.

citizens, who longed for an efficient and civil government; the more ambitious members of the rising Equestrian Order, who longed for political power; and such aristocrats as had fallen on evil times, or were for some reason or other at variance with those in power, and longed for dignitas.

When their power and the title to it were challenged, the ruling oligarchy, perhaps with complacent self-praise, or in an attempt to give their social and political supremacy an air of moral superiority, were pleased to consider and call themselves Optimates;[1] their opponents contemptuously called them Pauci, Factio paucorum, and the like.[2] Around the core of the nobilitas there were gathered together various supporters of the established order; nevertheless, they did not form a party in the modern sense of the word, nor had they a political programme distinctively their own.[3] Yet the majority of the Optimates had a common cause, and the identity, in the last resort, of their interests produced among them a certain cohesion despite all personal frictions, and a certain continuity of policy amid all the inconsistencies of a deliberate opportunism.[4]

The Populares were even less cohesive and less possessed of a common political programme than their opponents the Optimates. The name of Populares was given in antiquity to all manner of people with different, and sometimes divergent, aims and motives: reformers[5] and adventurers, upstarts and aristocrats, moderates and

---

[1] The earliest instance of "optimates" in a political sense is *Rhet. ad Herenn.* IV, 45. For the date of this treatise see W. Warde Fowler, *Journ. Phil.* X (1882), pp. 197 ff., who assigns it to the mid-eighties of the first century B.C. H. Strasburger's assumption (PW, XVIII, col. 774) that the words of C. Gracchus "Pessumi Tiberium fratrem meum optimum interfecerunt" (Charis. *G.L.* I, 240, 16 = frag. 16, Malcovati, II, p. 130) presuppose the currency of "optimates" as a political term, is probable but not certain. The antithesis in the quoted sentence may be self-contained, "pessumi" being evoked by "optimum" without at the same time foreshadowing the term optimates.

[2] C. Gracchus, frag. 52 (Malcovati, II, p. 142); Sallust, *Cat.* 39, 1; *Jug.* 31, 1–4; 42, 1; *Hist.* III, 48, 3 and 6 M; Cic. *Pro Sest.* 96.

[3] In his *Pro Sestio* Cicero, for obvious reasons, stretches unduly the meaning of Optimates, and neither his explanation of the term nor the exposition of policy can be accepted at their face value.

[4] See Cicero's remarks on opportunism in *Ad Fam.* I, 9, 21, and *Pro Planc.* 94. They would apply to many a politician in Cicero's times.

[5] Although the difference between them and the other Populares since Marius is only too obvious, the Gracchi cannot, for that reason, be excluded

D

extremists. What they all had in common was their tactics, namely, to seek the support of the Populus, hence their name. The episode of the Gracchi showed that the Popular Assembly could be a weighty counterpoise to the power of the nobility, entrenched as it was behind the authority of the Senate. But unlike the Gracchi who were, to some extent, genuine—even if misguided—democrats, the Populares on the whole thought of the People as a means, and not an end.[1] Their prime object was to break the monopoly of power of the ruling oligarchy. Hence the incessant invective against the dominatio, potentia, superbia, and libido of the pauci, the factio potentium, and the appeal to the People to restore its freedom.[2] The Optimates, for their part, countered their opponents with the assertion that it was they who protected freedom and republicanism.[3]

For the present purpose there is no need to follow the tortuous and chequered politics of Rome in their entire length. They will be discussed here only in so far as they bear, directly or indirectly, on the idea of libertas, and may conveniently be grouped under several major heads.

2. MAJOR POINTS AT ISSUE

(a) Senatus Auctoritas

A very illuminating piece of evidence for the character of the constitution the Optimates had in mind when they professed to defend the Republic is contained in Cicero's Pro Sestio (96–143). Accepting the provocative challenge "quae esset natio optimatium?"

from among the Populares, as they are by H. Last, C.A.H. IX, pp. 96, 114, 137, because in antiquity the Gracchi were regarded as model Populares; Cic. De Dom. 24: C. Gracchus qui unus maxime popularis fuit; Pro Sest. 105: Gracchos aut Saturninum aut quemquam illorum veterum qui populares habebantur. It is noteworthy that Cicero, Pro Sest. 103, begins his account of the Populares with L. Cassius, the initiator of the Lex Cassia Tabellaria (137 B.C.). Likewise, Sallust places the Gracchi at the beginning of the "mos partium et factionum", Jug. 41–2.

[1] Cf. H. Last, C.A.H. IX, pp. 137 ff.; W. Ensslin, Die Demokratie und Rom, Philologus LXXXII (1927), p. 327.

[2] See, e.g., Sallust, Jug. 31; 41–2; 85; Hist. I, 55; III, 48 M. More about those slogans will be said later.

[3] Sallust, Hist. III, 48, 22 M: Neque eos (sc. factionem nobilitatis) pudet, vindices uti se ferunt libertatis. Cic. Pro Sest. 136: Concludam illud de optimatibus eorumque principibus ac rei publicae defensoribus. Cf. also Pro Sest. 98.

Cicero outlined an idealized version of the political programme of the Optimates, a version, no doubt, calculated, as it were, for external consumption but nevertheless equally revealing by virtue of its contents and omissions.

Two passages of this lengthy exposition deserve especial attention:

Quid est igitur propositum his rei publicae gubernatoribus, quod intueri, et quo cursum derigere debeant? Id quod est praestantissimum, maximeque optabile omnibus sanis et bonis et beatis: cum dignitate otium. Hoc qui volunt, omnes optimates; qui efficiunt, summi viri et conservatores civitatis putantur.... Huius autem otiosae dignitatis haec fundamenta sunt, haec membra, quae tuenda principibus et vel capitis periculo defendenda sunt: religiones, auspicia, potestates magistratuum, senatus auctoritas, leges, mos maiorum, iudicia, iuris dictio, fides, provinciae, socii, imperii laus, res militaris, aerarium (98).

Concludam illud de optimatibus eorumque principibus ac rei publicae defensoribus.... Haec est una via, mihi credite, et laudis et dignitatis et honoris: a bonis viris sapientibus et bene natura constitutis laudari et diligi; nosse discriptionem civitatis a maioribus nostris sapientissime constitutam, qui cum regum potestatem non tulissent ita magistratus annuos creaverunt ut consilium senatus rei publicae praeponerent sempiternum, deligerentur autem in id consilium ab universo populo, aditusque in illum summum ordinem omnium civium industriae ac virtuti pateret; senatum rei publicae custodem, praesidem, propugnatorem collocaverunt; huius ordinis auctoritate uti magistratus, et quasi ministros gravissimi consilii esse voluerunt; senatum autem ipsum proximorum ordinum splendorem confirmare, plebis libertatem et commoda tueri atque augere voluerunt. Haec qui pro virili parte defendunt optimates sunt, cuiuscumque sunt ordinis; qui autem praecipue suis cervicibus tanta munia atque rem publicam sustinent, hi semper habiti sunt optimatium principes, auctores et conservatores civitatis (136–8).

The main points of this tendentious statement reveal a consistent line of thought: the goal of the Optimates is otium cum dignitate,[1] otium for the people, dignitas for the aristocrats;[2] the propertied classes are the supporters of this otiosa dignitas—an echo, no doubt,

---

[1] A closer examination of this phrase must be reserved for later notice.

[2] *Pro Sest.* 104: Nunc iam nihil est quod populus a delectis principibusque dissentiat; nec flagitat rem ullam neque novarum rerum est cupidus, et *otio suo et dignitate optimi cuiusque* et universae rei publicae gloria delectatur. Cf. *De Rep.* I, 52: Quibus (*sc.* optimatibus) rem publicam tuentibus beatissimos esse populos necesse est, vacuos omni cura et cogitatione aliis permisso otio suo, quibus id tuendum est neque committendum ut sua commoda populus neglegi a primoribus putet. Cf. also *Pro Sest.* 137.

of the concordia ordinum[1]—and the Senate its chief constitutional instrument. It is noteworthy that freedom of the people is either entirely ignored, as in the enumeration of the foundations on which the otiosa dignitas rests (98), or perfunctorily mentioned (137), and even so it is made to depend on the authority of the Senate, whereas the celebrated guardians of freedom, the tribunicium auxilium and provocatio, are not so much as mentioned. The description of the Roman *patrios politeia*—civitas a maioribus nostris sapientissime constituta (137)—is also very significant: the Senate is represented as always having been the dominating element of the constitution;[2] it is the guardian and champion of the State, the annual magistrates are its ministers, and the plebs is dependent on it for its liberty and welfare. In Cicero's view, the constitution of the free State centred round and depended upon the authority of the Senate.

Essentially the same tendency is present in Cicero's *De Re Publica* and *De Legibus*.[3] In the *De Re Publica* Cicero asserts that the vetus res publica attained the ideal of a mixed form of government,[4] the nature of which consists in "an even balance of rights, duties, and functions (ius, officium, munus), so that the magistrates have enough potestas; the council of eminent citizens, enough auctoritas; and the people, enough libertas".[5] But when Cicero translates the theoretical typology of governmental forms into practical terms of Roman constitutional law, and illustrates it with a historical example, the "even balance" becomes a preponderance of the Senate. For this is how he describes the vetus res publica:

Tenuit igitur hoc in statu senatus rem publicam temporibus illis, ut in populo libero pauca per populum, pleraque senatus auctoritate et instituto ac more gererentur, atque uti consules potestatem haberent tempore dumtaxat annuam, genere ipso ac iure regiam (II, 56).

Here, as in the *Pro Sestio*, the centre of gravity of the whole system is to be found in the Senate. Likewise, in the *De Legibus* (III, 10) Cicero lays down "eius (*sc.* senatus) decreta rata sunto".

[1] Cf. H. Strasburger, *Concordia Ordinum*.

[2] Cf. *De Dom.* 130, where auctoritas senatus means gubernatio senatus.

[3] More will be said of Cicero's political writings in the subsequent chapter. For the present, the barest outline will suffice.

[4] *De Rep.* I, 70; *De Leg.* II, 23.

[5] *De Rep.* II, 57. Cf. I, 45; 69.

It is worth pointing out that Cicero's description of the Roman constitution, and particularly that found in the *Pro Sestio*, bears a remarkable resemblance to Sulla's constitution. Sulla invested the Senate with the supreme control of the State,[1] and his Lex Cornelia de xx quaestoribus gave the Senate that representative character to which Cicero attached great importance.[2]

There is also another point to be observed. In theory the advantage of the mixed form of government is that it combines the merits of the three simple forms and at the same time prevents the degeneration of monarchy into tyranny, aristocracy into oligarchy, democracy into ochlocracy (*De Rep.* I, 69). But the whole tenor of the *De Re Publica* seems to suggest that Cicero's true motive in advocating what he believed to be a mixed constitution was the realization that that form of government was the only practical compromise which, on the one hand, allowed for a strong government while keeping absolutism at bay, and, on the other, made it possible to keep the people satisfied while it precluded democracy.[3] In fact, democracy is to be eliminated at all costs,[4] for behind the rule of the sovereign people lurks the would-be tyrant.[5]

It seems, therefore, to judge from the *Pro Sestio* and the *De Re Publica*, that Cicero's ideal constitution was meant to be, in the first place, an aristocratic republic, centred round the pre-eminent Senate, and hostile to absolutism and democracy alike. And if this is true of the moderate Cicero it is, with one proviso, a fortiori true of the extremist Optimates. Cicero, as a consistent homo novus, maintained that the ruling class represented in the Senate should be

---

[1] See H. Last, *C.A.H.* IX, pp. 280 ff. and pp. 286 ff.

[2] See *C.A.H.* IX, p. 287; PW, IV, col. 1559, 53 ff. Cic. *Pro Sest.* 137: Deligerentur autem in id consilium ab universo populo. *De Leg.* III, 27: Ex iis autem qui magistratum ceperunt, quod senatus efficitur, populare sane neminem in summum locum nisi per populum venire sublata cooptatione censoria.

[3] *De Rep.* I, 52: Sic inter infirmitatem unius temeritatemque multorum medium optimates possederunt locum, quo nihil potest esse moderatius.

[4] *Ib.* II, 39: Quod semper in re publica tenendum est ne plurimum valeant plurimi. And:...neque excluderetur (multitudo) suffragiis, ne superbum esset, nec valeret nimis, ne esset periculosum.

[5] *Ib.* I, 65 ff., particularly 68: Ex hac nimia licentia (populi), quam illi solam libertatem putant, ait ille (Plato) ut ex stirpe quadam existere et quasi nasci tyrannum.

drawn from all quarters according to personal merit,[1] whereas the Optimates, on the whole, showed an intransigent exclusiveness. But the difference between Cicero and the ruling nobility concerns the composition, not the function, of the Senate. The Senate was, and was looked upon as, the stronghold of the aristocracy in their struggle to retain their power.

It is a remarkable thing that, although its social background was by no means uniform, the Senate, on the whole, remained largely pro-Optimate in sentiment, except on such occasions as those on which the membership of the Senate was drastically changed, as for example by Cinna. It is perhaps not unduly cynical to say that two senators, one of whom sided with the Optimates and the other with the Populares, had more in common than two Populares, of whom one was a senator and the other was not.[2] It is therefore not at all surprising that the alliance between the Optimates and the Senate remained firm, and throughout the period the Optimates went on invoking the senatus auctoritas,[3] just as the Populares invoked the libertas populi Romani.

(b) Leges Agrariae

The social reform of the Gracchi was in many respects relevant to freedom, but the state of the available evidence makes it almost impossible to ascertain to what extent and in what manner "libertas" figured in the advocacy of the various proposals.[4] It would seem a reasonable assumption that the Leges Agrariae and Frumentariae (and perhaps also the Leges Iudiciariae[5]) were championed in the name of aequitas and aequum ius which, as has been seen, form an essential aspect of libertas but lend themselves to various interpretations.

---

[1] Pro Sest. 137; De Rep. I, 51. Cf. below, pp. 52 ff.

[2] In this respect it may be of interest to compare Cic. Phil. x, 3.

[3] See, e.g., Sallust, Hist. I, 77 M (Oratio Philippi); Cic. Pro Rab. perd. reo, 2; Pro Sest. 98; 137; 143; and the Philippics, passim. See also Cic. Brut. 164. It is noteworthy that Livius Drusus "ob eximiam adversus Gracchos operam 'patronus senatus' dictus", Suet. Tib. 3, 2. For Livius Drusus the younger see Cic. Pro Mil. 16; De Orat. I, 24; Diod. Sic. XXXVII, 10.

[4] Kloesel, Libertas, pp. 42–4, maintains that in the struggle for the Leges Agrariae "libertas" was the watchword of the plebeians, but the ancient authorities he cites, besides being partly irrelevant, fall short of proving his statement beyond doubt.   [5] See Flor. II, 1.

The underlying idea of the economic measures proposed by the Gracchi was that the people were entitled to a share in the common property, be it the State domain or the treasury. Tiberius Gracchus is said to have argued that it was only just that common property should be divided between the citizens—τὰ κοινὰ κοινῇ διανέμεσθαι.[1] In like manner the poor Romans complained that they were robbed of their share in the very land that had been acquired by their military exploits.[2] This coincides with the speech of Tiberius Gracchus—summarized by Plutarch, *Ti. Gracchus* 9, 5 f. —in which he complained that "the men who fight and die for Italy have a share in the air and light, but nothing else...they fight and die for the luxury and wealth of others, and, while they are called masters of the world, have not a single clod of their own".[3] The claim that a citizen was entitled to a home on the land he helped to acquire is perhaps echoed in Sallust, "Nam quid a Pyrrho Hannibale Philippoque et Antiocho defensum est aliud quam libertas et *suae cuique sedes* neu cui nisi legibus pareremus?" (*Hist.* I, 55, 4 M).

A faint echo of the propaganda of the Gracchi is perhaps heard, through Livy, in Florus (II, 1):

Inerat omnibus (sc. legibus agrariis, frumentariis, iudiciariis) species aequitatis: quid tam iustum enim quam recipere plebem sua a patribus, ne populus gentium victor orbisque possessor extorris aris ac focis ageret? Quid tam aequum quam inopem populum vivere ex aerario suo? Quid ad ius libertatis aequandae magis efficax quam ut senatu regente provincias ordinis equestris auctoritas saltem iudiciorum regno niteretur?

---

[1] Appian, *Bell. Civ.* I, 11.   [2] *Ib.* I, 10, 4.

[3] F. Taeger, *Untersuchungen zur römischen Geschichte und Quellenkunde: Tiberius Gracchus*, pp. 16 ff., who maintains that Tiberius's speech reflects the tenets of Stoicism which Tiberius learned from Blossius, seems to read too much into Plutarch's text. The main point of the speech is not that "es ist... ein grauenhafter Verstoss gegen die goettliche Weltordnung wenn die 'bestiae Italiae' die einfachsten, also gottgewollten Rechte geniessen, nicht aber die Buerger der Weltherrin Rom" (*op. cit.* pp. 17 f.), but that the citizens who fight and die for the Italian land "have not a single clod of earth that is their own" whereas all the fruits of their exploits fall to the rich. Had Gracchus really to look to the Stoic ethic for the idea of elementary justice which forms the essence of the very notions aequum ius and res publica? And as to Blossius, grave doubts about the Stoic origin of his democratic views have been expressed by D. R. Dudley, Blossius of Cumae, *J.R.S.* XXXI (1941), pp. 95 ff., who traces Blossius' democratic views to the Campanian tradition rather than to Stoicism.

All this perhaps goes farther back than to Livy's own reflections, since Livy, in some form or other, was acquainted with the pronouncements of the Gracchi.[1]

In so far as the Leges Agrariae and Frumentariae involved the distribution of common property, and not the improvement of civic rights, it was entirely in keeping with the ideas of res publica and aequum ius, if aequitas rather than libertas was paramount in the advocacy of the new measures.[2] But in view of the scarcity of first-hand evidence nothing can be asserted with certainty. If, however, the above conjecture concerning the Leges Agrariae is right, libertas in the propaganda of the Populares would seem to have had a purely political meaning.

The Optimates, no doubt, were unwilling to contemplate a reform of the tenure of the ager publicus because they and their followers held most of it. Gracchus must have known the sentiment prevalent in the Senate, and he probably knew that he could not expect a favourable reception for his Land Bill there. This may be the reason why he sought advice privately[3] but did not submit his Bill to discussion in the Senate prior to its introduction in the Assembly. This departure from the established constitutional practice, which was a blow at the senatus auctoritas, may have been one of the reasons why the Senate opposed the Bill. Gracchus made a last attempt to conciliate the Senate by submitting his proposals to it for discussion.[4] But the attempt failed, and Gracchus resorted to extreme means.

---

[1] Compare Flor. II, 2, 3, with Plut. *Ti. Gracchus* 9, 5 f.

[2] It is true that economic independence is a necessary prerequisite of freedom but if one applies this statement to the Late Roman Republic and infers from it the possible phraseology used by the advocates of the Leges Agrariae—as does Kloesel, *op. cit.* p. 43, following Poehlmann—the question arises whether or not this is projecting modern ideas into antiquity. As has been seen, the elementary meaning of libertas at Rome was the status of a person who is not a slave and who is a Roman citizen. And it is doubtful whether in the Gracchan period, when, on the one hand, nexum had already been abolished, and, on the other, the poorest citizen enjoyed rights denied to the richest foreigner or freedman, the interdependence between economic welfare and libertas would be as easily grasped as it is nowadays.

[3] Cic. *Acad. Prior.* II, 13; Plut. *Ti. Gracchus* 9, 1.

[4] Plut. *Ti. Gracchus* 11, 1–4.

(c) Popular Sovereignty

To crush the unyielding opposition of Octavius, Tiberius Gracchus resorted to an unheard-of measure: he had Octavius deposed by a vote of the Concilium Plebis. A few points of the speech in which he justified his conduct before the people are preserved in Plutarch, *Ti. Gracchus* 15 (cf. Appian, *Bell. Civ.* I, 12), and call for attention.

Two main arguments stand out in this speech: (*a*) A tribune is sacrosanct only in so far as he serves the people; therefore, should he wrong the people, he deprives himself of his office and of inviolability (§ 2). (*b*) Since it is the people who invest the tribune with power, the people can also divest him of his power, if he acts against the people's will, and they can transfer the power to another person (§§ 7–8).[1]

This theory, even if it were—as it presumably could not be—confined to the tribunate and the Concilium Plebis, would have sufficed, if adopted, to revolutionize by virtue of its two far-reaching implications the entire system of government at Rome.

As has been seen, the essential feature of the Roman magistracy was that while the magistrate was elected by popular vote he was not obliged to act as a delegate of the electorate. The moment a magistrate entered upon his office he acted, within the limits set by the constitution, by magisterial prerogative, and not by popular consent. The People chose the man, but they could not control his actions. The Senate, in later times, could express its opinion that a certain action was "contra rem publicam", but the People never could pass a vote of censure on a magistrate. Now the deposition of Octavius by popular vote, on the ground that he acted contrary to the will of the People, implied that the tribune at least was henceforward to be a mere delegate of the People. Government by the will of the

---

[1] It is apparently under the influence of F. Kern's "Gottesgnadentum und Widerstandsrecht" that Taeger, *op. cit.* pp. 18 ff. (see also p. 125 n. 162), finds in the speech of Gracchus the theory of "Widerstandsrecht". But obviously Gracchus mentioned Tarquin's expulsion, as well as the penalty inflicted on unchaste Vestals, only to adduce examples and precedents of disregarding sanctity in the case of wrongdoers, and not to propound the right of resistance to tyrants. He was concerned with the formal deposition of an inviolable magistrate who acted within his prerogative, which is a case entirely different from resistance to unjust rule.

sovereign Assembly would have been substituted for government
by magisterial prerogative supported by the senatus auctoritas.
And in view of the fact that the tribunes had the standing of maior
potestas with regard to all magistracies except the dictatorship,[1] the
implications of this innovation for the entire system of government
were far-reaching indeed.

Secondly, the principle of par potestas was interpreted in the way
that if colleagues disagreed the No was always stronger than the
Aye.[2] If, however, a tribune could override the veto of another
tribune by a decision of the sovereign Assembly, the institution of
par potestas, with regard to the tribunate at any rate, was undermined. It may be that Tiberius did not attack the principle of par
potestas explicitly,[3] but whatever he said or meant, his action
undermined that principle.

Overriding decision by the People was unusual, but not new. In
148 B.C. Scipio was elected consul contrary to the Lex Annalis, and
entrusted by popular vote with the command in Africa contrary to
the provision that the "provinciae" were to be distributed by lot.[4]
But there is a cardinal difference between the procedure in 148 and
133 B.C. In the former case the People—with the connivance of the
Senate—suspended the law, whereas in the latter, they deposed
a magistrate. And if the People always had the power to enact or
repeal laws, they never had the right to interfere with the magisterial prerogative, except by means of general laws. The government
of Rome, although elected by all the full citizens, was essentially
non-democratic because, once in power, it was largely independent
of the popular will. And this is why Gracchus's measure was
regarded as revolutionary.

Similarly, the idea that the tribunes were obliged always to follow
the People's will was obsolete rather than new.[5] But by reviving
this old principle in new circumstances, and by using it as a justification for the deposition of a tribune, Gracchus introduced a new

[1] See above, p. 23.   [2] See above, p. 22 n. 3.
[3] As Plutarch, *Ti. Gracchus* 11, 6, seems to suggest. Cf. H. Last, *C.A.H.* ix,
p. 27.
[4] Appian, *Lib.* 112.
[5] Polyb. vi, 16, 5: ὀφείλουσιν ἀεὶ ποιεῖν οἱ δήμαρχοι τὸ δοκοῦν τῷ δήμῳ
καὶ μάλιστα στοχάζεσθαι τῆς τούτου βουλήσεως. But this applies to the
period of the Struggle of the Orders.

element into the constitutional practice. It is hard to say whether or not his conduct was lawful, but it certainly was new and revolutionary, a nova res indeed.

Without the slightest sympathy for his opponents, one cannot help thinking that there was, in a sense, some truth in their allegation that Gracchus was seeking a "regnum". For if the Assembly was to be sovereign in the full sense of the word; if it was to have power over laws and tribunes alike; and if tribunes could be re-elected for any indefinite number of successive years, a tribune enjoying the favour of the urban populace would possess an incalculable and uncontrollable power.

In subsequent years several measures closely allied to the principle of popular sovereignty were proposed or passed. Gaius Gracchus introduced (and withdrew at his mother's request to spare Octavius) a measure providing that if the People deposed a magistrate, such magistrate should not be allowed to hold another office.[1] L. Cassius Longinus, tribune in 104 B.C., "plures leges ad minuendam nobilitatis potentiam tulit, in quibus hanc etiam ut quem populus damnasset cuive imperium abrogasset in senatu ne esset".[2] In the same year the Lex Domitia de sacerdotiis provided that Pontiffs and Augurs should be elected by a special Assembly and not, as hitherto, merely coopted by the colleges.[3] It is noteworthy that Sulla repealed this law, and Caesar had it re-enacted.[4] In 100 B.C., Antonius, pleading for C. Norbanus who was accused of high treason, said "Si magistratus in populi Romani potestate esse debent, quid Norbanum accusas, cuius tribunatus voluntati paruit civitatis?"[5] That was not the orthodox Roman view. In 67 B.C., Gabinius, when his proposal to grant Pompey a command against the Pirates was vetoed by a fellow tribune, resorted to the measure that Tiberius Gracchus applied against his opponent Octavius. Gabinius put to the vote a proposal to depose his unyielding colleague, who withdrew his veto only after seventeen Tribes had already voted for his deposition (Ascon. 72 C). About the same time, the tribune Cornelius introduced a bill (ne quis nisi per populum legibus solveretur) which, if passed in its

---

[1] Plut. C. Gracchus 4, 1–2.
[2] Ascon. 78, 10 f. C.
[3] See Cic. De Lege Agr. II, 19, and Ascon. 79, 25 f. C.
[4] See C.A.H. IX, pp. 163 f., 288, 487.
[5] Cic. De Orat. II, 167.

original form might have reasserted popular sovereignty in respect of proposals to give dispensation to individuals (Ascon. 58, 3 ff. c).[1]

(d) Leges Tabellariae

In view of the fact that the Assembly proved to be for the Populares a valuable instrument with which to attack the power of the Optimates, great importance was attached to the secret ballot, which was designed to secure the independence of the voters. It appears from Cicero—our chief authority for the Leges Tabellariae —that the secret ballot was championed in the name of libertas.[2] Cicero himself, realizing on the one hand that the secret ballot had an adverse effect on the predominance of the nobility, and on the other that the People considered secrecy of voting as an essential constituent of their freedom, proposed in his De Legibus (III, 33 f.) a naïve compromise to the effect that voting by ballots should continue but the ballots should be shown "optimo cuique et gravissimo civi" before they were cast. He added that that procedure would give the people "an appearance of liberty" while the auctoritas bonorum would be secured. Cicero's attempt to deal with the problem shows the importance that the People attached to the secret ballot[3] and the unwillingness of the Optimates to concede it. The Optimates opposed the Leges Tabellariae because uncontrolled voting might put an end to their influence on the electorate.[4] Presumably for the very same reason, the Populares insisted on uncontrolled voting.[5]

(e) Tribunicia Potestas

The careers of the Gracchi and of Saturninus—to quote only the most notable names—proved that the tribunate might become a formidable opponent of the Senate and the nobility. Once again,

[1] The idea of popular sovereignty is also vaguely expressed in Sallust, Jug. 31, 11 and 20; Hist. I, 55, 11 and 24 M; III, 48, 15–16 M; Cic. Pro Rab. perd. reo, 5.

[2] Cic. Pro Sest. 103; De Lege Agr. II, 4; De Leg. III, 39. The agitation for free suffrage is reflected to some extent in Livy II, 56, 3; IV, 3, 7; IV, 43, 12; VI, 40, 7.

[3] Cf. also Cic. Pro Planc. 16; Pro Corn. ap. Ascon. 78, 2 c.

[4] Cic. Pro Sest. 103; Brut. 97; De Amic. 41; De Leg. III, 34 and 36.

[5] Plut. Marius 4; Cic. De Leg. III, 35 and 38.

as during the Struggle of the Orders, the tribunate was looked upon as a revolutionary magistracy, and the Optimates imputed to it all the troubles of civil strife.[1] It was, therefore, naturally an essential part of Sulla's settlement to render the tribunate harmless. Sulla crippled the tribunate in two ways: first, by enacting that the tenure of the tribunate should permanently disqualify from holding any other office, he made the tribunate unattractive to enterprising and ambitious politicians. Secondly, he limited the scope of the tribunician intercessio,[2] and either restricted or abolished the right of the tribunes to initiate legislation.[3] By so doing, Sulla secured the position of the Senate, but at the same time he provided the opponents of his settlement with an appealing catchword for their agitation. For just as Sulla's measures concerning the tribunate were not isolated enactments but part of a comprehensive scheme, so the struggle of the Populares for the restoration of the tribunician prerogative aimed at the overthrow of Sulla's entire system.

In regard to the restoration of the tribunician powers there was, as might be expected, much talk about libertas and servitium on the part of the Populares.[4] But their agitation on that occasion shows that the freedom of the people was not the real aim of the Populares.

Licinius Macer agitated in 73 B.C. for the restoration of the tribunician power on the ground that it was "the guardian of all the rights of the Plebs".[5] This description of the tribunate is traditional,[6] but it usually applied to the ius auxilii, of which Sulla did not deprive the tribunes, not to political power. The tribunate originally was the guardian of personal rights, but Macer dismissed the idea that personal rights sufficed to constitute freedom.[7] His real object was "opes nobilitatis pellere dominatione" and he regretted that he held

[1] Sallust, *Hist.* I, 77, 14 M; Cic. *De Leg.* III, 19–22; Flor. II, 1, 1.

[2] Cic. *II in Verr.* I, 155. Cf. H. Last, *C.A.H.* IX, p. 292.

[3] See Livy, Epit. LXXXIX; Cic. *De Leg.* III, 22; *C.A.H.* IX, p. 293.

[4] See especially the speech of the tribune Licinius Macer, Sallust, *Hist.* III, 48 M. And also *ibid.* I, 55 and II, 24.

[5] Sallust, *Hist.* III, 48, 1 M: Vindices paravisset (plebs) omnis iuris sui tribunos plebis. *Ib.* § 12: Vis tribunicia, telum a maioribus libertati paratum.

[6] See above, p. 26.

[7] Sallust, *Hist.* III, 48, 26 M: Verum occupavit nescio quae vos (sc. Quirites) torpedo...cunctaque praesenti ignavia mutavistis, abunde libertatem rati, scilicet quia tergis abstinetur et huc ire licet et illuc, munera ditium dominorum.

but "a shadow of a magistracy".[1] He obviously wished for the unrestricted intercessio and ius agendi, but he spoke of the people's freedom. Similarly, Aemilius Lepidus, who started the agitation for the restoration of the tribunician powers in 78 B.C., is said to have stated that the choice lay between servitium and dominatio.[2] The frequent appeals to freedom on the part of the Populares seem to have been an expedient which served to stir up the passions of the People, who were reluctant to plunge into political strife.[3] It is also unlikely that the demand to restore the pristine powers of the tribunes was meant to further the power of the People.[4] It is noteworthy that Cicero, whose personal experience made him no friend of the tribunate, argued that, on balance, it was in the interests of the Senate to retain the tribunician powers undiminished,[5] and there is much to be said for this view.

It would, therefore, seem that the insistence of the Populares on the restoration of the tribunician powers was in the first place a move to gain an instrument for their struggle for political power with a view to overthrowing senatorial hegemony. They deliberately misrepresented the issue as if the rights of the plebs were at stake. Although their agitation was successful,[6] it is doubtful whether they expressed the genuine feeling of the People. But, at any rate, they made the slogan vindicatio libertatis a household phrase in the political struggle of the closing period of the Republic.

(f) Equality of Opportunity for the Homines Novi

The issue over the question whether the consulship should be equally accessible to the nobiles and homines novi,[7] or reserved for the nobiles only, was a prominent feature in the controversy between

---

[1] *Ib.* §3: inanis species magistratus. For the manner in which the tribunate was employed after the full restoration of its powers, see Sallust, *Cat.* 38, 1.

[2] Sallust, *Hist.* I, 55, 10 M: Hac tempestate serviundum aut imperitandum, habendus metus est aut faciundus, Quirites.

[3] The attitude of the People towards the political rivalries during the Late Republic will be discussed in the next chapter.

[4] As the passage in Sallust, *Hist.* III, 48, 15 M, would suggest.

[5] See *De Leg.* III, 23. Cf. Livy II, 44.

[6] See Ascon. 67, 1 f. c. But see Sallust, *Hist.* III, 48, 8 M.

[7] On the significance of this term see J. Vogt, *Homo novus, ein Typus der römischen Republik*, Stuttgart, 1926; W. Schur, Homo novus. Ein Beitrag zur Sozialgeschichte der sinkenden Republik, *Bonner Jahrbücher* CXXXIV (1929),

the Optimates and Populares.[1] Libertas, it is true, is not explicitly mentioned in the claims and arguments advanced by the homines novi; nevertheless it is directly involved in the issue. For although the controversy waxed hottest over the particular question of eligibility to the consulship, it resulted in the formulation of the general principle that access to all offices should depend in the first place on the personal qualities of the candidate, and not on his origin and social standing.

The homines novi laboured under a social handicap, not under legal discrimination. Neither Cicero nor Sallust[2] base the case for the homines novi on their formal right to hold the consulship, for, in fact, no one denied that right. Since the fourth century all citizens of appropriate age, character, and past office, where this was required, were eligible for all the offices that constituted the normal cursus honorum.[3] But despite the formal position in law, the nobles, as a rule, exerted all their influence to debar the homines novi from the consulship.[4] They maintained that descendants of consulars only, or, at least, sons of senators,[5] were fit for the consulship, whereas other people were "unworthy"—indigni[6]—of the honour, disqualified by reason of birth. It was, therefore, not a question of right but of worthiness or, as the Romans would say, dignitas.[7]

In the face of the attempt on the part of the Optimates to shut out the homines novi from the exclusive clique of the nobilitas, the

pp. 54–66; H. Strasburger, in PW, XVII, col. 1223–8, s.v. novus homo; M. Gelzer, Die Nobilität der römischen Republik, pp. 22 f., 27 f., 40 f.

[1] See H. Last, C.A.H. IX, p. 138.

[2] Jug. 85. Schur's statement (op. cit. p. 55) that Sallust offers nothing but a stylistically remodelled version of Cicero's utterances seems a gratuitous assumption.

[3] Exceptis excipiendis: plebeians only were eligible for the tribunate; likewise, certain special offices, as for example the office of interrex, could be held only by patricians.

[4] Cic. De Lege Agr. II, 3; Sallust, Jug. 63, 6.

[5] See Gelzer, op. cit. p. 28. Cf. Vogt, op. cit. p. 24 n. 4. As Gelzer, pp. 40 f., has shown, only fifteen homines novi are known to have attained the consulship during the three hundred odd years between the consulate of L. Sextius (366 B.C.) and that of Cicero (63 B.C.).

[6] Sallust, Cat. 35, 3: Non dignos homines honore honestatos videbam (Catiline complains). Cf. Cat. 23, 6 and Jug. 63, 7.

[7] See Livy IV, 3, 7; Cic. Pro Mur. 15 f. Cf. M. P. Charlesworth, Pietas and Victoria, J.R.S. XXXIII (1943), p. 2, and the inscriptions there cited.

homines novi claimed that personal merit, and not ancestry, should be the criterion of a person's worthiness for all offices, including the consulship; that in respect of access to the honores proved ability should count for as much as inherited nobility.[1]

Livy, projecting the propaganda of the homines novi into a fictitious speech by Canuleius, brings in the question of free suffrage.[2] In a sense, Livy may have been right: the freedom of suffrage is curtailed if there is no reasonable freedom to nominate candidates. But it is very doubtful whether Livy realized this at all. In fact, the statement that liberum suffragium means "ut quibus velit (populus Romanus) consulatum mandet" is true only in so far as it applies to the choice between recognized and qualified candidates. If, however, it was meant literally, it is a misrepresentation of the Roman practice, and entirely out of tune with the real wishes of the homines novi. For when Cicero said (*De Lege Agr.* II, 3) that in electing him despite his novitas the People had triumphed over the nobles, he was only paying a flattering compliment to the electorate; otherwise he never represented the issue as one between the nobility and the people. He clearly indicated that it was an issue between those who, from the day of their birth, found their place ready for them, and those who aspired to make their position.[3] The nobility tended to narrow down the limits of the ruling oligarchy, whereas the homines novi sought to broaden the ranks of the governing class: they strove to break the exclusiveness of the nobility, not its pre-eminence. It was Cicero's belief that the tenure of the consulship put him on equal footing with the nobles.[4] For all their hostility to the nobiles of their own time, the homines novi were by no means opposed to nobilitas as such. But while the Optimates wished to see the nobilitas as an exclusive clique perpetuating its own hereditary position, the homines novi wished for a broadened nobility drawn from all quarters according to merit. They demanded an equal opportunity for new aspirants to dignitas and nobilitas, not an egalitarian levelling down of the nobility.

---

[1] Moribus non maioribus, Cic. *In Pis.* 2. Cf. H. Last, *C.A.H.* IX, pp. 138 f.
[2] Livy IV, 3, 7.
[3] Cic. *In Pis.* 2 f.; *De Lege Agr.* II, 100; *II in Verr.* III, 7; IV, 81; V, 180 f. Cf. Sallust, *Jug.* 85.
[4] *Ad Fam.* III, 7, 5.

From the standpoint of the res publica the importance of the claims of the homines novi lies in the fact that they resulted in the advocacy of equal opportunity regardless of ancestry—a truly Roman idea harmonizing with the aequum ius and aequae leges— and, judged by the prevalent views in the Republican period, in a new conception of nobilitas, namely aristocracy of merit, not of birth, or as Cicero put it "nobilitas nihil aliud...quam cognita virtus".[1]

The new or rather the renewed original concept of nobilitas propounded by Cicero and Sallust[2] was to gain a firm foothold under the Early Empire when the principal ideas of the homines novi prevailed.[3] Cicero, for all his expressed opinions, found it presumably quite impossible, or undesirable, to call "nobilis" anyone except the descendants of consulars;[4] Velleius Paterculus described Cicero as a "vir novitatis nobilissimae",[5] an expression that, strictly speaking and judging by Cicero's own usage, is an oxymoron. Marius was said to have laboured under the lack of ancestral imagines;[6] Seneca, a man "equestri et provinciali loco ortus",[7] roundly declared that "Non facit nobilem atrium plenum fumosis imaginibus. Nemo in nostram gloriam vixit, nec quod ante nos fuit nostrum est. Animus facit nobilem, cui ex quacumque condicione supra fortunam licet surgere."[8] And two generations after Seneca the new concept of nobility was set out in Juvenal's eighth Satire, the gist of which, in Juvenal's own words, is "Tota licet veteres exornent undique cerae Atria, nobilitas sola est atque unica virtus" (l. 19 f.)—a fitting motto, strongly reminiscent of Cicero and Sallust, for the new imperial nobility.

(g) Senatus Consultum Ultimum

A particular and long-standing issue in which senatus auctoritas and libertas were matched against each other was the dispute between the Optimates and Populares over the implications and

---

[1] See above, p. 37 n. 3. Cf. Sallust, *Jug.* 85, 17.   [2] *Jug.* 85, 29–30.

[3] This fact appears nowhere more clearly than in the Fasti Consulares of the Early Empire. See, e.g., the list of consuls in Syme's *Roman Revolution*, pp. 525 ff.

[4] Gelzer, *op. cit.* pp. 22 ff. and 26 ff.

[5] Vell. Pat. II, 34, 3.   [6] Sallust, *Jug.* 85, 25.

[7] Tac. *Ann.* XIV, 53, 5.   [8] *Epist.* 44, 5. Cf. *De Benef.* III, 28, 2.

E

effects of the Senatus Consultum de Re Publica Defendenda, commonly known as the S.C. Ultimum.[1]

The S.C. Ultimum was a measure designed to meet grave domestic emergencies. Until the end of the third century B.C. recourse was had in cases of emergency to the dictatorship. But it was probably no fortuitous coincidence that the dictatorship fell into disuse about the same time as the Senate gained ascendancy.[2] For although constitutional practice now subjected it to the provocatio,[3] and perhaps to other limitations too,[4] the dictatorship remained a formidable power, and the appointment of a dictator, despite the specification of the task set before him, meant that for six months—unless he deemed fit to resign sooner—the whole State was subjected to a temporary autocracy instituted at the discretion of one consul, or, if rarely, by popular vote.[5] Cicero's pronounced dislike of the "Sullanum regnum", and the opposition of the Optimates to the proposal that Pompey be made dictator, or sole consul, are indicative of the Senate's attitude towards the dictatorship.[6]

To avoid recourse to this distasteful and uncontrollable magistracy, the Senate resorted to another expedient: it passed a decree advising the magistrates, in the first place the consuls, to defend the State "lest harm befalls it". The passage of a S.C. Ultimum by itself raises no constitutional problems. As any other Senatus Consultum, the S.C. Ultimum was, strictly speaking, a resolution, not a law, and, unless the motion was vetoed by par maiorve potestas, the Senate might pass any resolution it wished. It is therefore quite in keeping with Roman constitutional practice that no one ever questioned the right of the Senate to pass a S.C. Ultimum. On one occasion Caesar

---

[1] For a detailed discussion of its formal wording and legal implications see above all G. Plaumann, Das sogenannte senatus consultum ultimum, die Quasidiktatur der späteren römischen Republik, *Klio* XIII (1913), pp. 321–86. Also Mommsen, *Staatsrecht* III, pp. 1240 ff., and H. Last, *C.A.H.* IX, pp. 82 ff.

[2] The last dictator before Sulla was appointed in 202 B.C., see Mommsen, *op. cit.* II³, p. 169, and also Plaumann, *op. cit.* p. 355. Sulla's dictatorship "legibus scribundis et rei publicae constituendae", as well as the dictatorship of Caesar, resembled the power of the Decemvirs rather than of the dictators "rei gerundae causa".

[3] See Festus, *s.v.* optima lex (p. 216, ed. Lindsay). Cf. Mommsen, *Staatsrecht* II³, p. 164; Plaumann, *op. cit.* p. 353.

[4] Namely par potestas, see Plaumann, *loc. cit.*

[5] See Livy XXVII, 5, 16 f.; and above, n. 3.   [6] Cf. below, pp. 61 ff.

(*Bell. Civ.* I, 7, 5 f.) argued that the situation did not justify the passage of a S.C. Ultimum, but even so he did not question the Senate's right to pass such a resolution.

Strictly speaking the Senate could not impose upon the magistrates any course of action; in theory the consuls were not bound to obey the S.C. Ultimum any more than any other Senatus Consultum, and there is even some likelihood that a S.C. Ultimum was passed, or at least moved, in 133 B.C., but the consul to whom it was addressed refused to implement it.[1] The value of a S.C. Ultimum lay not in its being a peremptory injunction, but in something different.

A S.C. Ultimum was a declaration by the Senate that the State was in real danger and that therefore unusual measures for its protection were justified. Moreover, as any other S.C., the S.C. Ultimum could only be passed after the consul had laid the matter before the House and had it discussed,[2] and the debate in the Senate was mentioned in the preamble of the S.C. Ultimum as the reason why it was passed at all.[3] Therefore, even if the Senate did not supplement its S.C. Ultimum with a declaration stating that specified persons committed specified acts "contra rem publicam", the S.C. Ultimum itself, despite the fact that as a rule no names were mentioned in it, pointed out the quarters from which the State was threatened, and implied that certain citizens, having adopted a hostile attitude towards the State, should be treated as hostes. A specific declaration that so-and-so "contra rem publicam fecit" and thereby made himself an enemy of his country (hostis) is only an elaboration of an element present in the original, and as a rule unspecified, S.C. Ultimum,[4]

[1] See Val. Max. III, 2, 17; IV, 7, 1; Plut. *Ti. Gracchus* 19, 3 f.; *Rhet. ad Herenn.* IV, 68; Mommsen, *Staatsrecht* III, p. 1242; Plaumann, *op. cit.* p. 359.

[2] Verba de r. p. facere; de r. p. referre. See Plaumann, *op. cit.* p. 341.

[3] De ea re ita censuere, Cic. *Phil.* VIII, 14. See also *Phil.* V, 34; and Plaumann, *op. cit.* p. 340.

[4] Cf. Mommsen, *Staatsrecht* III, pp. 1242 ff.; and H. Last, *C.A.H.* IX, pp. 87 ff. A different view of the relation between the S.C. Ultimum and the indication of specified hostes is advanced by Plaumann (p. 344) who concludes: "Mit der Hostis-Erklärung hat das S.C. de re publica defendenda systematisch und seinem Ursprunge nach nichts zu tun." Yet even he admits that "die beiden Akte häufig innig verbunden sind" and that "das S.C. de r. p. defendenda sich de facto ja meist gegen eine bestimmte Person richtete" (p. 343). The reason he offers for the separation of measures intrinsically

since the only justification for passing such a decree is the presence of hostes within the State.[1]

In theory the S.C. Ultimum does not infringe any existing laws nor violate the freedoms of the citizens, because, in theory, it is directed against people who by their own acts have placed themselves beyond the pale of Roman citizenship. But, in practice, a clear-cut line could rarely be drawn between hostes and cives, and on occasion there was much to be said for the view that on the strength of the S.C. Ultimum the magistrates arrogated to themselves unconstitutional powers, and, in contravention of the rights of formal trial and appeal, put to death the political opponents of the government of the day. Since the Populares were apt to be the victims of such treatment, it fell to them to combat the implications of the S.C. Ultimum.

The peculiar character that the issue over the S.C. Ultimum assumed was due to the fact that the direct responsibility for any unconstitutional act committed on the strength of a S.C. Ultimum rested with those who committed such acts, whereas the ultimate responsibility rested with the Senate which passed the Last Decree. Therefore, if a S.C. Ultimum resulted in acts of violence, its opponents could indict the persons who committed such acts on a charge of violation of civic rights, whereas its supporters could defend them with the plea that they acted for the safety of the State and on the authority of the Senate. And thus it came about that, although no Roman questioned the right of the State to defend itself, the long-standing issue over the S.C. Ultimum was fought out under the banner of senatus auctoritas on the part of the Optimates, and in the name of libertas on the part of the Populares. In this respect three instances are of particular interest: the trial of Opimius in 120 B.C.; the last stage of the trial of Rabirius in 63 B.C.; and the debate on the punishment of Catiline's associates in the same year.

Cicero summarized the arguments for the prosecution and the defence of Opimius as follows: Carbo, for the defence, admitted the

belonging together is that "man kommt zu keinem systematischen Verständniss dieser Massregel, wenn man sie nicht von den historischen Begleitumständen loslösst". The soundness of his method in this particular case may safely be considered a matter of opinion.

[1] An example of a motion for a S.C. Ultimum is the speech of Philippus, Sallust, *Hist.* I, 77 M, especially § 22.

act of putting C. Gracchus to death, but justified it on the ground
that it was committed "pro salute patriae" and "ex senatus con-
sulto";[1] whereas Decius, for the prosecution, argued that on no
account and under no circumstances do the laws allow a citizen to be
put to death without trial.[2] So far as Cicero's summary goes, it
appears that the prosecution did not raise the question whether there
really existed a danger to the State. The issue was represented as one
between higher legality based on reasons of State and backed by the
authority of the Senate, on the one hand, and personal liberty resting
on civic rights, on the other.

Cicero's largely extant speech in defence of Rabirius is valuable
in that it states Cicero's view of the political implications of the trial
of Rabirius, and provides some clues for the reconstruction of the
arguments put forward by the prosecution. Between the lines of
Cicero's direct retort to Labienus, the prosecutor, some of the
latter's arguments can be read (§§ 11–13). It would seem that
Labienus dwelt on the provisions of the Lex Porcia and Lex
Sempronia concerning provocatio, and on libertas. Cicero, for the
defence, stated that the indictment of Rabirius was a blow at the
senatus auctoritas, and an attempt to deprive the State of means of
protection in grave emergencies.[3] And although Hortensius, the
other counsel for the defence, sought to refute the charge of com-
plicity in the murder of Saturninus, Cicero admitted that Rabirius
was in possession of arms with a view to killing Saturninus (18–19),
but he argued that Rabirius was right in doing so, since he complied

---

[1] It is noteworthy that Scipio Africanus, when interpellated by Carbo about
the murder of Tiberius Gracchus, replied "iure caesum videri", see Cic.
De Orat. II, 106; Livy, Epit. LIX; Vell. Pat. II, 4, 4. It seems that "iure" in this
context means "justifiably" rather than "legitimately".

[2] Cic. De Orat. II, 106 and 132; Partit. Orat. 104 ff.

[3] Pro Rab. perd. reo, 2 ff.; 35; cf. Orator, 102, and also Dio Cass. XXXVII,
26, 1–2. E. G. Hardy, Political and Legal Aspects of the Trial of Rabirius in
Some Problems in Roman History, Oxford, 1924, pp. 102 and 106, is of course
right in maintaining that the impeachment of Rabirius was not an attack on the
validity and legality of the S.C. Ultimum. Needless to say, no lawcourt could
pronounce upon the validity and legality of a duly passed S.C. But the question
which the trial of Rabirius raised, although by circuitous methods, was
whether a S.C. Ultimum, however valid and legal, justified the execution
without trial of seditious citizens. It is for this reason, above all, that
Hardy's statement that Cicero misrepresented the nature of the trial requires
qualification.

with the S.C. Ultimum (20 ff.). It seems therefore that, in so far as the S.C. Ultimum is concerned, the arguments put forward by Labienus and Cicero were of the same character as those put forward by the prosecution and defence of Opimius some sixty years before, namely civic rights versus reasons of State and the authority of the Senate.

Caesar's criticism of the implications of the S.C. Ultimum—in his speech on the punishment of Catiline's associates, as reported by Sallust, *Cat.* 51—went deeper than that of his predecessors.

Summary punishment on the strength of a S.C. Ultimum was an innovation—so Caesar argued—incompatible with the Roman constitution (§§ 8; 17; 41), a timely reminder to those who represented it as a mos maiorum. But he did not leave the matter at opposing reasons of State with claims of legality, as Decius and Labienus seem to have done. He admitted that whatever was done to the conspirators would be justified (§ 26, cf. §§ 15, 17, 23), but he raised the fundamental question whether in resorting to unconstitutional measures for its own protection the State was not courting graver disasters than those it sought to encounter.

The implications of the S.C. Ultimum have two aspects, one concerning magisterial power, and the other, civic rights, and Caesar dwelt on both. Once the practice is established that on the strength of a S.C. Ultimum the consul may assume unlimited power over the life and death of citizens, there is nothing left to stop the consul from proscriptions (§§ 25–36). The value of the Lex Porcia and its like lies in the fact that they stand between the citizen and political vindictiveness, and for this reason, above all else, he disapproves of the proposed dispensation (§§ 40–1).[1]

It seems, therefore, that Caesar did not insist on legality for its own sake, but pointed out that the State could not afford to dispense with the established checks on magisterial power, nor with the safeguards of personal freedom. Without the safeguards of freedom the State would drift to arbitrariness and lawlessness.[2]

[1] Cf. Cic. *In Cat.* IV, 10. It may be worth while quoting here Thomas Paine's saying: "He that would make his own liberty secure, must guard even his enemy from oppression; for if he violates this duty, he establishes a precedent that will reach to himself."

[2] Cicero's banishment may be passed over as of little consequence from the standpoint of the controversy about the S.C. Ultimum. For although Cicero

There is ample reason to assume that the attacks of the Populares on the S.C. Ultimum were inspired by considerations other than idealistic; nevertheless, it seems that nothing in their platform justified their claim to be the champions of freedom better than their insistence on the inviolability of the provocatio as against magisterial action supported or instigated by the auctoritas of the Senate.

(h) Potestates Extraordinariae

The controversy over extraordinary executive powers was perhaps the most important feature of domestic politics in the Late Republican period. The Republican constitution contained elaborate rules concerning the tenure of offices,[1] which, as has been seen, were considered an essential check on magisterial power, and thereby an effective safeguard of freedom.[2] A potestas extraordinaria is either a special office conferred by a special law, or a regular office attained or exercised contrary to, or through dispensation from, any of the existing rules concerning the tenure of offices, as, for example, the Lex Annalis.[3]

Cicero's remark that "extraordinarium imperium populare atque ventosum est, minimeque nostrae gravitatis, minime huius ordinis" (*Phil.* XI, 17), in so far as it expresses the attitude of the Optimates and Populares to extraordinary powers, is in the main true; for whatever their motives, the Optimates were on the whole opposed to extraordinary potestates and imperia.

It was doubtless in the interests of the Senate and the ruling class to prevent any member from becoming so strong as to be independent

---

went into self-imposed exile as a consequence of the Clodian plebiscite which outlawed anyone who condemned a citizen to death without trial, the privilegium that subsequently banned Cicero gave as pretext the forgery of a S.C., not the execution of citizens without trial. It may, however, be mentioned in passing that Cicero's enemies inveighed against his "regnum", *Ad Att.* I, 16, 10 and *Pro Sulla*, 21 and 25; his "tyranny", *Pro Sest.* 109 and *De Dom.* 75 and 94; and his arbitrary power, Plut. *Cic.* 23, 2; cf. also Ps.-Sallust, *In Cic.* 5. Perhaps his own experience was at the back of Cicero's mind when in his *De Leg.* III, 8 he laid down with regard to the consuls "ollis salus populi suprema lex esto".

[1] Cic. *De Lege Agr.* II, 24; *Dig.* L, 4, 14, 5.

[2] Cf. Livy XXXIX, 39, 6: Nec iure ullo nec exemplo tolerabili liberae civitati aedilis curulis designatus praeturam peteret.

[3] See Cic. *Brut.* 226; *De Harusp. Resp.* 43. Cf. Mommsen, *Staatsrecht* I[3], pp. 20 ff.

of the Senate and the nobility. They were therefore opposed to
the continuation and iteration of offices, and Cato the Elder about
the year 151 B.C. supported a measure "ne quis consul bis fieret".[1]
But with the expansion of the Roman empire and the increasing
demand for commanders and administrators, it became on occasions
necessary to dispense with the rigid rules that regulated the tenure
of offices, as for example in the case of Scipio's unconstitutional
election to the consulship and to the command against Carthage, or
Marius' successive commands granted to avert the danger of the
invasion of the Cimbri and Teutones.[2]

Since the Gracchi and Marius, with the growing power of the
popular vote and the advent of a professional army, there was present
in an extraordinary power, especially if it was a military command,
the danger of personal government. The holder of an imperium
extraordinarium was placed in power by the popular will and then
largely left free to act according to his own notion of expediency.
And since the armies owed their allegiance in the first place to their
commanders to whom they looked to secure for them grants and the
equivalent of pensions, the position of the government, the Senate,
and constitutional republicanism became insecure. Inasmuch as
there were no effective means of control, extraordinary power might
easily become inordinate power, incompatible with freedom and
savouring of autocracy. This fact explains the choice of terms that
were used in the agitation against extraordinary powers. Tiberius
Gracchus was accused of having wished for a "regnum".[3] Similar
allegations were made about Saturninus.[4] Cinna's régime was called
dominatus and tyrannis.[5] Sulla's dictatorship was considered
a dominatio, tyrannis, servitium, and regnum.[6]

Sulla sought to eliminate extraordinary and uncontrollable powers,
hence the importance that he—and also Cicero—attached to the

---

[1] Malcovati, *op. cit.* I, p. 200, cf. *ibid.* pp. 71 ff., and Mommsen, *op. cit.* I³,
p. 521 n. 1.

[2] Appian, *Lib.* 112; Cic. *De Prov. Cons.* 19.

[3] Cic. *De Amic.* 40; Flor. II, 2, 7; Sallust, *Jug.* 31, 7; Plut. *Ti. Gracchus*
14, 3.

[4] Flor. II, 4, 4.

[5] Cic. *Phil.* I, 34; II, 108; Sallust, *Hist.* I, 64 M; Ascon. 23, 24 C.

[6] Sallust, *Hist.* I, 31; 55, 1, 7; 57; III, 48, 1, 9 M; Cic. *De Lege Agr.* I,
21; II, 81; *Phil.* II, 108; V, 44; *Ad Att.* VIII, 11, 2; Appian, *Bell. Civ.* I, 3.

Lex Annalis.[1] But events proved stronger than his constitution. When in 77 B.C. objection was raised to entrusting Pompey, a mere knight at that time, with a proconsular command against Sertorius, it was found that there was no alternative, and he was sent to Spain, as Philippus said, "pro consulibus".[2] By so doing the Optimates themselves made a breach in Sulla's provisions, and the question of extraordinary commands again became acute. In 74 B.C. a "curatio infinita totius orae maritimae" was conferred on the praetor M. Antonius in order that he might wage war against the pirates.[3]

A decisive turning-point in the struggle against the extraordinaria imperia came in 67 and 66 B.C. In 67 there was passed, despite resistance by senatorial leaders, the Lex Gabinia, which conferred far-reaching powers upon Pompey to suppress piracy, and in the next year there followed the Lex Manilia, which entrusted him with an equally great command to end the war with Mithridates. Cicero, at that time speaking for the Populares, represented the opposition to these laws as opposition to the will of the People.[4] But this was far from being the case. The Optimates opposed the laws on the ground that so strong a power in the hands of one man was too strong for the liberty of the State: Q. Catulus "dissuadens legem (sc. Gabiniam) in contione dixisset esse quidem praeclarum virum Cn. Pompeium, sed nimium iam liberae fieri rei publicae, neque omnia in uno reponenda".[5]

The term regnum with regard to extraordinary power crops up again in Cicero's speeches against the Agrarian Bill of Rullus in 63 B.C. He calls the special commission proposed by that Bill a "regnum decemvirale".[6] Soon afterwards Cicero himself was subjected to abuse as "rex" on account of having illegally executed Catiline's associates.[7] Cato the Younger did not cease to inveigh

[1] See H. Last, *C.A.H.* IX, pp. 288 f.; Cic. *De Leg.* III, 9.

[2] Cic. *De imp. Cn. Pompei*, 62; *Phil.* XI, 18.

[3] Ps.-Ascon. 259, 6 Stangl; Vell. Pat. II, 31.

[4] Cic. *De imp. Cn. Pompei*, 63 ff.

[5] Vell. Pat. II, 32, 1. Cf. Cic. *ibid.* 52 and 60; Plut. *Pomp.* 30.

[6] Cic. *De Leg. Agr.* I, 24; cf. II, 8, 15, 20, 24, 33, 43, 54, 57, 75, 99. It is interesting that the emperor Claudius described as "decemvirale regnum" the rule of the Decemvirs, see Dessau, *I.L.S.* 212, col. I, l. 33. Livy employed similar terms: decem regum species erat, III, 36, 5, cf. III, 38, 2 and 39, 7–8.

[7] See above, p. 60 n. 2. Catiline himself is also said to have aimed at a "regnum", see Sallust, *Cat.* 5, 6.

against extraordinary powers even under the Triumvirate,[1] and the nobles were unwilling to grant extraordinary powers to Pompey.[2] Feeling against extraordinary power must have been strong, if Caesar, in order to reassure his opponents, declared on entering Rome in 49 B.C. "se nullum extraordinarium honorem appetisse" (*Bell. Civ.* I, 32, 2). It is, indeed, a noteworthy fact—sometimes overlooked by the advocates of "Pompey's Principate"—that Cicero described as a "regnum" not only Caesar's régime but also that contemplated by Pompey.[3]

It appears that throughout the Late Republic, with the exception of Sulla's dictatorship, the Optimates were opposed to the establishment of the extraordinariae potestates which were championed with popular support by the Populares. This struggle is the background against which the various descriptions of such powers must be placed. The odious term regnum signifies a power, or a position, which, even if formally legal, is incompatible with the spirit of the republican constitution, but not necessarily monarchy.[4] As a term of political invective arising from the controversy between the Optimates and Populares it was not used in the literal sense. And therefore, incidentally, unless there are other cogent reasons for believing that Caesar wanted to establish a monarchy, this cannot be properly deduced from the mere fact that he was called "rex", and his régime, "regnum".

From all that has hitherto been said it appears that no new ideas or principles were developed in the course of the contest between the Optimates and Populares. Certain aspects of libertas were on occasion stressed by either side, and consequently gained prominence. But there was nothing in the doctrines, or rather pleas, of either side that was not present, explicitly or implicitly, in the traditional conception of freedom. There can be no doubt that principles were

---

[1] Cic. *De Sest.* 60. Cf. *De Dom.* 22.

[2] Cic. *Ad Att.* I, 19, 4; IV, 1, 7; *Ad Q. Fr.* III, 8, 4 and 9, 3; Brutus ap. Quintil. *Inst.* IX, 3, 95.

[3] See, e.g., *Ad Att.* VIII, 11, 2.

[4] See Cic. *II in Verr.* V, 175; Livy II, 41, 5–9; III, 58, 5; VI, 41, 3. The odious connotation of the term regnum derives from its association with Tarquin, see Cic. *De Rep.* I, 62: Quid? tu non vides unius inportunitate et superbia Tarquinii nomen huic populo in odium venisse regium? And also Livy VI, 40, 10: Tarquinii tribuni plebis, with which cf. 40, 7 and 41, 3.

involved in the controversy, but it is in the highest degree doubtful whether those principles were championed for their own sake. It would rather seem that with very few exceptions—Ti. Gracchus, Cato and Cicero—each side strove for power, and for power alone, while constitutional principles and institutions were means and not ends. Sallust's verdict was right:

Quicumque rem publicam agitavere, honestis nominibus, alii sicuti populi iura defenderent, pars quo senatus auctoritas maxuma foret, bonum publicum simulantes pro sua quisque potentia certabant.[1]

But the struggle between the Optimates and Populares, although it contributed no new ideas to the conception of libertas, proved to be a factor of immense importance in its history, for the very reason that it was a struggle for power devoid of higher motives. That struggle shattered the institutions on which libertas rested, as well as the confidence of the Romans in those institutions, and thereby it contributed greatly to the disintegration of the old form of government which was the embodiment of Roman libertas.

[1] Cat. 38, 3. Cf. Jug. 41; Tac. Hist. II, 38; Ann. III, 27, 1–28, 1.

THE DECLINE OF THE TRADITIONAL FORM OF GOVERNMENT

1. The Struggle of the Italians for Civic Rights

Of the two cardinal notions that Roman libertas comprised, namely the republican constitution and the rights inherent in Roman citizenship, the former, on the showing of the extant evidence, was by far the more prominent in the presentation of libertas by politicians and political writers at Rome during the Late Republican period. Except on such occasions as those on which the Populares upheld the civic right of provocatio against magisterial action supported by a S.C. Ultimum,[1] libertas as a political watchword in the struggle of factions in Rome meant in the first place a form of government, and not the rights and liberties of the individual citizen. This tendency in the conception of libertas is due, not to a slackening of the appreciation of personal freedom, but to the fact that, while the rights inherent in Roman citizenship seemed firmly established, the traditional form of republican government underwent a severe test, and as time went on it became more and more doubtful whether that form of government was adequate, and whether it would continue at all.

But unlike the politicians in the city of Rome who regarded libertas as a certain form of government, the Latins and Allies who rose against Rome to assert their freedom seem to have had in mind civic rights above all else. In the extant sources, and particularly the Latin ones, which view the issue mainly from the Roman standpoint, the Allies are represented as having simply demanded civitas.[2] Since however various things go under that head, viz. social status, personal rights, political rights, it would be more illuminating to know, if possible, for what purpose the Allies sought Roman

---

[1] See above, pp. 55 ff.
[2] See Appian, *Bell. Civ.* I, 21, 87; 34, 152; 49, 213; Vell. Pat. II, 14, 1; 15, 2; Flor. II, 6, 3; *Liber de Vir. Illustr.* (ed. Pichlmayr), 66, 11; Ascon. 67, 23 f. c; Plut. *Cat. Min.* 2, 1; Diod. Sic. XXXVII, 2, 2; 11.

citizenship. Granted that there were other contributory causes, what was the immediate motive of the rising of Fregellae in 125 B.C. and of the Social War that began in 91 B.C.? Was it national independence or political freedom? For the Romans, although they had one word—libertas—for both notions,[1] did not fail to see that independence and freedom were separable and distinctively different things.[2]

To begin with the second question. The chief of the Samnites at the battle of the Colline Gate (82 B.C.) is said to have declared "numquam defuturos raptores Italicae libertatis lupos, nisi silva in quam refugere solerent esset excisa".[3] If this dictum is authentic, —and there is no good reason to impugn its authenticity—what does "Italica libertas" mean? The Samnites, and especially those who fought at the Colline Gate, may well have interpreted libertas as complete independence,[4] but in so far as the Social War was fought for, or in the name of, libertas,[5] it is unlikely that all the Allies meant libertas in the sense of independence. For although the secessionists formed an Italian confederacy with a capital of its own, national independence was not what the Allies desired most, nor was it an end in itself. They seceded because they despaired of being peacefully granted Roman citizenship, that is to say they broke away from Rome because she would not admit them into the Roman State, and not because they wanted to stay out.[6] This conclusion is supported both by the manner in which the Italian problem was finally settled, namely by admitting the Italians to Roman citizenship, and by the fact that before the war broke out the Allies demanded citizenship, not national sovereignty, and after the outbreak of the

[1] Independence is sometimes described as suis legibus vivere or esse, see Livy XXV, 16, 7; 23, 4; XXX, 37, 1; XXXIII, 31–32; XXXVII, 54, 26.

[2] For a detailed discussion of the enfranchisement of Italy see H. Last in *C.A.H.* IX, pp. 41 f., 45 f., 78 f., 174 f., 201 f.; A. N. Sherwin-White, *The Roman Citizenship*, Oxford, 1939, pp. 126 f.; R. Gardner, *C.A.H.* IX, pp. 185–200.

[3] Vell. Pat. II, 27, 2.

[4] Cf. H. Last, *C.A.H.* IX, p. 273; Sherwin-White, *op. cit.* p. 126.

[5] As Strabo, V, 4, 2, (241), says it was: δεόμενοι τυχεῖν ἐλευθερίας καὶ πολιτείας μὴ τυγχάνοντες ἀπέστησαν καὶ τὸν Μαρσικὸν καλούμενον ἐξῆψαν πόλεμον.

[6] Cic. *Phil.* XII, 27: Non enim ut eriperent nobis socii civitatem, sed ut in eam reciperentur petebant.

war many stopped fighting as soon as they were offered Roman citizenship.

The much-desired Roman citizenship[1] was sought, as will presently be seen, for the sake of two things: safeguards for personal liberty, and equal partnership in the res publica. Of these two objects the former could be, and eventually was, achieved without national independence, whereas the latter was, in view of the Roman idea of res publica, clearly inconsistent with national separatism; it was however in the end combined with municipal autonomy.

Shortly before the rising of Fregellae in the year 125 B.C., M. Fulvius Flaccus introduced a bill "de civitate *Italiae* danda et de provocatione ad populum eorum qui civitatem mutare noluissent".[2] The proposal that those who did not wish to have Roman citizenship should be granted the ius provocationis instead shows, among other things, that the Roman citizenship was sought, not only for its own sake, i.e. as a recognition of status, but because it carried with it the protection of personal liberty against the Roman magistrates. If subjection to the unchecked imperium of Roman magistrates could result in such outrageous maltreatment of Italian citizens as in the incidents which C. Gracchus related in a public speech,[3] no wonder the fasces were looked upon by the unenfranchised as a symbol of a cruel subjection.[4] It is noteworthy that in 123 B.C. Livius Drusus the elder proposed a measure the object of which, according to Plutarch (*C. Gracchus* 9, 5), was ὅπως μηδ' ἐπὶ στρατιᾶς ἐξῇ τινα Λατίνων ῥάβδοις αἰκίσασθαι. If Plutarch is right, Drusus proposed to grant the Latins a right the Romans themselves did not enjoy, commanders in the field not being as a rule bound by the laws concerning provocatio.[5] It may be that one reason, among others, for introducing this proposal was the belief, or hope, that the Latins would not insist on full Roman citizenship if they were exempt from corporal punishment.

The proposal of Flaccus deserves especial notice; for although it came to nothing, it marks the first attempt in Roman history to

---

[1] See Ascon. 67, 23 f. c. and Diod. Sic. XXXVII, 2, 2.
[2] Val. Max. IX, 5, 1.　　　　　　　　　[3] Ap. Gell. *N.A.* x, 3, 3 f.
[4] Diod. Sic. XXXVII, 12, 3: οὐ γάρ εἰμι 'Ρωμαῖος ἀλλ' ὅμοιος ὑμῶν ὑπὸ ῥάβδοις τεταγμένος περιστονῶ τὴν Ἰταλίαν, said a Latin to Italians.
[5] Cic. *De Leg.* III, 6. Cf. Mommsen, *Staatsrecht* III, pp. 352 ff.

recognize the ius provocationis—the mainstay of personal freedom —as a right of all free Latins and Italians, and not an exclusive privilege of Roman citizens. Needless to say, this proposal falls short of recognizing the Rights of Man, even if Man means a free man and not simply a human being; but in spite of the fact that the idea of the Rights of Man, in the modern sense, was not so much as known at Rome in the second century B.C., and that personal rights were regarded as privileges of citizenship or concessions ad personam in the case of strangers, Flaccus recognized the need of making the safeguards of a person's life and dignity available to all free Italians regardless of Roman citizenship, and in recognizing this he was far ahead of his own times. It would probably be an error to suppose that Flaccus was inspired by any theories; what he sought was a practical compromise; but that seems to be precisely how Rome made almost all her great discoveries in the sphere of public law—in a quest for workable compromises.

The other thing the Allies hoped to gain by the acquisition of full Roman citizenship was equal partnership in the State and the empire, or, as Appian (*Bell. Civ.* I, 34, 152) put it, ἐπιθυμεῖν τῆς 'Ρωμαίων πολιτείας ὡς κοινωνοὺς τῆς ἡγεμονίας ἀντὶ ὑπηκόων ἐσομένους. The Allies, while they bore more than their due share in building up the strength of Rome and her empire, were denied the right of equal partnership,[1] and were regarded in Rome as strangers liable at any time to be expelled from the city by consular decree.[2] The violent controversy that raged after the Social War over the question whether the enfranchised Allies should be enrolled in all the thirty-five tribes or in eight of them only, or perhaps form a group of either eight or ten new tribes which should vote last,[3] shows that the Allies were not content with a formal recognition of equal status but demanded a man-for-man equality with the Romans. That is why they would not agree to be segregated in a small number of tribes,

[1] Vell. Pat. II, 15, 2; Flor. II, 6, 3.

[2] Cic. *Pro Sest.* 30; Ascon. 67, 20 ff. C.

[3] Appian, *Bell. Civ.* I, 49, 214 f.; 53, 231. Vell. Pat. II, 20: Cum ita civitas Italiae data esset ut in octo tribus contribuerentur novi cives, etc. According to the different meanings of the verb contribuo Velleius' statement may mean that the Allies were either to be incorporated into eight (existing) tribes or to be united so as to form eight (new) tribes, cf. *Thes. Ling. Lat., s.v.* contribuo, col. 777, 47 ff. See also Appian, *Bell. Civ.* I, 55, 243 and Livy, Epit. LXXVII.

since in view of the Roman system of voting, whereby each tribe voted separately and for the purpose of establishing the final majority each tribe counted as one vote regardless of the number of actual voters it comprised, such a segregation meant that despite their superiority in numbers the Allies would be outvoted by the Romans.[1]

There is also another thing to be observed. On admission to Roman citizenship the Allies did not cease to retain their separate and partly autonomous municipal form of organization. Indeed, as the bill of M. Fulvius Flaccus shows, some of the Allies were unwilling to acquire Roman citizenship in 125 B.C., probably for fear that their incorporation into the citizen body of Rome would mean the end of their own municipal communities as political entities.[2] Their determination to retain their own municipal "commonwealths" shows, among other things, that in demanding admission to Roman citizenship the Allies aimed at partnership, not in the communal life of the city of Rome, as the selfish urban populace thought they did, but in the res publica universa, as Cicero called it,[3] of which Rome itself was only to be the capital.

It appears therefore that in the opinion of the Allies, at least as it is represented from the Roman point of view, Roman citizenship meant in the first place safeguards of personal liberty, and a share in the res publica. And if this is what they meant by libertas, they were quite in tune with the Roman tradition.

2. SUBVERSIVE FACTORS

The transformation of the Populus Romanus which resulted from the extension of Roman citizenship to all free Italians was a decisive turning point in Roman history; since however it was not supplemented by any measures, as for example a different system of popular voting, that would meet the needs of the new situation, Rome herself, from a constitutional point of view, failed to benefit by the advantageous potentialities latent in the enfranchisement of

[1] See the passages cited in the previous note and also Appian, *Bell. Civ.* I, 64, 287.

[2] See H. Last, *C.A.H.* IX, pp. 46 f. There was in certain Italian towns opposition to the fusion of citizenship even after 89 B.C.; see Cic. *Pro Balbo*, 21.

[3] *Ad. Q. Fr.* I, 1, 29; cf. *De Leg.* II, 5.

Italy, and the forces that were slowly but persistently undermining the traditional republican constitution remained unchecked. Chief among those forces during the last century of the Republic were the Popular Assembly, on the one hand, and those politicians who sought by popular support and with military backing to establish their own pre-eminence in the State, on the other.

In Roman constitutional law the Popular Assembly and the People are identical, and the power of the Assembly as a constitutional organ rested entirely on the assumption that the Assembly actually was the People in corpore. So long as the Assembly could in practice be approximately co-extensive with the Populus Romanus Quiritium the constitutional theory had a factual foundation, and, what is still more important, in the Assembly a substantial portion of the citizen body could within certain limits bring their will to bear on public affairs, if they so desired. During the Late Republican period, however, the situation underwent a complete change. After the franchise had been extended to all Italians south of the Po, it was for practical reasons no longer possible that even a substantial portion of the populus Romanus universus should regularly attend the Assemblies at Rome, the only place where lawful comitia Populi Romani or concilia plebis Romanae could be convened. On occasions of particular importance voters might flock to Rome even from distant regions, but as a rule the Assemblies were largely attended by voters who lived at Rome or near by. This state of affairs was particularly harmful because, roughly since the end of the second century B.C., the metropolitan population was by no means representative of the interests and sentiments of the municipales and country folk. A considerable portion of the plebs urbana consisted of the so-called proletarii, who possessed little more than a vote for hire, and cared for little else than the cheap corn doled out by the government and the free entertainment provided by the munificence of magistrates—"panem et circenses". And in so far as the traditional form of republicanism was in the Roman view equivalent to political freedom, the greater the power of the plebs urbana the more real the danger to libertas. For if the Assembly which was both the electorate and the supreme legislature consisted to a large extent of people unschooled in politics, ignorant of the real issues at stake, and demoralized and venal at that, a daring and successful demagogue

F

might obtain from the Assembly the sanction of almost anything. From a constitutional point of view, the Late Republican Assemblies, by virtue of their readiness to delegate extraordinary magisterial powers or to enact Bills of doubtful legality, became a subversive and disruptive factor.

It would be idle to vindicate the actions of the Popular Assemblies in the Late Republic on the alleged ground that after all they voiced the will of the sovereign People. For if about the middle of the second century B.C. there was a measure of truth in Polybius' statement that the Popular Assembly constituted a democratic element in the Roman constitution,[1] this was no longer so in the first century, at any rate after the enfranchisement of Italy. After that date the Assemblies voiced the opinion of the majority of the Roman People very seldom, if at all. It was a political calamity that a gulf should exist between "tota Italia", which really was the Populus Romanus Quiritium, and the Popular Assembly at Rome, which acted as if it alone were the Roman People—a function of which the Assembly was no longer worthy or capable.[2] The Assembly became less and less an organ of government, and more and more an instrument of factious bickering; and as such it provided many opportunities for jobbery and demagogy, but few, if any, for genuine democracy.

Therefore, to regard the Populares as progressives or democrats on the ground that they sought the support of the Assembly rather than of the Senate is to misconceive both the Populares and the Assembly. The motive of the Populares in seeking the support of the Assembly was political expediency, not concern for democracy. The fact that they were wont to speak of the Populus Romanus, its rights and its liberty, should deceive no one. To call the Assembly Populus Romanus was, by republican usage, correct; but every contemporary knew what was behind that appellation, and, as a matter of fact, neither the Optimates nor the Populares had much respect for the plebs urbana. Cicero says that in 63 B.C. the popularis Rullus commended to the Senate his Agrarian Bill declaring that the plebs urbana had to be "drained away" from the city because its

---

[1] Polyb. VI, 11, 12; 14, 3 f.
[2] See Cicero's biased but not unfounded remarks in his *De Dom.* 89 f.

influence on State affairs was too great.[1] Since Cicero's statement is contained in a speech against Rullus addressed to the People, it is uncertain whether Cicero reported Rullus' own words without wilful distortion; but it is by no means unlikely that Rullus actually advanced such an argument, even if presumably not in those words.[2] Cicero himself wrote about the Land Bill proposed by the tribune Flavius in 60 B.C. that he thought it might "bail out the bilge-water of the City".[3] But agrarian reform, in so far as it was meant to remedy the anomalous position of the plebs urbana, may have relieved the evil but did not remove it. An idea of the voting power that "illa contionalis hirudo aerarii, misera ac ieiuna plebecula"[4] possessed can be gained from the fact that by the time of Caesar's dictatorship the number of those who received corn at public expense swelled to 320,000 and was reduced by the dictator to 150,000.[5] Even the latter figure points to some 25,000 potential voters. And Caesar's first consulate and Clodius's tribunate show in what manner and for what purpose the urban populace might be employed. Thus the fact that the constitutional function of the Populus Romanus devolved to a large extent on the "faex Romuli"[6] jeopardized libertas, in the sense of constitutional republicanism, for in those circumstances direct democracy of necessity became demagogy which provided the aspirants for dominatio with an appearance of legality.

If the Popular Assembly might give the would-be potentates a legal sanction, the army gave them a backing of strength. The fact that, after the creation by Marius of an almost professional army, Rome failed to inspire her fighting men with a sense of unwavering loyalty to the State and the lawful government of the day proved to be a disaster, especially for political freedom. Within a generation after the new form of army organization had been established Rome was taken by a Roman army; and the same happened several times during the following years. It is significant for the state of mind at

---

[1] Cic. *De Lege Agr.* II, 70: Urbanam plebem nimium in republica posse; exhauriendam esse.

[2] If the second *Epistula ad Caesarem senem de Republica* were written at its dramatic date, the passage, chap. 5, 4 ff., would be of great interest in respect of the attitude of the Populares to the plebs urbana.

[3] *Ad Att.* I, 19, 4.

[4] *Ib.* I, 16, 11.

[5] Suet. *Div. Jul.* 41, 3.

[6] Cic. *Ad. Att.* II, 1, 8.

Rome, and for what the Romans expected of the army commanders, that shortly before Pompey's return from the East in 62 B.C. it was rumoured that he would march on Rome and substitute his own arbitrary rule for the constitution of the Free State.[1] The Romans must have felt that they were at the mercy of the army and its commanders.

As dictator, Sulla had sought to eliminate the dangers both of the army and of the Popular Assembly by imposing checks on the legislative initiative of the tribunes and the legislative powers of the Assembly, on the one hand, and by subjecting the army commanders to senatorial control, on the other.[2] But, as has been seen, his measures did not last long, and after the year 70 B.C. the situation was much the same as it had been before Sulla's constitutional settlement.

The growing menace of domination by self-seeking politicians inspired Cicero during his consulship to advocate the "concordia ordinum", an alliance between the Senate and the Equestrian Order, and its broader version the "consensus omnium bonorum", an alliance of all law-abiding citizens for the purpose of preserving the established order and protecting it against any unconstitutional designs.[3] He also tried to win over Pompey for the Senate,[4] no doubt in order that constitutionalism might have the support of his prestige and his veterans. But in 60 B.C. the concordia ordinum was shattered,[5] and Pompey, frustrated by the Senate and alienated from it,[6] entered a compact with Caesar and Crassus to have their own way over the head of the Senate.

3. CONTENTIO LIBERTATIS DIGNITATISQUE

The First Triumvirate was a decisive turning point in the history of libertas for more reasons than that it was—as Cicero and Asinius Pollio rightly observed[7]—the ultimate source of the Civil War. It

---

[1] Vell. Pat. II, 40, 2; Plut. *Pomp.* 43; Dio Cass. XXXVII, 20, 4 1.

[2] On the scope of Sulla's measures see H. Last, *C.A.H.* IX, pp. 288–98.

[3] See H. Strasburger, *Concordia Ordinum*, especially pp. 13 f., 39, 59 f., 71 f.

[4] *Ad Att.* I, 19, 7; II, 1, 6.   [5] *Ib.* I, 18, 3; II, 1, 8.

[6] Dio Cass. XXXVII, 49; Appian, *Bell. Civ.* II, 9; Plut. *Pomp.* 46, 3–4; *Cato Min.* 31, 1; Cic. *Ad Att.* I, 19, 4; II, 1, 6; I, 18, 6.

[7] Cic. *Ad Fam.* VI, 6, 4. For Pollio's view see Horace, *Odes* II, 1, 1 f., and R. Syme, *The Roman Revolution*, p. 8.

is true that at the time of the Triumviral domination the régimes of Marius, Cinna, and Sulla were well within living memory; but, unlike the military despotism of Cinna and of Sulla, the Triumvirate enjoyed, at any rate at the beginning, the support of the army, the urban populace, and those who, like many of the Equites, were discontented with senatorial rule.[1] Besides, the Senate had never before faced an opponent as powerful as the Triumvirate, whose grip on the State was none the less firm for the absence of proscriptions. "Tenemur undique," wrote Cicero in 59 B.C., "neque iam quominus serviamus recusamus."[2]

There was also another difference between the position of the Triumvirs and that of Cinna or Sulla: the latter, each in his turn, emerged victorious in a civil war; the former established their domination by a secret compact between themselves—dominatio ex fide, as Florus called it[3]—and the fact that three politicians could enter a compact with the view of forcing their own idea of effective government on the State,[4] and subsequently realize their design with comparatively little trouble, showed the weakness of the State and the ineffectiveness of its institutions in domestic affairs. No wonder, therefore, that a constitutionalist like Cicero, when he realized what the situation was, spoke of the State on a note of despair, "Vincere incipit timorem dolor sed ita ut omnia sint plenissima desperationis";[5] and, "De re publica quid ego tibi subtiliter? tota periit".[6] The only hope for restoration, Cicero thought, was an eventual breach in the coalition[7]—a view, right in itself, that all too clearly shows the precarious existence of the free constitution when power was with those who were out of humour with the established order.

But although the constitution was flouted by the Triumvirs, public opinion was not suppressed, and the centuries-old tradition of political freedom inspired a vocal, if politically powerless,

---

[1] Cic. Ad Att. II, 21, 1; 16, 2; 9, 2, with which cf. I, 18, 3 and II, 1, 8.

[2] Ib. II, 18, 1.   [3] Flor. II, 13, 13.

[4] Suet. Div. Jul. 19, 2: Societatem cum utroque iniit, ne quid ageretur in re publica quod displicuisset ulli e tribus. Cf. Dio Cass. XXXVII, 57. Suetonius seems to be essentially right although of course he does not record the agreement in its actual phrasing.

[5] Ad Att. II, 18, 2 (59 B.C.).

[6] Ib. II, 21, 1 (59 B.C.).

[7] Ib. II, 7, 3 (59 B.C.): Una spes est salutis—istorum inter istos dissensio.

opposition. Bibulus, Caesar's colleague in the consulship, publicly attacked both Caesar and Pompey in his edicts, which were very popular.[1] Varro launched against the Triumvirate a pamphlet entitled *The Three-Headed Monster* (*Tricaranus*).[2] The elder C. Curio in his speeches assailed Caesar's private and public life,[3] and his son gained popularity by open opposition to the Triumvirate.[4] There were also other signs of disapproval and dissatisfaction.[5] Public opinion turned against the potentates,[6] but this had hardly any appreciable effect except that it angered Pompey and Caesar,[7] and possibly, among other reasons, induced Caesar to intimidate his opponents: armed men were posted about in the Forum;[8] when Cicero in the course of a speech in defence of his former colleague C. Antonius made some critical remarks about the condition of the State,[9] Caesar promptly assisted Clodius's traductio ad plebem,[10] and in the next year Clodius as tribune paid off old scores and had Cicero outlawed and banished;[11] Cato was sent on a mission to Cyprus whereby his "free tongue was plucked out".[12]

In 56 B.C., when there appeared signs of dissension in the Triumvirate, hopes ran high for a while, only to give way, after the Conference at Lucca, to utter despair:

Quae (res communes) quales sint non facile est scribere. Sunt quidem certe in amicorum nostrorum potestate, atque ita ut nullam mutationem umquam hac hominum aetate habitura res esse videatur.[13]

Quid multa? Tenent omnia idque ita omnis intellegere volunt.[14]

---

[1] *Ad Att.* II, 14, 1; 15, 2; 19, 2 and 5; 20, 4 and 6; 21, 4; Plut. *Pomp.* 48; Suet. *Div. Jul.* 9, 2; 49, 2.

[2] Appian, *Bell. Civ.* II, 9. Cf. C. Cichorius, *Römische Studien* (1922), p. 211.

[3] Suet. *Div. Jul.* 9, 2; 49, 1; 52, 3; Cic. *Brut.* 218 ff.

[4] *Ad Att.* II, 18, 1; cf. 8, 1; 12, 2.

[5] The young C. Cato in a public speech called Pompey "privatus dictator", *Ad Q. Fr.* I, 2, 15. For other instances of discontent see *Ad Att.* II, 19 and 21.

[6] *Ad Att.* II, 19, 2; 20, 4.   [7] *Ib.* II, 19, 3; 21, 4.

[8] Plut. *Caes.* 14; Cic. *Ad Att.* II, 24, 4.

[9] Suet. *Div. Jul.* 20, 4; Dio Cass. XXXVIII, 10, 4.

[10] Cic. *De Dom.* 41; *De Prov. Cons.* 45–6; *Ad Att.* II, 12, 1–2.

[11] For detailed evidence for Cicero's banishment see T. Rice Holmes, *The Roman Republic* I, pp. 317 f., 328 f.; and E. Meyer, *Caesars Monarchie und das Principat des Pompejus*[3] (1922), pp. 95 ff.

[12] Cic. *De Dom.* 22; *Pro Sest.* 60.

[13] *Ad Fam.* I, 8, 1 (Jan. 55 B.C.).

[14] *Ad Q. Fr.* II, 7, 3 (Feb. 55 B.C.).

Amisimus, mi Pomponi, omnem non modo sucum atque sanguinem sed etiam colorem et speciem pristinae civitatis. Nulla est res publica quae delectet, in qua quiescam.[1]

Angor, mi suavissime frater, angor nullam esse rem publicam.[2]

Under the Triumviral régime, Cicero, and doubtless not he alone, realized that many things he must have been wont to take for granted were gone: he lost his auctoritas, his dignitas, his freedom of speech; and even his personal safety became precarious.[3] In 59 B.C. Cicero expressed his fear that not only private persons but even magistrates would no longer be free,[4] and subsequent events confirmed his gloomy outlook.[5] The coalition of the powerful statesmen destroyed the power of the Senate,[6] and endangered its freedom. It is noteworthy that in 56 B.C., while speaking about the assignment of the consular provinces, Cicero told the Senate that, although the consul (Marcellinus) argued "ne citerior Gallia nobis invitis alicui decernatur...perpetuoque posthac ab iis qui hunc ordinem oppugnent populari ac turbulenta ratione teneatur", he (Cicero) would not for a moment suspect that Caesar "per quem ordinem ipse amplissimam sit gloriam consecutus ei ne libertatem quidem relinquat".[7] It seems that the view was expressed in the Senate that the continuous presence of Caesar's army in Gaul jeopardized the freedom of the Senate, and it is a stroke of irony that Cicero, the untiring champion of the Senate, was compelled, possibly against his better judgement, to cast doubts on the soundness of that view.

What, in the opinion of contemporaries, caused the Triumviral compact and the Civil War that in the end was to be its outcome when a coalition of three became a rivalry of two? All ancient authorities agree that the motive was the desire for power and pre-eminence, or, as the Romans would say, potentia and dignitas. "Caesare dignitatem conparare, Crasso augere, Pompeio retinere cupientibus, omnibusque pariter potentiae cupidis, de invadenda re publica facile convenit", says Florus of the First Triumvirate.[8]

---

[1] *Ad Att.* IV, 18, 2 (54 B.C.).

[2] *Ad Q. Fr.* III, 5 and 6, 4 (Oct. or Nov. 54 B.C.).

[3] *Ad Fam.* I, 8, 3–4; *Ad Att.* IV, 5, 1; IV, 6, 1–2; *Ad Q. Fr.* III, 5 and 6, 4.

[4] *Ad Att.* II, 18, 2.   [5] See Cic. *In Vat.* 22.

[6] Cic. *Ad Fam.* VI, 6, 4.   [7] *De Prov. Cons.* 39.

[8] Flor. II, 13, 11. Cf. Dio Cass. XXXVII, 55, 3–56, 4. Cf. also Suet. *Div. Jul.* 50, 1 (Pompey's "potentiae cupiditas").

After the death of Crassus in 53 B.C. two dynasts, each suspicious of the other and jealous of his own dignitas,[1] shared all power, and the situation of republicanism—which now became the most prominent aspect of libertas—was such that concord between the two meant suppression of the Senate, while discord meant civil war.[2] As the ancients saw it, the Civil War was a struggle for dignitas: Pompey would tolerate no equal, Caesar would not brook a superior.[3] Caesar himself admitted that he valued his dignitas more than his life, and that it was in defence of his dignitas that he appealed to armed force.[4] Cicero was convinced that Caesar and Pompey alike strove for nothing else but power, and absolute power at that. Each of them fought for his own aggrandizement at the expense of the State.[5] Thus dignitas, which was pursued without regard for

---

[1] Flor. II, 13, 14: Iam Pompeio suspectae Caesaris opes et Caesari Pompeiana dignitas gravis.

[2] Cic. Ad Fam. VI, 6, 4; Phil. II, 23. Cf. Ad Fam. VIII, 14, 2.

[3] Lucan I, 125: Nec quemquam iam ferre potest Caesarve priorem Pompeiusve parem. Flor. II, 13, 14: Nec ille (Pompey) ferebat parem, nec hic (Caesar) superiorem. Dio Cassius (XLI, 54, 1) transposes it: Πομπήϊος μὲν οὐδενὸς ἀνθρώπων δεύτερος, Καῖσαρ δὲ καὶ πρῶτος εἶναι ἐπεθύμει. Caesar, Bell. Civ. I, 4, 4: Ipse Pompeius...quod neminem dignitate secum exaequari volebat totum se ab amicitia (Caesaris) averterat. Vell. Pat. II, 33, 3: Nam neque Pompeius ut primum ad rem publicam adgressus est quemquam omnino parem tulit et in quibus rebus primus esse debebat solus esse cupiebat. Cf. also Quintil. Inst. XI, 1, 80: Ligarium...non pro Cn. Pompeio, inter quem et Caesarem dignitatis fuerit contentio...stetisse.

[4] Bell. Civ. I, 9, 2: Sibi semper primam fuisse dignitatem vitaque potiorem. Ib. I, 7, 7: Hortatur (Caesar milites) ut eius existimationem dignitatemque ab inimicis defendant. Cf. ib. III, 91, 2. And also Cic. Ad Att. VII, 11, 1; Pro Lig. 18; Pro Marc. 25; De Off. I, 26; Hirtius, Bell. Gall. VIII, 52, 4; 53, 1; Suet. Div. Jul. 30, 5; Plut. Anton. 6, 3.

[5] Ad Att. VII, 3, 4: De sua potentia dimicant homines hoc tempore periculo civitatis; VIII, 11, 2: Dominatio quaesita ab utroque est.... Genus illud Sullani regni iampridem appetitur, multis qui una sunt cupientibus.... Sed neutri σκοπός est ille ut nos beati simus; uterque regnare vult. See also X, 4, 4. Flor. II, 13, 14: sic de principatu laborabant. Seneca, Ep. 14, 13: "Quid tibi vis, Marce Cato? Iam non agitur de libertate; olim pessumdata est. Quaeritur utrum Caesar an Pompeius possideat rem publicam. Quid tibi cum ista contentione?" De Benef. II, 20, 2: Ubi viderat (viz. Brutus) tot milia hominum pugnantia non an servirent, sed utri. Tac. Hist. I, 50, 3: Prope eversum orbem etiam cum de principatu inter bonos certaretur, etc.; Hist. II, 38, 1: Post quos (viz. Marius and Sulla) Cn. Pompeius, occultior non melior, et nunquam postea nisi de principatu quaesitum.

other people's libertas, proved to be a destructive factor in Roman public life.

Difficile autem est, cum praestare omnibus concupieris, servare aequitatem, quae est iustitiae maxime propria. Ex quo fit ut neque disceptatione vinci se nec ullo publico ac legitimo iure patiantur, existuntque in re publica plerumque largitiones et factiosi ut opes quam maximas consequantur, et sint vi potius superiores quam iustitia pares.[1]

Quidquid eiusmodi est in quo non possint plures excellere in eo fit plerumque tanta contentio ut difficillimum sit sanctam servare societatem. Declaravit id modo temeritas C. Caesaris, qui omnia iura divina atque humana pervertit propter eum quem sibi opinionis errore finxerat principatum.[2]

In fact, a "contentio libertatis dignitatisque"—to use a phrase of Livy[3]—became the dominant feature of Roman domestic politics, and dignitas of a kind incompatible with libertas prevailed.

4. THE FOUNDATION OF FREEDOM IN CICERO'S THEORY OF GOVERNMENT

What follows is concerned to examine some salient features of Cicero's *De Re Publica* and *De Legibus* against the background of his times and in the light of his own political experience with a view to ascertaining whether Cicero's political doctrine bore on the problem of political freedom in the last decades of the Republican period, and if so, in what manner.

In spite of the general terms that he occasionally used in the *De Re Publica*, it is obvious that in that treatise Cicero did not theorize on statecraft in general but rather sought to remedy the evils that beset the Roman State of his own times.[4] This intention can be read between the lines of the *De Re Publica* itself, notably the preface to book v, and it also appears from the fact that in the *De Legibus*, the avowed purpose of which is to draw up a code of

---

[1] Cic. *De Off.* I, 64.
[2] *Ib.* I, 26. Cf. *In Cat.* III, 25.   [3] IV, 6, 11.
[4] Cf. V. Pöschl, *Römischer Staat und Griechisches Staatsdenken bei Cicero* (1934), especially pp. 171 ff. Pöschl, however, interprets Cicero's *De Re Publica* as a philosophical forerunner of the Principate inspired by Plato's *Republic*. See also K. Sprey, *De M. Tullii Ciceronis Politica Doctrina*, Zutphen, 1928, pp. 258 ff.

laws to suit the form of government that he described in the *De Re Publica*,[1] Cicero deals, specifically and exclusively, with the laws of Rome.

The *De Re Publica* was composed between the years 54 and 51 B.C. with the experience under the First Triumvirate and the effect of the Conference at Lucca fresh in Cicero's mind. The *De Legibus* was in part composed after the Civil War under Caesar's autocratic régime, and very much with Cicero's own career and fortunes in mind.[2] At the time Cicero wrote the *De Re Publica* the familiar system of government was no longer its own self: the dynasts, for the sake of their own dignitas, seized almost all power, and conducted public affairs according to their own view of efficient government; the constitution was partially disregarded, freedom was curtailed, and on the whole the interests of those in power prevailed. Even so, Cicero did not lose faith in the vitality of the traditional constitution which he believed to be the best form of government,[3] and he attributed the decline of the excellent "vetus res publica", not to any deficiency of the system itself, but to the failure of the Romans to maintain their good old institutions.[4] With such convictions, and with the lessons drawn from recent history in his mind, Cicero approached the question what the best form of government ought to be.

Cicero began his disquisition by defining "res publica" as "res populi", "populus" being a "coetus multitudinis iuris consensu et utilitatis communione sociatus".[5] The full implications of this definition appear in a passage of book III (43 ff.) in which Cicero

---

[1] See *De Leg.* I, 15; 20; II, 14; 23; III, 4; 12–13. And also *ib.* I, 37: Ad res publicas firmandas et ad stabiliendas urbes sanandosque populos omnis nostra pergit oratio. The *De Legibus* was perhaps less topical than the *De Republica*, see *De Leg.* III, 29.

[2] For detailed evidence for the dates of composition see H. W. How, Cicero's Ideal in His *De Republica*, *J.R.S.* xx, pp. 25 ff., and C.W. Keyes in his edition of the *De Rep.* and *De Leg.* (Loeb), pp. 2 ff. and 289 ff.

[3] *De Rep.* I, 70; II, 56; *De Leg.* II, 23. [4] *De Rep.* V, 2.

[5] *De Rep.* I, 39. For a discussion of the Stoic sources of this definition see M. Pohlenz, Cicero De Re Publica als Kunstwerk, *Festschrift Richard Reitzenstein*, 1931, pp. 82 f., and Id. *Antikes Führertum*, 1934, p. 5 n. 2; and R. Stark, *Res Publica*, Göttingen Diss. 1937, pp. 5 ff. For a somewhat different view of the literary sources of this passage in Cicero see Pöschl, *op. cit.* pp. 10 ff. Cicero's sources are also discussed by Sprey, *op. cit.* pp. 116 ff.

lays it down on the strength of the above definition that a State governed by a despot, or an oligarchy, or the multitude, is in fact not a res publica at all, because it ceases to be a res populi.[1] It appears, therefore, that in Cicero's view the very notion of res publica postulates that the State should be the common weal of the entire people, not of any section only; further, that all the people should have a share in the conduct of State affairs; and, finally, that the State should be based on an agreed acceptance of laws equally binding on all. This, however, is not to say that, if it is to be a genuine res publica, the State ought to be a democracy; for in Cicero's opinion democracy had the ring of ochlocracy,[2] and was therefore in principle as sectional as oligarchy or despotism. In the opinion of the present writer, Cicero's intention may be better explained by a passage of the *De Officiis*, I, 85:

Omnino qui rei publicae praefuturi sunt duo Platonis praecepta teneant: unum, ut utilitatem civium sic tueantur ut quaecumque agunt ad eam referant, obliti commodorum suorum; alterum, ut totum corpus rei publicae curent ne, dum partem aliquam tuentur, reliquas deserant.... Qui autem parti civium consulunt, partem negligunt, rem perniciosissimam in civitatem inducunt, seditionem atque discordiam. Ex quo evenit ut alii populares, alii studiosi optimi cuiusque videantur, pauci universorum. Hinc apud Athenienses magnae discordiae; in nostra re publica non solum seditiones sed pestifera etiam bella civilia.

On the strength of the passages of the *De Re Publica* and *De Officiis* just mentioned it may be concluded that, if a State is to be a genuine res publica and immune against civil strife, no sectional interest should be allowed to dominate the State. It would even seem that the notion of res publica postulates respect for interests other than one's own, just as libertas postulates respect for rights other than one's own.[3] And, if that is so, the similarity is not

---

[1] *De Rep.* III, 43: Ubi tyrannus est ibi non vitiosam...sed...nullam esse rem publicam. *Ib.* 44: Vides igitur ne illam quidem quae tota sit in factionis potestate posse vere dici rem publicam. *Ib.* 45: Cum per populum agi dicuntur et esse in populi potestate omnia, cum de quocumque volt supplicium sumit multitudo...potesne tum, Laeli, negare rem esse illam publicam?...Tum Laelius: Ac nullam quidem citius negaverim esse rem publicam quam istam quae tota plane sit in multitudinis potestate.

[2] See *De Rep.* I, 65 ff. and III, 45.

[3] Cf. above, p. 8.

accidental; for is not the res publica the political expression of libertas and, conversely, is not libertas the essence of res publica?[1]

Provided the argument is sound so far, the doctrine of the mixed form of government in Cicero assumes a significance beyond the purely academic sphere. The "mixed form of government" is only a terminological pattern which epitomizes the distribution of power in the State (as distinct from the Separation of Powers). The essential feature of the excellent vetus res publica was a balance of rights, duties, and functions as a result of which the government had enough executive power (potestas), the Senate enough authority, and the people enough freedom.[2] Such a balance of rights, duties, and functions that are matched against each other, and it alone, can prevent the establishment of despotism, or oligarchy, or ochlocracy, all of which, each in its own way, represent the domination of a sectional interest. Cicero was convinced that only a mixed form of government with its system of checks and balances can secure freedom. He made it quite clear that, good though monarchy and aristocracy may be, they are incompatible with the freedom of all, because they deprive a section of the polity of a share in the conduct of public affairs.[3] It seems, therefore, that in Cicero's view all can be free only in a State in which power is distributed between all (needless to say a right is power in a constitutional sense). It is true that Cicero does not accord to all elements in the State an equal amount of power,[4] but this is by no means inconsistent with the Roman concept of freedom, which includes equality before the law but not

[1] The passage *De Rep.* III, 43 ff. is interpreted by R. Stark, *Res Publica*, pp. 44 ff., as implying that a res publica must be a "Rechtsstaat". This is no doubt true, but at the same time it is obvious that the idea of a "Rechtsstaat" does not by itself suffice to explain Cicero's idea of a genuine res publica. For a "Rechtsstaat" may exist under any form of legitimate and constitutional government, whereas a res publica, in Cicero's opinion, is wedded to one particular constitution. Stark declares that "über die Verfassungsform besagte der Terminus (viz. res publica) an sich nichts" (p. 33) which shows that he must have missed the constitutional significance of the notion. V. Pöschl, *op. cit.* pp. 132 ff. (and to some extent also Pohlenz, *Reitzenstein Festschrift*, p. 95), interprets the same passage in the light of Plato's idea of justice. Whatever the merits of that interpretation, it falls short of explaining the political significance of Cicero's statement.

[2] *De Rep.* II, 56–7. Cf. I, 69.

[3] *Ib.* I, 69; III, 46–7; I, 55; II, 43.

[4] Cf. above, p. 42. See also K. Sprey, *op. cit.* pp. 222 ff.

complete egalitarianism of rights.[1] The essential thing is to have, not equal rights, but enough rights on which to found freedom. And the system of checks and balances which results from distribution of power is the only way to secure concern for all interests and respect for all rights, and therefore it is the only way to maintain freedom. For only in a State in which power is not concentrated in the hands of one person, or a sectional group of persons, can there be rule of law equally binding on all, upon which in the last resort freedom rests.[2]

But if this is the case, several questions arise. What is the nature of those laws on which freedom can be founded? What is the source of law? What is it that makes laws binding?

In Rome all popular enactments (populi iussa and plebis scita) were leges, and in all matters, save matters divine,[3] the legislative power, i.e. the populus or plebs with the concurrence of a competent magistrate, was above the law, in the sense that it had the power to repeal any law or to amend it by a new enactment.[4] But if the people is the lawgiver and the ultimate source of law, and if all valid laws are equally binding, a grave antinomy seems inevitable: Is everything just that was placed on the Statute book?

Iam vero illud stultissimum, existimare omnia iusta esse, quae sita sint in populorum institutis aut legibus. Etiamne si quae leges sint tyrannorum? Si triginta illi Athenis leges inponere voluissent, aut si omnes Athenienses delectarentur tyrannicis legibus, num idcirco eae leges iustae haberentur? Nihilo, credo, magis illa quam interrex noster tulit, ut dictator, quem vellet civium, aut indicta causa, inpune posset occidere.[5]

Further, is every valid enactment absolutely binding regardless of its content?

---

[1] Cf. above, pp. 9 ff. and especially pp. 13 ff.

[2] Cf. above, pp. 7 ff. For a somewhat similar view of Cicero's doctrine see J. Kaerst, Scipio Aemilianus, die Stoa und der Prinzipat, in *N. J. f. Wiss.* v (1929), pp. 661 f.

[3] See Mommsen, *Staatsrecht* III, 335.

[4] Livy VII, 17, 12: In XII tabulis legem esse ut quodcumque postremum populus iussisset id ius ratumque esset. Cf. the caput tralaticium de impunitate in the Lex de Imperio Vespasiani. On the repeal of laws see Cic. *Ad Att.* III, 23, 2; 15, 6; *Cum Senat. Grat.* 8.

[5] *De Leg.* I, 42. The law referred to is that of L. Valerius Flaccus concerning Sulla's dictatorship. Cf. *De Lege Agr.* III, 5 and *II in Verr.* III, 82.

Quid, quod m ulta perniciose, multa pestifere sciscuntur in populis? quae non magis le gis nomen adtingunt quam si latrones aliquas consensu suo sanxerint. N am neque medicorum praecepta dici vere possunt, si quae inscii inperi tique pro salutaribus mortifera conscripserunt, neque in populo lex, cuic uimodi fuerit illa, etiamsi perniciosum aliquid populus acceperit.[1]

But if some laws are good and others bad, what is the criterion to judg e them by? And if bad laws are not laws at all, despite the fact that they were formally enacted by the legislature, what is it that makes good laws binding and bad ones null and void? Some such questions must have exercised Cicero's mind, for, as will presently be seen, his statement of the nature and the force of law offers an answer to such questions. Seeking to explain the nature of law, Cicero introduced into Roman political thought what appears to be a new, though not original, theory, namely the doctrine of natural law, which is expounded at some length in book II of the *De Legibus*, and with which Cicero must have dealt to some extent in the *De Re Publica*, as witness the fragment § 33 of book III.

Following the teaching of the Stoics, Cicero asserts that the various laws peoples possess derive their power from the primal, everlasting, and immutable law which is divine or natural reason;[2] that Law is the distinction between things just and unjust made in agreement with Nature, which is the standard of all human laws;[3] and that the purpose of true laws is the safety of citizens, preservation of States, and the tranquillity and happiness of human life.[4]

It is not necessary here to discuss the merits, or lack of them, of Cicero's doctrine of natural law. For the present purpose the signifi-cance of this doctrine in Cicero's theory of government lies in the fact that it testifies to his desire to find a firm basis for the rule of law and thereby for the commonwealth and freedom. There is in the *De Legibus* a remark that throws much light on Cicero's intention. Immediately before the beginning of his proposed code of laws he stated that natural law could be neither repealed nor abrogated, and that the laws he was about to propose would be of the kind that

---

[1] *De Leg.* II, 13.
[2] *Ib.* II, 8–9, 11, 13–14; *De Rep.* III, 33.
[3] *De Leg.* II, 13. Cf. II, 11 *ad fin.* and also I, 28.
[4] *Ib.* II, 11.

would never be repealed.[1] Cicero seems to have been aware of the conflict between the conceptions of law as will and law as reason, and he tried to resolve the conflict by making natural law (i.e. law as reason) the formative and controlling standard of statutory law (i.e. law as will). If Cicero really believed that the code he proposed was an embodiment of natural law, it was a somewhat naïve belief. But even if naïve, his assertion is in the highest degree significant, because it means that in Cicero's opinion the fundamental laws of Rome ought to be unalterable, that is to say, the fundamental laws, i.e. the constitution, ought to be above the ordinary legislative power.[2]

It seems that the political experience both of his own and of the preceding age led Cicero to the conclusion that legality did not alone suffice to secure the freedom and well-being of the State and its citizens. He thought the constitution ought to have a moral basis and a moral purpose, and, as such, it ought to have permanent validity irrespective of political expediency or the changing moods of the people. It may well be doubted whether the doctrine of natural law provided the best solution of the problem that confronted Cicero, but it certainly provides a solution in that it makes human laws depend on absolute values independent of man. For if indeed "legum idcirco omnes servi sumus ut liberi esse possimus"(*Pro Cluent.* 146) we must have the assurance that the laws will be a just and enlightened master.

However, as Aristotle pointed out, good laws, if they are not obeyed, do not constitute good government.[3] During Cicero's own lifetime illegality became almost endemic, and he did not fail to see that that was due, not to a shortcoming of the laws, but to a failure of men, "nostris vitiis non casu aliquo rem publicam verbo retinemus, re ipsa iam pridem amisimus" (*De Rep.* v, 2). Rome had, so Cicero thought, the best constitution a State could have; nevertheless he agreed with Ennius that her true strength was the quality of her

---

[1] *Ib.* II, 14: Lex autem illa, cuius vim explicavi, neque tolli nec abrogari potest.—Q. Eas tu igitur leges rogabis videlicet, quae numquam abrogentur? —M. Certe, si modo acceptae a duobus vobis erunt.

[2] For similar interpretations of Cicero's view see C. W. Keyes, Original Elements in Cicero's Ideal Constitution, *A.J.Ph.* XLII (1921), p. 311; F. Cauer, *Ciceros politisches Denken*, Berlin, 1903, pp. 28 ff.; Sprey, *op. cit.* pp. 217 ff.

[3] *Polit.* IV, 8, p. 1294a, 3.

people, "Moribus antiquis res stat Romana virisque". And the moral decay of the people brought about the decline of Rome's excellent constitution.[1]

The source of trouble was the all too ambitious pursuit of dignitas.[2] Excessive dignitas became a destructive factor, because in its pursuit the moral basis on which dignitas must rest was disregarded. Cicero's indignation at the news of Caesar's advance after the outbreak of the Civil War is worth quoting:

> Quaeso, quid est hoc? aut quid agitur? Mihi enim tenebrae sunt. Cingulum, inquit, nos tenemus; Anconem amisimus; Labienus discessit a Caesare. Utrum de imperatore populi Romani, an de Hannibale loquimur? O hominem amentem et miserum, qui ne umbram quidem umquam τοῦ καλοῦ viderit! Atque haec ait omnia facere se dignitatis causa. Ubi est autem dignitas, nisi ubi est honestas? Honestum igitur habere exercitum nullo publico consilio, occupare urbes civium quo facilior sit aditus ad patriam, χρεῶν ἀποκοπάς, φυγάδων καθόδους, sexcenta alia scelera moliri?[3]

It would be unfair to Cicero to attribute his moral indignation wholly and solely to the impact of the news. It is noteworthy that of all Republican writers Cicero alone conceived dignitas as a sense of unselfish and unconditional duty, and not merely as a title to respect and political pre-eminence.[4] This is all the more important in view of what Cicero says in the fifth and sixth books of his *De Re Publica* about the princeps civitatis, the Elder Statesman, whose wisdom and moral authority should guide the State. It seems from the scanty fragments of those books that, on the one hand, Cicero expected the people to show honour to the princeps,[5] but, on

---

[1] *De Rep.* v, 1 ff. A similar view is expressed by Sallust, *Cat.* 9 f.; 52, 19; *Hist.* 1, 7, 11–12, 16 M. Cf. Horace, *Odes* III, 24, 35.

[2] *De Off.* 1, 26 and 64, quoted above. Cf. Sallust, *Hist.* 1, 7 M: Nobis primae dissensiones vitio humani ingenii evenere, quod inquies atque indomitum semper inter certamina libertatis aut gloriae aut dominationis agit.

[3] *Ad Att.* VII, 11, 1.

[4] See *Pro Cluent.* 150; *Pro Sest.* 48; *Ad Att.* VII, 17, 4; *Phil.* I, 14 f. This aspect of dignitas in Cicero's writings is fully discussed by H. Wegehaupt, *op. cit.* pp. 24 f. Wegehaupt, however, does not seem to be right in his criticism (p. 38) of R. Reitzenstein, *Gött. Nach.* 1917, p. 434, who stressed the other aspect of dignitas, namely a title to respect and honour, which is very prominent in Caesar.

[5] *De Rep.* v, 9.

the other, he demanded of him devotion to duty and unselfish service to the commonwealth,[1] the reward for such service being in his opinion, not worldly aggrandizement, but everlasting fame and eternal bliss in after life, as foreshadowed in Scipio's Dream.[2] This seems to be what Cicero thought the pursuit of dignitas ought to be.

Therefore, it seems that far from being an advocacy and theoretical justification of an institutional principate[3] of the kind that was established by Augustus and allegedly coveted by Pompey,[4] the *De Re Publica* is a vindication of the vetus res publica and a call to the statesmen of the day for a change of heart; it is not the harbinger of the approaching Principate, but, with the *De Legibus*, the swan-song of Republican constitutionalism based on the idea that "libertas in legibus consistit". As Cicero himself realized, the leading figures in Roman politics did not share his moral idealism.[5] Although there is evidence that the *De Re Publica* had a warm reception,[6] Cicero's was a voice crying in the wilderness.

5. LIBERTAS UNDER INCIPIENT AUTOCRACY

As a phase in the history of political freedom at Rome Caesar's dictatorship can, and should, be approached from two different points of view: the character of that régime is one, the attitude of the republicans towards it is the other.

A tradition which has outlived its originators describes Caesar as a virtual, or at least a would-be, monarch. But, speculations on his aims apart, Caesar's "regnum" was essentially no more regal than the "regnum Sullanum".[7] As has been seen,[8] "regnum" was a derogatory term of political invective, and was profusely used after the Gracchi. It had no doubt its roots in the aversion to kingship that prevailed in Republican Rome ever since the expulsion of the

---

[1] *Ad Att.* VIII, 11, 1. Cf. *De Off.* I, 85.   [2] *De Rep.* VI, 13 and 29.

[3] It is noteworthy that in *Ad Q. Fr.* III, 5 and 6, 1, Cicero defines the subject of his *De Re Publica* as "de optimo statu civitatis et de *optimo cive*".

[4] As asserted by E. Meyer, *Caesars Monarchie und das Principat des Pompeius*[3], pp. 177 ff. Sprey, *op. cit.* pp. 191 ff., thoroughly refuted Meyer's theory.

[5] *Ad Att.* VII, 11, 1; VIII, 11, 1 f.   [6] *Ad Fam.* VIII, 1, 4.

[7] See F. E. Adcock, *C.A.H.* IX, pp. 718–35, esp. 727.

[8] Above, pp. 62 ff.

G

last Tarquin, but with regard to Roman domestic politics in the Late Republic "regnum" connoted unconstitutional power rather than institutional kingship. But although Caesar's position was not altogether unprecedented, it was none the less anomalous and inconsistent with the traditional concept of a free State. A dictatorship for life with its overriding powers and unlimited scope could not but paralyse the whole Republican system, no matter what pains were taken to preserve its form. Par potestas and potestas ad tempus were the chief exponents of republicanism and political freedom at Rome.[1] It is true that occasions on which one man held all power were within living memory,[2] but in the case of Caesar such power was granted for life; this was unprecedented and, in the eyes of constitutionalists, an arrogation of despotic power.[3]

To the strict republicans Caesar, for all his clemency and friendliness, was an oppressive tyrant, who destroyed the republican institutions and suppressed freedom.[4] They killed Caesar in the name of libertas and for the purpose of restoring the res publica. Thanks especially to Cicero's correspondence, it is possible to form some idea of what res publica and libertas meant to a Roman of Cicero's social standing and political persuasion.

The impression one gains from the Latin literature of the Republican period in general, and from Cicero's writings in particular, is that to a Roman senator the res publica was at the same time a form of government and a way of life. Free political activity among his equals was as a rule considered to be the senator's vocation and his aim in life. The display of one's abilities and free competition for honour and glory were felt to be the life-blood of republicanism.[5]

[1] See above, pp. 22 ff.

[2] Cic. *Phil.* v, 17: Cinnam memini, vidi Sullam, modo Caesarem: hi enim tres post civitatem a L. Bruto liberatam plus potuerunt quam universa res publica. Cf. also *ib.* II, 108.

[3] *Ib.* I, 3: Dictaturam quae vim iam regiae potestatis obsederat.

[4] E.g. *Ad Att.* x, 4, 2: Nec iam recusat sed quodam modo postulat ut, quem ad modum est, sic etiam appelletur tyrannus. Cf. *Phil.* I, 4, 6, 13, 15; II, 34, 64, 87, 96, 108, 110, 117; *De Off.* III, 83.

[5] Cic. *Phil.* XIV, 17: Magnus est in re publica campus, ut sapienter dicere Crassus solebat: multis apertus cursus ad laudem. Seneca, *Ep.* 98, 13: Honores reppulit pater Sextius, qui ita natus, ut rem publicam *deberet* capessere, etc. Cf. also Cic. *Pro Archia*, 29.

People who held such views could, to some extent, be conciliated by Caesar's clemency only so long as they hoped that he would use his enormous power for the purpose of reconstituting the shattered Republic,[1] and that they would be called on to act at least as masons, if not as architects, in the work of reconstruction.[2] But evidence was mounting that Caesar did not intend to reconstitute the State, to say nothing of restoring the old order. It must have been rumoured at Rome that he said the res publica was a sham not worth having;[3] he certainly acted alone without paying much attention even to the advice of his associates.[4]

One might publish with impunity laudations of Cato, the martyr of freedom,[5] but freedom of speech in the Senate was gone,[6] and participation in the debates—a thing that to many a senator must have seemed a most important element in Roman government— became useless.[7] Caesar wanted people to cooperate but made it clear that he would not gladly listen to advice that was not in tune with his intentions.[8] The dictator was no longer a magistrate socially equal to members of the senatorial class: it was difficult to see him,[9] it was tiresome to entertain him as guest.[10] He was given unusual honours verging on the superhuman; he did not show due respect to the Senate;[11] he gave offence, perhaps inadvertently, by appointing a consul suffect for one day;[12] and the episode of Laberius may have been a painful reminder that the dignity of a Roman knight was not secure against degradation by a whim of the autocrat. There was truth in Laberius' line, "Porro, Quirites, libertatem perdimus".[13]

[1] See Cic. *Pro Marcello*, and *Ad Fam.* IV, 4, 3; VI, 10, 5; IX, 17, 2; XIII, 68, 2.

[2] Cic. *Ad Fam.* IX, 2, 5.   [3] Suet. *Div. Jul.* 77.

[4] Cic. *Ad Att.* X, 4, 9; *Ad Fam.* IV, 9, 2.

[5] To Cicero's "Cato" and other "Catones" that followed it Caesar replied with the pen only, see Tac. *Ann.* IV, 34, 7.

[6] See *Ad Fam.* IV, 9, 2; IX, 16, 3 (46 B.C.); IV, 14, 1 (46 B.C.).

[7] *Ib.* IX, 15, 4.

[8] As happened in the case of Cicero's συμβουλευτικός, see E. Meyer, *op. cit.* pp. 438 ff.

[9] Cic. *Ad Att.* XIV, 1, 2; 2, 3; *Ad Fam.* IV, 7, 6; VI, 13, 3; 14, 2.

[10] Cic. *Ad Att.* XIII, 52, 2.

[11] Suet. *Div. Jul.* 78, 1.   [12] Cic. *Ad Fam.* VII, 30.

[13] See Macrob. II, 7, 1–4. Cicero seems to have recalled the opening lines of Laberius' poem—Necessitas, cuius cursus transversi impetum Voluere multi effugere, pauci potuerunt, Quo me detrudit paene extremis sensibus!— in his *De Off.* I, 114: Sin aliquando necessitas nos ad ea detruserit quae nostri

Autocracy lay heavily on the Roman nobility because it cut to the heart of their cherished notions and way of life. What Brutus the tyrannicide expounded, probably in 53 B.C., by way of principle, became grim reality under Caesar: "Praestat enim nemini imperare quam alicui servire: sine illo enim vivere honeste licet, cum hoc vivendi nulla condicio est."[1] Even Epicureans like Cassius found that they could not, under Caesar's autocracy, remain in quietist aloofness from politics.[2] It is noteworthy that Cassius went Epicurean in 46 B.C., the year when there was hope of conciliation with a kind master.[3] But apparently it did not take him long to discover that escapism was not the course for a Cassius to take: "C. Cassius in ea familia natus, quae non modo dominatum sed ne potentiam quidem cuiusdam ferre potuit."[4] The letters of M. Brutus to Cicero and to Atticus in which he speaks of Cicero's attitude to Octavian reveal indirectly his own attitude to autocracy.[5] He hates domination that is above the law.[6] He cannot bear to think that his safety should depend on the goodwill of anybody;[7] was not the purpose of the rising against the dynast to prevent such an existence?[8] To live a precarious life, to endure submission and to suffer insults is worse than exile, worse even than death.[9] It appears from those letters, as well as from his dictum quoted above, that Brutus was inspired by

---

ingenii non erunt. The whole episode must have impressed him, although he wrote at that time (*Ad Fam.* XII, 18, 2): Equidem sic iam obdurui ut ludis Caesaris nostri animo aequissimo viderem T. Plancum, audirem Laberi et Publili poemata.

[1] In a speech De Dictatura Pompei, quoted in Quintil. IX, 3, 95. See also Asinius Pollio, in *Ad Fam.* X, 31, 3 (16 March 43 B.C.): Cuius facti iniustissima invidia erudire me potuit quam iucunda libertas et quam misera sub dominatione vita esset. Ita si id agitur ut rursus in potestate omnia unius sint, ei me profiteor inimicum, nec periculum est ullum quod pro libertate aut refugiam aut deprecer.

[2] See A. Momigliano, *J.R.S.* XXXI (1941), pp. 151 ff.

[3] In 45 B.C. when Caesar went to war in Spain, Cassius wrote to Cicero, *Ad Fam.* XV, 19, 4: Peream nisi sollicitus sum ac malo veterem et clementem dominum habere quam novum et crudelem experiri.

[4] Cic. *Phil.* II, 26.

[5] *Ad Brut.* I, 16 and 17. For a discussion of the authenticity of these letters —which is accepted here—see R. Y. Tyrrell and L. C. Purser, *The Correspondence of Cicero*, vol. VI, pp. CXI ff.

[6] *Ib.* 17, 6 and 16, 5.

[7] 16, 1.

[8] 16, 4.

[9] 16, 1 *ad fin.* and 6.

the realization that existence under tyranny can be bought only at the price of personal freedom and dignity.[1]

Such sentiments as those described above do not explain all the motives that inspired the conspiracy against Caesar, but they go some way towards explaining the spirit in which the conspiracy was conceived.

If it was hoped that the removal of the autocrat would by itself restore republican freedom, disillusionment soon set in. "Quem ad modum tu praecipis," wrote Cicero to Atticus in April 44, "contenti Idibus Martiis simus, quae quidem nostris amicis, divinis viris, aditum ad caelum dederunt, libertatem populo Romano non dederunt."[2] And again: "Equidem doleo quod numquam in ulla civitate accidit, non una cum libertate rem publicam recuperatam."[3] There was more truth than he realized in Cicero's judgement that the assassination of Caesar was undertaken with much courage and little wisdom.[4] The liberation of the Republic was doomed to fail, not because, as Cicero thought, the liberators failed to strike down Antony, but because they failed to perceive that Caesar's régime was a result of the disintegration of the old Republic, not its cause.

6. Freedom versus Order and Security

Owing to the character of our literary sources we have some acquaintance with the views and sentiments of leading personalities, whereas what the ordinary people thought is largely a matter of conjecture and generalization. But since, apart from enforced collaboration or bought sympathies, the support freely given by the people to either cause was by no means a negligible factor in the political struggle of the Late Republic and may have appreciably affected its outcome, it is essential to ascertain so far as possible what the people in general really wanted, so that we can better appreciate the stand they took in the matter of republicanism and political freedom. The evidence for this is unfortunately very scanty and largely indirect; nevertheless it throws some light on the question.

In some passages of Sallust and Cicero that may fairly be regarded as specimens of propagandist statements either of the Populares or

[1] 16, 5 *ad fin.*, 17, 6. Cf. 17, 5.
[2] *Ad Att.* XIV, 14, 3.
[3] *Ib.* XIV, 4, 1.
[4] *Ib.* XIV, 21, 3; XV, 4, 2.

the Optimates, an undercurrent of rebuke to their followers for insufficient support occasionally runs alongside of the invective against their acknowledged opponents. That rebuke, as will presently be seen, arose from the fact that while politicians agitated for libertas or dignitas the ordinary and less politically-minded people desired peace, order, security, tranquillity.

Aemilius Lepidus, who fomented a movement against the Sullan régime in the year 78 B.C., is credited with the following statements:

Itaque illa quies et otium cum libertate quae multi probi potius quam laborem cum honoribus capessebant, nulla sunt: hac tempestate serviundum aut imperitandum, habendus metus est aut faciundus, Quirites.

And:

Quae [viz. the Sullan settlement] si vobis pax et composita intelleguntur, maxuma turbamenta rei publicae atque exitia probate, adnuite legibus inpositis, accipite otium cum servitio... Mihi... potior visa est periculosa libertas quieto servitio.[1]

Licinius Macer, who in 73 B.C. agitated for the restoration of the tribunician power, is said to have addressed the people in a similar vein:

Quod ego vos moneo quaesoque (Quirites) ut animadvortatis neu nomina rerum ad ignaviam mutantes otium pro servitio appelletis. Quo iam ipso frui, si vera et honesta flagitium superaverit, non est condicio; fuisset, si omnino quiessetis.

And:

Verum occupavit nescio quae vos torpedo, qua non gloria movemini neque flagitio, cunctaque praesenti ignavia mutavistis, abunde libertatem rati, scilicet quia tergis abstinetur et huc ire licet et illuc.[2]

It seems that the attempts to foment a popular rising collided with the people's desire of otium, and therefore the demagogues represent otium as an indolent acceptance of servitium or as neglect of libertas. But this is not the case. Otium means leisured life or a course of life avoiding active participation in politics,[3] but it also

---

[1] Sallust, *Hist.* I, 55, 9–10 and 25–6 M.
[2] *Ib.* III, 48, 13 and 26. Cf. *Jug.* 31, 2.
[3] *Hist.* I, 55, 9; Cic. *Pro Cluent.* 153; *Pro Rab. Post.* 17.

means a state of security[1] and peace,[2] and it approaches in meaning to pax and tranquillitas, with which it is often coupled.[3]

That the people were concerned above all for otium, in the sense of peaceful security, is also borne out by Cicero. In his speeches against the Land Bill of Rullus Cicero said: "Etenim, ut circumspiciamus omnia, quae populo grata atque iucunda sunt, nihil tam populare quam pacem, quam concordiam, quam otium reperiemus."[4] And: "Quis enim umquam tam secunda contione legem agrariam suasit, quam ego dissuasi?...Ex quo intellegi, Quirites, potest, nihil esse tam populare quam id, quod ego vobis in hunc annum consul popularis affero, pacem, tranquillitatem, otium."[5] With every allowance for exaggeration and deliberate confusion of the issues, it seems that Cicero would not have spoken as he did had he not felt that he knew the true sentiments of his listeners. Further, on the eve of the Civil War, Cicero wrote: "An faeneratores, an agricolas (bonos putas), quibus optatissimum est otium? Nisi eos timere putas, ne sub regno sint, qui id numquam, dummodo otiosi essent, recusarunt."[6] And again, shortly after the outbreak of the War: "Multum mecum municipales homines loquuntur, multum rusticani. Nihil prorsus aliud curant nisi agros, nisi villulas, nisi nummulos suos."[7] It appears therefore that the ordinary people wanted peace and security; if possible, "cum libertate"; if not, they seem to have been inclined to prefer otium to what was considered to be libertas.

A similar mood must have existed also among senators who by reason of their social standing were expected to show much concern for their dignitas. In his *Pro Sestio*, and elsewhere, Cicero stated that the ideal of the Optimates was "cum dignitate otium".[8] In that phrase "otium" may mean private leisure, as it does in fact in the

---

[1] See Horace, *Odes* II, 16, 1–4.

[2] Caes. *Bell. Civ.* I, 5, 5; Cic. *Phil.* I, 16; II, 113; VIII, 11; *Ad Att.* XIV, 21, 2; XV, 2, 3; *Ad Brut.* I, 15, 4.

[3] E.g. Cic. *De Lege Agr.* II, 102; *Phil.* V, 41; *Pro Mur.* 78; 86. Some fine remarks on the Roman idea of peace will be found in Harald Fuchs, *Augustin und der antike Friedensgedanke, Neue philologische Untersuchungen*, 3. Heft, Berlin, 1926, pp. 182–205.

[4] I, 23.   [5] II, 101 ff.

[6] *Ad Att.* VII, 7, 5 (Dec. 50 B.C.).

[7] *Ib.* VIII, 13, 2 (1 March 49 B.C.).

[8] *Pro Sest.* 98. Cf. *Ad Fam.* I, 9, 21.

preface to the *De Oratore* (I, I, I). But the long list of the essentials of the "otiosa dignitas" which he gives in the *Pro Sestio* (98) clearly shows that what Cicero had in mind, in that speech at any rate, was, in the first place, otium in the sense of public peace and order, not private leisure. And as regards dignitas he states clearly that it is the object of the aristocrats (optimi cuiusque) while otium is the advantage of the people in general.[1] It seems therefore that in the *Pro Sestio* otium cum dignitate means peace for all and distinction for some.[2] In regard to this ideal of otium cum dignitate Cicero, with an obvious allusion to recent events, says:

> Maioribus praesidiis et copiis oppugnatur res publica quam defenditur, propterea quod audaces homines et perditi nutu impelluntur...boni nescio quo modo tardiores sunt et...ad extremum ipsa denique necessitate excitantur; ita ut nonnumquam cunctatione ac tarditate, dum otium volunt etiam sine dignitate retinere, ipsi utrumque amittant.[3]

Just as the Populares sought to persuade the People that otium without libertas was not otium at all, so Cicero tried to convince some of the ruling class that an accommodation at the price of their dignitas is no accommodation at all, for if they surrender their dignitas for the sake of otium they will not have otium either. Like the Popularis Licinius Macer, who scornfully remarked that the People mistook slavery for otium, Cicero said in his second *Philippic*:

> Quam volent illi cedant otio consulentes, tamen a re publica revocabuntur. Et nomen pacis dulce est, et res ipsa salutaris. Sed inter pacem et servitium plurimum interest. Pax est tranquilla libertas.[4]

From all that has been said it would appear that there were people, both senators and ordinary citizens, who during the difficult period

---

[1] *Pro Sest.* 104. Cf. above, p. 41.

[2] In this sense he uses otium and dignitas in *Phil.* x, 3: Cur, cum te et vita et fortuna tua ad otium et ad dignitatem invitet, ea probas...quae sint inimica et otio communi et dignitati tuae? See also E. Remy, Dignitas cum otio, *Musée Belge* XXXII (1928), pp. 113 f., who interprets dignitas in the sense of dignitas imperii rather than dignitas optimi cuiusque. For an entirely different interpretation of "otium cum dignitate" see H. Wegehaupt, *Die Bedeutung und Anwendung von dignitas*, pp. 53–60.

[3] *Pro Sest.* 100. Cf. *ib.* 98: Neque ullum amplexari otium quod abhorreat a dignitate. And also *Ad Fam.* I, 7, 10 *ad fin.*

[4] *Phil.* II, 113. Cf. *Phil.* VIII, 12: Sed quaeso, Calene, quid tu? Servitutem pacem vocas?

of civil discord wished for peace and security above all else. And this circumstance may partially explain why the attempts to maintain the traditional form of government failed.

Cicero's assertion to the contrary notwithstanding,[1] it is on the whole true that after the assassination of Caesar the Roman People showed little enthusiasm for the cause of republican freedom. Why did this happen? There was no doubt much weariness and indifference resulting from the Civil Wars and the long years of domestic strife. But it would be an over-simplification of the issue to ascribe the lack of enthusiasm for the cause of freedom solely to a failure of nerve. After all, the people responded when Italy was, or seemed to be, in danger; but they failed to respond when republicanism was in danger. The reason for this seems to be that gradually the conviction struck root that what was offered under the name of libertas was not worth fighting and dying for. Such a view may have been inspired by certain considerations which deserve notice.

It has already been said that during the Late Republican period libertas as a political watchword meant in the first place republicanism. The tenacity with which the Romans adhered for centuries to the republican form of government derived not from an ideological preference for any form of government but from the fact that at Rome republican institutions not only prevented the establishment of monarchy but provided effective guarantees of personal liberty. During the closing period of the Republic, however, republicanism and personal freedom were no longer allied in the same sense as they were before. Republicanism came more and more to mean a wild competition for power, a pursuit of dignitas with complete disregard for other people's rights. The defenders of republicanism were primarily concerned for the auctoritas senatus and the constitutionalism of the imperia and potestates. But to the lives of ordinary people it was of slight moment whether the Senate was or was not free, or whether the magistracies did or did not conform to the standards of rigorous constitutionalism. It was in the lawcourts and in the smooth working of the rapidly growing system of civil law that the interests of personal liberty really lay, but it was only too obvious that without peace and order freedom became nugatory, or

[1] *Ad Fam.* x, 12, 4; *Phil.* III, 32.

to use Cicero's own words, "libertas sine pace nulla est".[1] At Rome the rule of law was, and was considered to be, the foundation of freedom. But although the republican form of government was designed to establish the rule of law and order, during the closing decades of the Republic the rule of law became precarious, and at times it was replaced by the law of the stronger. Freedom without the rule of law was inconceivable at Rome, but the laws could no longer be relied upon, "invalido legum auxilio quae vi, ambitu, postremo pecunia turbabantur".[2]

Roman republicanism had sought to secure distribution of power in a manner that admitted of a strong government and at the same time safeguarded personal freedom. But, for reasons that have been discussed above, the system of checks and balances broke down, and Rome was faced with the grave fact that the form of government considered to be the embodiment of political freedom was ill suited to secure law and order. The conflict between libertas, in the sense of republicanism, and order lasted too long to be seen as a transitory crisis, and gradually people may have come to the conclusion that, since distribution of power failed to secure law and order, it was worth looking for other means to achieve the same end. Those who lived to see recurrent civil wars as inescapable concomitants of the old form of government may have thought that a new dispensation that would ensure peace was worth having even at the price of the old constitution.[3] And this may be one of the reasons why the Romans, for all their love of freedom, accepted in the end a form of government the salient feature of which was permanent concentration of power in the hands of one man. "Omnem potentiam ad unum conferri pacis interfuit."[4]

---

[1] *Ad Brut.* II, 5, 1.

[2] Tac. *Ann.* I, 2, 2. Cf. Cic. *Phil.* VIII, 11; *Pro Mil.* 18; Lucan I, 171–82; Tac. *Ann.* III, 27, 1–28, 2 ("non mos non ius").

[3] Favonius, the intimate friend of Cato, thought χεῖρον εἶναι μοναρχίας παρανόμου πόλεμον ἐμφύλιον, Plut. *Brut.* 12, 3.

[4] Tac. *Hist.* I, 1, 1.

THE AUGUSTAN PRINCIPATE
IN RELATION TO LIBERTAS

1. PAX ET PRINCEPS

Even Tacitus, who found much to criticize in the Augustan Principate, did not deny it one great achievement, the restoration of peace:
"Sexto...consulatu Caesar Augustus, potentiae securus, quae
triumviratu iusserat abolevit, deditque iura quis pace et principe
uteremur."[1] And in an earlier work he indicated that the coincidence
of peace and the Principate was not accidental, "postquam bellatum
apud Actium...omnem potentiam ad unum conferri pacis interfuit".[2] It is no doubt a fact of great moment for our estimate of the
Principate that Augustus himself laid as much stress on the restoration of peace as on the restoration of the Republic.[3] And indeed it
seems that the Romans, in so far as they had a free choice at all,
willingly accepted the Principate, not because they believed that
it was tantamount to the old Republican form of government, but
above all because they realized that the new dispensation offered
a prospect of lasting peace.

A people exhausted with fratricidal wars[4] needed and desired
internal peace, stability, and order more than anything else. The
decisive victory of Actium put an end to civil war. But while
victories may bring peace, they cannot alone secure it. Sulla was
victorious; he claimed to have established peace,[5] yet it did not last

---

[1] *Ann.* III, 28, 3; cf. I, 2, 1; *Dial.* 38, 2 *ad fin.* Philo, *Legat. ad Gaium,*
39, 309.

[2] *Hist.* I, 1, 1. Cf. *Ann.* IV, 33, 2. See also Lucan I, 670; Appian, *Bell.
Civ.* I, 6, 24.

[3] Witness, e.g., the legend P A X on the coin on which Augustus is styled
libertatis p. R. vindex (see H. Mattingly, *Coins of the Roman Empire in the
British Museum,* vol. I, p. 112, no. 691, and plate 17, 4); the reference in the
Res Gestae, 13, to the closing of the temple of Janus; the dedication of the
Ara Pacis Augustae.

[4] Horace, *Epodes* XVI, 1 f.: Altera iam teritur bellis civilibus aetas Suis et
ipsa Roma viribus ruit.

[5] See Sallust, *Hist.* I, 55, 24 M.

long. Caesar also was victorious, and the peace his victories brought
was short-lived too. How could the hard-won peace be made to
last? This was the heart of the problem that faced the Romans after
Actium.

We have seen that in the Roman view, so far as it could be
ascertained, the domestic troubles that beset the Late Republic were
due to a rivalry for personal aggrandizement rather than to a conflict
between divergent policies based on irreconcilable principles. The
Civil War in particular was regarded as a contest for primacy
between Pompey and Caesar, a contest for dignitas and principatus.
It may therefore have seemed to the Romans that civil strife and
civil wars would continue as long as ambitious men strove to advance
their own dignitas by all means and at all costs, and as long as there
existed conditions favourable to such pursuits. Cicero called for
a change of heart. But it is easier to alter political institutions than
to change human nature.[1] And in this respect the Principate offered
a solution to the problem that defied Republican statesmanship and
destroyed the Republic.[2]

If rivalry for dignitas was the root of civil strife, and if that rivalry
was made possible by the fact that both civil and military power was
distributed among many agents, a supremacy of one man, so firmly
established as to leave no room for temptation to ambition, let alone
for a trial of strength, seemed to remove the major source of civil
war. Such ideas were not new at Rome. Sallust makes Aemilius
Lepidus say of Sulla: "Neque aliter rem publicam et belli finem ait
(Sulla), nisi maneat expulsa agris plebes, praeda civilis acerbissima,
ius iudiciumque omnium rerum penes se, quod populi Romani
fuit."[3] Similarly, Caesar used to say: "Non tam sua quam
rei publicae interesse uti salvus esset; se iam pridem potentiae
gloriaeque abunde adeptum; rem publicam, si quid sibi eveniret,
neque quietam fore et aliquando deteriore condicione civilia bella
subituram."[4] And history proved him to be right. It was no doubt

---

[1] Seneca, De Benef. II, 20, 2, says Brutus erred if he thought "civitatem in
priorem formam posse revocari amissis pristinis moribus".

[2] Cf. R. Syme, The Roman Revolution, p. 315.

[3] Hist. I, 55, 24 M. If this remark were representative of Sulla's views, it
would lend much point to Caesar's criticism, "Sullam nescisse litteras, qui
dictaturam deposuerit", Suet. Div. Jul. 77.

[4] Suet. Div. Jul. 86, 2.

under the stress of recurrent civil war that the Romans came to the conclusion "non aliud discordantis patriae remedium fuisse quam ut ab uno regeretur".[1]

It seems therefore that the Romans responded favourably to the establishment of the Principate, not because they erroneously believed that it meant no change in the old order, but precisely because they were well aware of the immense change that took place: instead of a quivering balance of discordant powers and an armed truce between competing dignitates, there emerged an accumulation of power at the top, and a dignitas surpassing all beyond challenge. One cannot help thinking that Mommsen, although he missed the actual reading of the *Res Gestae*,[2] was nearer the truth of the matter when he conjectured "praestiti omnibus *dignitate*" in Augustus's famous definition of his place in the State.

As has been seen in the previous chapter, the Republic in its last stage laboured under two interdependent difficulties: the one was a "contentio libertatis dignitatisque"; the other, a conflict between libertas and otium; and the second was the result of the first. The Principate by its very existence put an end to the rivalry for dignitas; it brought the "dulcedo otii";[3] but what happened to libertas?

---

[1] Tac. *Ann.* I, 9, 5. Cf. *Ann.* IV, 33, 2; *Hist.* I, 1, 1 and 16, 1. See also Seneca, *De Clem.* I, 4. E. Schönbauer, Untersuchungen zum römischen Staats- und Wirtschaftsrecht, Wesen und Ursprung des Prinzipats, *Z.d.Sav.- Stif. Rom. Abt.* XLVII (1927), pp. 310 ff., maintains that the favourable disposition of the Romans to the Principate resulted from the influence of Platonic and Aristotelian political ideas which were transplanted to Rome by Panaetius the Stoic and inspired first Scipio the Younger and later Cicero. (For this view cf. J. Kaerst, *N.J.f.Wiss.* V (1929), pp. 653 ff.) Formative influence of Stoicism upon the Principate is assumed by A. v. Domaszewski, Die philosophische Grundlage des Augusteischen Principats, in *Bilder und Studien aus drei Jahrtausenden, Gothein Festgabe*, 1925, pp. 63–71. But why vainly search in Stoic philosophy for the lessons the Romans had been taught in the hard school of civil war? Cf. R. Syme, *op. cit.* pp. 321 ff.

[2] 34, 3. See *Res Gestae Divi Augusti ex monumentis Ancyrano et Apolloniensi, iterum ed. Th. Mommsen* (1883), p. 144.

[3] Tac. *Ann.* I, 2, 1. See also Virgil, *Ecl.* I, 6 ff., with which compare Seneca, *Ep.* 73, 8 and 10–11.

2. "LIBERTATIS VINDEX": AN OUTWORN PHRASE

The *Res Gestae Divi Augusti*[1] opens with a statement about the liberation of the commonwealth from factious domination, and closes with a statement about the restoration of the government to the Senate and People of Rome, and the honours conferred on Augustus in recognition of that service. This arrangement of the *Res Gestae* makes it almost inevitable that the reader should tend to take both statements together. And in fact it seems that in recent times the beginning of the *Res Gestae* has occasionally been read and interpreted in the light of its end,[2] with the result that its opening sentence has been considered to be an enunciation of Augustus's political creed and constitutional intentions. In view of its direct bearing on the subject of this study it is necessary to examine the scope of the statement about the liberation of the commonwealth as well as the extent to which it may reasonably be accepted at its face value.

Annos undeviginti natus exercitum privato consilio et privata impensa comparavi, per quem rem publicam a dominatione factionis oppressam in libertatem vindicavi. Eo [nomi]ne senatus decretis honorificis in ordinem suum m[e adlegit C. Pansa et A. Hirtio] consulibus, consularem locum s[ententiae ferendae tribuens et i]mperium mihi dedit.[3]

Since the adverbial "eo nomine" at the beginning of the second sentence refers both to the raising of an army and to the liberation of the commonwealth, the first sentence can only refer to the events of the last months of the year 44 B.C., and it is difficult to see how, without reading into them too much, the words "rem publicam a dominatione factionis oppressam in libertatem vindicavi" could refer to the battles of Mutina and Philippi[4] or still less Actium.[5] The senatorial decrees of the year 43 B.C., which Augustus mentions, were moved by Cicero, whose speeches delivered on that occasion

---

[1] Referred to here in the edition by Jean Gagé, *Res Gestae Divi Augusti*, Paris, 1935 (= Gagé, RG).

[2] See, for instance, Gagé, RG, pp. 73 ff.; E. G. Hardy, *The Monumentum Ancyranum*, Oxford, 1923, p. 27; H. Kloesel, *Libertas*, p. 58; V. Ehrenberg, Monumentum Antiochenum, *Klio* XIX (1925), p. 203.

[3] *Res Gestae*, I, 1–2.   [4] See Mommsen, *Res Gestae²*, p. 3.

[5] See Hardy, *Mon. Anc.* p. 27; Ehrenberg, *op. cit.* p. 203.

are extant.[1] Cicero made it clear beyond doubt that what he meant by the "liberation of the State" was the fact that Octavian with the Legio Martia and the Fourth Legion caused Antony to withdraw from Rome.[2] And he praised Octavian as a heaven-sent deliverer who "rem publicam privato consilio liberavit".[3] All Augustus did in his *Res Gestae* was to repeat as closely as possible Cicero's own words. Now, if to call the short relief provided by Octavian to the Senate a "liberation of the commonwealth" seemed somewhat extravagant even at Rome, the extravagance was in the first place Cicero's, and many must have known that. But they must have also known that soon after that "liberation" the liberator marched on Rome and extorted a consulship for himself; that he severely punished the people of Nursia who erected a monument to their citizens slain in the battle of Mutina and inscribed upon it that they fell for liberty;[4] that he entered into a compact with the oppressor; and that that compact was followed by proscriptions.[5] Had Augustus only wished to proclaim that he was the liberator of his country he could have pointed to greater and more solid achievements than his successful move in 44 B.C., which was quite insufficient to justify so high a claim. But it may be that Augustus did not write the first sentence of his *Res Gestae* with a view to establishing his reputation as the restorer of freedom, or that his contemporary readers were not disposed to accept it in that sense, if he did.

Augustus's intention becomes clear if the passage in question is viewed against the background of what happened late in 44 and early in 43 B.C., with which period that passage deals, and not in the light of the year 27 B.C. and after, with which it has nothing to do.

[1] See Cic. *Phil.* III, 37 ff. especially 38 *ad fin.* Cf. IV, 4; V, 46.
[2] *Phil.* III, 4; IV, 4; V, 23 and 42.
[3] See *Phil.* III, 3–5; IV, 2–4; V, 42–6. Cf. XIV, 25.
[4] Suet. *Div. Aug.* 12.
[5] Posterity did not forget nor gloss over Octavian's early career. It is noteworthy that, in a work addressed to Nero, Seneca should have said: Divus Augustus fuit mitis princeps, si quis illum a principatu suo aestimare incipiat; in communi quidem rei publicae gladium movit. Cum hoc aetatis esset, quod tu (Nero) nunc es, duodevicesimum egressus annum, iam pugiones in sinum amicorum absconderat, iam insidiis M. Antonii consulis latus petierat, iam fuerat collega proscriptionis, *De Clem.* I, 9, I. See also Tac. *Ann.* I, 10, 1–3.

When Octavian first entered Roman politics he was often spoken of as "puer", which he resented.[1] As an old man he recalled, not without pride, that as a youth of nineteen he raised an army on his own initiative and with his own means. Contemporaries did not need to be told that in this he surpassed even Pompey the Great.[2] But his extraordinary feat was not above criticism by constitutional purists. Augustus and his contemporaries, as well as posterity, knew only too well that, in spite of Pompey's notable precedent, "exercitum privato consilio comparare" was, strictly speaking, high treason.[3] And the view that unfriendly critics might take of Octavian's action may be gathered from Tacitus: "Ceterum cupidine dominandi concitos per largitionem veteranos, paratum ab adulescente privato exercitum, corruptas consulis legiones."[4] The only justification of that illegal action, even if it may have received a coating of retrospective whitewash, could be its motive and results. The soundness of such justification may be questionable, but the principle which underlies it was certainly acceptable to the Romans. Was it not the greatest Republican constitutionalist who said "L. Brutus...qui, cum privatus esset, totam rem publicam sustinuit, primusque in hac civitate docuit in conservanda civium libertate privatum esse neminem"?[5] And in fact Cicero gave his opinion as to whether Octavian's undertaking was justified or not. In his Fourth *Philippic* Cicero says:

Nec enim, Quirites, fieri potest, ut non aut ii sint impii, qui contra consulem exercitus comparaverunt, aut ille hostis, contra quem iure arma sumpta sunt. Hanc igitur dubitationem, quamquam nulla erat, tamen ne qua posset esse, senatus hodierno die sustulit. C. Caesar, qui rem publicam libertatemque vestram suo studio, consilio, patrimonio denique tutatus est et tutatur, maximis senatus laudibus ornatus est.[6]

The real doubt that the senatorial resolutions removed was whether or not Octavian's action was justified; and it is not unlikely that Cicero was answering unfriendly criticism of Octavian's action although he pretended that it was above reproach.

---

[1] Suet. *loc. cit.*   [2] See Cic. *Phil.* v, 43–4.

[3] Cf., e.g., the motion for a S.C. Ultimum against Aemilius Lepidus, Sallust, *Hist.* I, 77, 22 M.

[4] *Ann.* I, 10, 1.   [5] *De Rep.* II, 46. Cf. *Phil.* XI, 28.

[6] *Phil.* IV, 2.

Augustus, who in his *Res Gestae* emphasized the fact that he strictly observed the constitution,[1] certainly wished that contemporaries and posterity alike should be in no doubt about the legality of his political beginnings. The reasoning implicit in his statement is something like this: I raised an army on my own initiative, but I did it for the welfare of the commonwealth; witness the Senate which approved of what I had done and honoured me on that account. And Cicero's well-known *Philippics*[2] made things easy for Augustus.

As regards the phrase "rem publicam a dominatione factionis oppressam in libertatem vindicavi", it seems that the ancients, who were familiar with the political vocabulary of the Late Republican period, were probably not disposed, and perhaps not even expected, to attach to it great importance, let alone to take it literally. The phrases "dominatio factionis" and "rem publicam (or populum Romanum) in libertatem vindicare" were too much used and too often misused to retain their original content. A few examples will suffice:

P. Scipio, qui ex dominatu Ti. Gracchi privatus in libertatem rem publicam vindicavit (Cic. *Brut.* 212);

Ti. et C. Gracchus...vindicare plebem in libertatem...coepere (Sallust, *Jug.* 42, 1);

Neque eos (viz. the Optimates) pudet, vindices uti se ferunt libertatis (Sallust, *Hist.* III, 48, 22 M);

Se non malefici causa ex provincia egressum sed...ut se et populum Romanum factione paucorum oppressum in libertatem vindicaret (Caesar, *Bell. Civ.* I, 22, 5);

Tuus...pater (viz. Pompey) istuc aetatis cum esset et animadvertisset rem publicam ab nefariis sceleratisque civibus oppressam...Italiam urbemque Romam in libertatem vindicavit (*Bell. Afr.* 22, 2);[3]

L. Flaccus...laudem patriae in libertatem vindicandae praetor adamarit (Cic. *Pro Flacco*, 25);

Video Milonem, vindicem vestrae libertatis (Cic. *Pro Sest.* 144).[4]

---

[1] *Res Gestae*, 5–6.   [2] Tac. *Dial.* 37, 6.

[3] Cf. Cic. *De imp. Cn. Pompei*, 30. But a different view of Pompey's action is taken in *Phil.* V, 44.

[4] Milo's victim, Clodius, must have also posed as liberator, see Cic. *De Dom.* 110 and 131. It may be worth while mentioning that after the execution of Catiline's associates, Metellus Celer introduced a Bill demanding Pompey's return: ὡς δὴ καταλύσοντα τοῦ Κικέρωνος δυναστείαν, Plut. *Cic.* 23, 4; the phrase sounds something like "ut rem publicam dominatione M. Tulli oppressam in libertatem vindicaret". Dio Cass. XLIII, 44, 1, says that in 46 B.C.

As the above examples show, "vindicatio in libertatem" (in a political sense) was used to denote opposite extremes. During the Late Republic it was a much used political catchword and became as vague as libertas itself. It was the kind of "speciosum nomen"[1] which every one was glad to use because of its emotional value, but it retained little of its original positive meaning. It seems that at best it denoted a public-spirited intention and little, if anything, else. And it seems likely that Augustus used this phrase in his *Res Gestae* for this very reason; "rem publicam in libertatem vindicavi" was the conventional way of saying: I worked for the public good. And, at any rate, Augustus's words at the beginning of his *Res Gestae* cannot, without strong support from other evidence (which does not seem to exist), bear the weight that has occasionally been put on them.

It also ought to be pointed out that although *prima facie* Augustus's phrase seems to be reminiscent of the phraseology of the Populares, this impression is not necessarily true. As has been seen, the Optimates did not fall behind the Populares in their professions to be "vindices libertatis". The only word that may have a peculiarly "popularis" tinge is "factio". But through excessive use this word also lost its original meaning of an oligarchical clique,[2] and became a somewhat vague term of political abuse.[3] Augustus in his *Res Gestae* refrained from mentioning Antony by name. He could not possibly use in chapter 1 the circumlocution he used elsewhere[4] and write "a dominatione eius cum quo bellum gesseram". "Factio" was

Caesar the dictator was hailed as liberator: αὐτόν τε (sc. τὸν Καίσαρα) ἐλευθερωτὴν (= vindicem libertatis?) καὶ ἐκάλουν καὶ ἐς τὰ γραμματεῖα ἀνέγραφον, καὶ νεὼν ἐλευθερίας δημοσίᾳ ἐψηφίσαντο. Many more instances, some of which are irrelevant, will be found in W. Weber's *Princeps, Studien zur Geschichte des Prinzipats*, 1936, n. 557, pp. 138–9.

[1] Tacitus (*Hist.* IV. 73, 3) put into the mouth of Cerialis the following remark about the Germans: Ceterum libertas et speciosa nomina praetexuntur; nec quisquam alienum servitium et dominationem sibi concupivit, ut non eadem ista vocabula usurparet.

[2] In the first century A.D. both Velleius Paterculus and Valerius Maximus use the term factio with regard to the Populares, see Vell. Pat. II, 18, 6, and Val. Max. III, 2, 17; IV, 1, 13.

[3] Sallust, *Jug.* 31, 15: Sed haec inter bonos amicitia, inter malos factio est. Cf. the references cited in the *Thes. Ling. Lat.* vol. VI, col. 137, 12 ff., and also *s.v.* factiosus, 138, 31 ff.

[4] *Res Gestae*, 24, 1.

a very handy substitute for Antony,[1] and it misled no one, except some modern scholars.[2]

In like manner, undue constitutional significance has been attributed to the well-known coin of the year 28 B.C. on the obverse of which Augustus is styled Imp. Caesar Divi f. cos. VI libertatis p. R. vindex.[3] There is, in the opinion of the present writer, more likelihood that this legend refers to the victory at Actium, that is to say, to the liberation of the Roman people from the danger of Cleopatra's domination, than to the restoration of the Republic[4] which only began to take place in 28 B.C. The reasons for this assumption are these: first, on the obverse is represented a laurel-wreathed head of Augustus, and on the reverse the goddess Pax holding a caduceus and trampling upon a torch. The laurel wreath on the obverse and the symbol of peace as well as the legend P A X on the reverse suggest victory in war, and not restoration of the constitution. Secondly, the fact that the legend "libertatis p. R. vindex" appears on a coin struck in 28 B.C. does not by itself imply that it refers to an event that occurred in the same year. The legend "Aegypto capta" appears on dated coins of the years 28 and 27 B.C.,[5] although the conquest of Egypt did not take place in either year. "Civibus servateis" appears in 27 B.C.,[6] and "ob civis servatos" some time after 23 B.C.,[7] although both legends refer to the pardon of the vanquished in the Civil War. Therefore, the vindication of Roman freedom referred to on the above coin need not be associated

---

[1] That he meant Antony and no one else appears from Vell. Pat. II, 61, 1: Torpebat oppressa dominatione Antonii civitas; and from Cic. *Phil.* v, 6; 44; VI, 3; VIII, 5; XII, 14–15; *Ad Fam.* x, 1, 1; *Ad Brut.* I, 15, 5.

[2] Hardy, *Mon. Anc.* p. 27, thought "factio" referred to the Liberators. This is untenable in view of *Res Gestae* ch. 1, ll. 3–5 and ch. 2, ll. 10–12. Kloesel, *Libertas*, p. 58, assumed that Augustus had in mind "die senatorische Reaktion", which is inconceivable, to say the least, in view of Augustus's subsequent statement about the honours he received from the very same Senate. It is true "factio" is a collective noun, but Antony had followers.

[3] See above, p. 97 n. 3.

[4] So Mommsen, *Res Gestae*[2], p. 145. Mommsen's view has been generally accepted, even by numismatists, see H. Mattingly and E. A. Sydenham, *The Roman Imperial Coinage*, I, p. 60 n. 1; also M. Grant, *From* Imperium *to* Auctoritas, pp. 384 and 424.

[5] Mattingly and Sydenham, *op. cit.* p. 61, no. 19 and p. 62, no. 21.

[6] *Op. cit.* p. 62, no. 22.

[7] *Op. cit.* p. 64, no. 55, tentatively assigned by the editors to 19–15 B.C.

exclusively with events of the year 28 B.C. Thirdly, the very idea of libertatis vindex implies the existence of an oppressor. Who, it may be asked, oppressed the freedom of the Roman people in the year 28 B.C.? Is it likely that Octavian was styled libertatis p. R. vindex because he rescinded his own triumviral enactments?[1] And even so, is there any positive evidence that the coin was struck (in the mint of Ephesus) after that event?

Since the war against Antony and Cleopatra was waged in the name of Roman freedom and independence, there seems to be every likelihood that this coin is a specimen of the issues that commemorated the victory at Actium. Common sense, apart from the comparative study of coin-types, suggests that in dating legends and types one has to bear in mind that dies in the mint might not always catch up with the latest developments of political propaganda.

It might have amused Augustus had he seen that a facsimile of the obverse of the coin with the legend libertatis p. R. vindex significantly adorns the title-page of a book on the Augustan Principate.[2] He would perhaps have preferred to see there the reverse with the legend PAX.

But be that as it may, those who believe that the opening sentence of the *Res Gestae* and the coin of 28 B.C. enunciate the programme of Augustus have to face the plain fact that, for all its emotional value, it is as vague, elusive, and evasive as the "programme" of Caesar at the outbreak of the Civil War. Phrases like "rem publicam in libertatem vindicare" and "libertatis populi Romani vindex" were used primarily to obscure political issues and not to enunciate positive programmes. And, therefore, to judge the Augustan Principate on the strength of such conventional and vague pronouncements, if indeed they are pronouncements, is to misjudge it.

[1] Tac. *Ann.* III, 28, 3.
[2] M. Hammond, *The Augustan Principate*, 1933.

3. Res Publica Restituta in Theory and in Fact

ἐγίγνετό τε λόγῳ μὲν δημοκρατία, ἔργῳ δὲ ὑπὸ τοῦ πρώτου ἀνδρὸς ἀρχή.

Thucydides, ii, 65, 9.

In his *Res Gestae* Augustus asserts that, when he had put an end to civil wars, he surrendered the absolute power, which by universal consent he had been exercising, and transferred the administration of the commonwealth to the free disposal of the Senate and People of Rome (rem publicam ex mea potestate in senatus populique Romani arbitrium transtuli). Officially no doubt the constitutional settlement of the year 27 B.C. was represented as a restoration of the Republic, witness "pacato orbe terrarum res[titut]a re publica" in the contemporary *Laudatio Turiae*,[1] or "corona quern[a uti super ianuam domus Imp. Caesaris] Augusti poner[etur senatus decrevit, quod rem publicam] p. R. rest[i]tui[t]" in the Fasti of Praeneste.[2] And Velleius Paterculus (II, 89, 3) went so far as to declare:

Finita vicesimo anno bella civilia, sepulta externa, revocata pax, sopitus ubique armorum furor, restituta vis legibus, iudiciis auctoritas, senatui maiestas, imperium magistratuum ad pristinum redactum modum, tantummodo octo praetoribus adlecti duo. Prisca illa et antiqua rei publicae forma revocata.

On the other hand, historians of a later date took an entirely different view of what, under Augustus, purported to be a restoration of the Republic. Tacitus said:

Posito triumviri nomine consulem se ferens et ad tuendam plebem tribunicio iure contentum, ubi militem donis, populum annona, cunctos dulcedine otii pellexit, insurgere paulatim, munia senatus magistratuum legum in se trahere.[3]

Suetonius briefly, and somewhat obscurely, remarked:

De reddenda re publica bis cogitavit...sed reputans et se privatum non sine periculo fore et illam plurium arbitrio temere committi, in retinenda perseveravit, dubium eventu meliore an voluntate.[4]

---

[1] *C.I.L.* VI, no. 1527, p. 333, l. 25.

[2] *C.I.L.* I², p. 231, on the Ides of January. Cf. Ovid, *Fasti* I, 589: Redditaque est omnis populo provincia nostro Et tuus Augusto nomine dictus avus.

[3] *Ann.* I, 2, 1. Cf. III, 28, 3; I, 3, 1; 4, 1; 3, 7; *Hist.* I, 1, 1.

[4] Suet. *Div. Aug.* 28, 1.

And Dio Cassius was convinced that Augustus established a real monarchy: Οὕτω μὲν δὴ τὸ τοῦ δήμου καὶ τῆς γερουσίας κράτος πᾶν ἐς τὸν Αὔγουστον μετέστη, καὶ ἀπ' αὐτοῦ καὶ ἀκριβὴς μοναρχία κατέστη· μοναρχία γάρ...ἀληθέστατα ἂν νομίζοιτο.[1]

In view of the fact that before the establishment of the Principate "res publica" was the principal embodiment of political "libertas", the new régime might be regarded either as restoration or as suppression of liberty according as it was a restoration or a suppression of the traditional form of government. This question, however, should not, even if it could, be decided on the strength of the extant appraisals of the Principate by the ancients. For if the contemporaries of Augustus are open to the charge of disingenuous flattery, his later critics may have been inclined to judge the Augustan Principate not on its own merits but in the light of its subsequent development under his successors.

Fortunately there is enough conclusive evidence to pass judgement on the nature of the "res publica restituta" without relying on questionable testimonials. It is quite obvious that, since the Princeps was the new and salient element in the reconstituted State, the extent to which the new dispensation amounted to a restoration of the traditional res publica depends in the first place on the extent to which the position of the Princeps was consistent with the Roman idea of a free State.[2]

---

[1] LIII, 17, 1. Cf. LII, 1, 1; LIII, 11, 5.

[2] Several scholars have considered the constitutional resettlement under Augustus to be a restoration of the Republic. See G. Ferrero, *The Greatness and Decline of Rome*, trans. by H. J. Chaytor, IV (1908), pp. 121–42; 235–55; and especially 134–6; Ed. Meyer, Kaiser Augustus, *Kl. Schr.* I² (1924), pp. 425 ff., esp. 455 ff.; F. B. Marsh, *The Founding of the Roman Empire*², Oxford, 1927, pp. 212–29, 290–3; H. F. Pelham, The Early Roman Emperors, *Essays*, Oxford, 1911, pp. 31 ff.; M. Hammond, *The Augustan Principate*, esp. pp. 4–5, 21 ff., 195–7. For various other interpretations of the Augustan Principate see Th. Mommsen, *Römisches Staatsrecht* II³, part 2, and III, pp. 1252 ff.; D. McFayden, *The Rise of the Princeps' Jurisdiction within the City of Rome*, Washington Univ. Stud., Humanistic Series, X (1923), no. 2, pp. 181 ff.; H. Dessau, *Geschichte der römischen Kaiserzeit*, I (1924), pp. 15–62; M. Rostovtzeff, *The Social and Economic History of the Roman Empire* (1926), pp. 38 ff.; E. Schönbauer, Untersuchungen zum römischen Staats- und Wirtschaftsrecht, Wesen und Ursprung des Prinzipats, *Z.d. Sav.-Stif. Rom. Abt.* XLVII (LX) (1927), pp. 264–318, esp. 288 ff.; T. Rice Holmes, *The Architect of the Roman Empire*, I (1928), pp. 180 ff., 263 ff.; W. Kolbe,

Augustus described his own position after the restoration of constitutional government: "Post id tempus auctoritate omnibus praestiti, potestatis autem nihilo amplius habui quam ceteri qui mihi quoque in magistratu conlegae fuerunt."[1] For the sake of clarity his potestas and auctoritas will be examined separately, although they were interdependent and formed in effect one thing.

In so far as potestas means formal right to exercise power and not the actual ability to do so, Augustus's statement about his potestas is unassailable provided it defines the nature of his power in each single magistracy (although his tribunicia potestas was not a magistratus in the strict sense), and not the limit of the sum total of all the powers he held. As consul his was a consularis potestas equal to that of his colleague consul; Agrippa and, after his death, Tiberius were Augustus's colleagues in the tenure of the tribunicia potestas; as a holder of imperium proconsulare Augustus possibly possessed a potestas of the same kind as that of any other proconsul.[2]

Under the Republic the Romans set great store by the principle of par potestas, which they regarded as a cardinal constituent of Roman republicanism and freedom. It is therefore only natural that Augustus would have the Romans believe that his own power was in no way inconsistent with that principle. He was certainly anxious to remove any doubt about the constitutionality of his position in the State, and recorded that he refused the offices of dictator, consul for life, ἐπιμελητὴς τῶν τε νόμων καὶ τῶν τρόπων ἐπὶ μεγίστη ἐξουσία μόνος, as well as any power inconsistent with the established constitutional practice, ἀρχὴ παρὰ τὰ πάτρια ἔθη διδομένη.[3] In so far, therefore, as Augustus meant to say that he held no

Von der Republic zur Monarchie, in *Das Erbe der Alten*, Heft 20 (1931), pp. 39–65; Sir Henry Stuart Jones, *C.A.H.* x (1934), chaps. v–vi; F. E. Adcock, *ib.* pp. 583 ff.; H. Last, *C.A.H.* xi (1936), pp. 399 ff.; A. von Premerstein, Vom Werden und Wesen des Prinzipats, *Abh. Bay. Akad.* Heft 15 (1937); R. Syme, *The Roman Revolution* (1939), esp. pp. 313 ff.; M. Grant, *From Imperium to* Auctoritas, esp. pp. 408 ff.

[1] *Res Gestae*, 34, 3.

[2] For the purpose of this study it is of little consequence whether Augustus held an imperium proconsulare maius in all the provinces or not. There is therefore no need here to discuss this subject. For the latest discussion see M. Grant, *op. cit.* pp. 424 ff.; H. Last, 'Imperium maius': a Note, *J.R.S.* xxxvii (1947), pp. 157 ff.

[3] *Res Gestae*, 5 and 6.

non-collegiate potestas his statement is true. But the juxtaposition of "auctoritate omnibus praestiti potestatis autem nihilo amplius habui" etc. implies much more than that. The obvious inference from the antithesis of auctoritas and potestas is that the entire potestas of Augustus was not greater than that of his colleagues in office. And this is so manifestly untrue that only the uninformed in antiquity, or the dogmatic in more recent times, could believe it. For apart from the fact that Augustus enjoyed supremacy by virtue of his auctoritas (the implications of which will be seen presently), his potestas was not confined to one magistracy at a time, as was the normal constitutional practice, but consisted in an accumulation of various magisterial prerogatives which, so far as his own power was concerned, deprived collegiality of its substance. Augustus held concurrently a permanent though nominally renewed tribunicia potestas, by virtue of which alone he enjoyed of right the standing of maior potestas with regard to the consuls,[1] an imperium proconsulare which carried with it the command of the best part of the Roman army,[2] and, although he was not a consul, he had the right "senatum habere, relationem facere, remittere, senatus consulta per relationem discessionemque facere".[3] It is therefore quite clear that the potestas held by Augustus far outstripped the limit set by normal constitutional practice. There was no potestas to match his own, nor was it intended that there should be one. And it was no comfort to constitutionalists of the strictest school, if any survived, that the

---

[1] Tacitus (*Ann.* III, 56, 2) rightly says of the tribunician power: Id summi fastigii vocabulum Augustus repperit, ne regis aut dictatoris nomen adsumeret ac tamen appellatione aliqua cetera imperia praemineret. Augustus himself declares that he performed the task of cura legum et morum by virtue of his tribunician power, see *Res Gestae*, 6. What an orthodox republican might have thought of the continuous tenure of the tribunician power may be gathered both from the fact that Ti. Gracchus was accused of aiming at a "regnum", and from Livy VI, 41, 3: Omitto Licinium Sextiumque, quorum annos in perpetua potestate tamquam regum in Capitolio numeratis; and III, 21, 2: Magistratus continuari et eosdem tribunos refici iudicare senatum contra rem publicam esse.

[2] Suetonius, *Div. Aug.* 47, 1; Dio Cass. LIII, 12, 2. Cf. R. Syme, *The Roman Revolution*, p. 326; and H. Stuart Jones, *C.A.H.* x, p. 128.

[3] S.C. de Imperio Vespasiani, Bruns, *Fontes*[7], 1, p. 202, ll. 3–5. From the phrase "ita uti licuit divo Augusto" can only be deduced the historical fact that Augustus was allowed to act in the manner described in the S.C.; the word licuit, however, does not by itself imply that the power to act in that manner was conferred on him by law. Cf. H. Last, *C.A.H.* XI, pp. 406 f.

powers of the Princeps were granted by the Senate and People.[1] Some scholars[2] seem to have attached undue importance to this fact. Were not, according to Roman tradition, the old kings of Rome installed as a rule "auctoribus patribus atque iussu populi"?[3] The conferment of power by the Senate and People did not by itself set any limit to that power, it only made the tenure of that power lawful, and marked it off from tyranny, in the sense of unconstitutional seizure of power. It must always be remembered that, in the eyes of the Romans, their political freedom began when the executive power was made annual and collegiate.[4] And the powers of the Princeps, though delegated, were permanent,[5] and, for all practical purposes, irrevocable.[6] By a very ingenious separation of magisterial prerogatives from the actual tenure of the corresponding magistracies, Augustus held various powers without as a rule being an annual magistrate. Thus, whatever its appearance, the potestas of the Princeps retained none of the essentials of a regular Republican magistracy: it was an accumulation of prerogatives inadmissible in normal Republican times, and in its scope dangerously similar to the power of a dictator;[7] it had no equal, and therefore was not amenable to administrative control; it was effectively for life, and therefore responsible to no one while the Princeps lived.[8]

Augustus's own description of his potestas is an understatement, to say the least. It was reserved to Tiberius to speak out the truth about the potestas of the Princeps:

[1] See Dio Cass. LIII, 12, 1.

[2] E.g. G. Ferrero, *op. cit.* IV, p. 134, who asserts that the powers of Augustus were "resembling those of the Federal President in America". And also F. B. Marsh, *op. cit.* pp. 224 ff.

[3] See Livy I, 17, 9; 22, 1; 32, 2; 35, 6; 41, 7; 49, 3; Cic. *De Rep.* II, 35.

[4] Livy II, 1, 7; IV, 24, 4; Sallust, *Cat.* 6, 7.

[5] For the character of the imperium proconsulare see Mommsen, *Staatsrecht* II³, pp. 793 f., 854; and von Premerstein, *op. cit.* pp. 234 ff.

[6] The principles concerning the abrogation of power from the Princeps will be found in Mommsen, *op. cit.* II³, p. 1132.

[7] For a directly opposed view see V. Ehrenberg, *Klio* XIX (1925), p. 206.

[8] A senior Roman magistrate could not be called to account during his term of office. It is true that Augustus and Tiberius rendered an account from time to time, but there was no constitutional means whereby the Princeps could be compelled to do so, cf. Suet. *Calig.* 16, 1. Moreover, all magistrates and senators had to take an oath to preserve the acta of the Princeps. Cf. Mommsen, *op. cit.* I³, p. 621; II³, pp. 906 ff.

Dixi et nunc et saepe alias, patres conscripti, bonum et salutarem principem, quem vos tanta et tam libera potestate instruxistis, senatui servire debere, et universis civibus saepe, et plerumque etiam singulis.[1]

The manner in which the Princeps ought to exercise his power must be reserved for later notice, but as regards the nature of that power Tiberius was certainly right in saying that it was "a potestas so great and so unrestricted".

So much for the potestas of Augustus. There remains to be seen what was the scope of his auctoritas. The words "auctoritate omnibus praestiti" have been much discussed ever since the discovery of the Monumentum Antiochenum which brought to light the true reading "auctoritate" instead of the conjectured "dignitate" of earlier days. On the strength of those words it has been assumed in recent times that the supremacy of the Princeps was in no way inconsistent with the Republican idea of freedom. For Augustus, so the argument goes, claimed nothing that was not permissible under the Republic; auctoritas derives solely from the force of personality; it is not legally enforceable, and may be freely accepted or disregarded; a preeminent auctoritas, therefore, does not collide with freedom.[2] This theory that Augustus's primacy by virtue of his auctoritas was entirely consistent with Roman Republican ideals, if true, would be of great consequence from the point of view of libertas, and must therefore be carefully examined.

A remark by Brutus may help to elucidate the relation between auctoritas and libertas. Writing to Cicero in the year 43 B.C. he says "...cuius (Cicero's) tantam auctoritatem senatus ac populus Romanus non solum esse patitur sed etiam cupit quanta maxima in libera civitate unius esse potest".[3] It is obvious from this remark that in Brutus's opinion there existed, or ought to exist, an upper limit beyond which an individual's auctoritas cannot extend in a free State. The reason for this view is not far to seek. It derived, not from the belief that a free State could not tolerate an outstanding personality, but from the realization, or rather knowledge, that auctoritas was power, in the sense that influence and the right to

---

[1] Suet. *Tib.* 29.
[2] R. Heinze, Auctoritas, *Hermes* LX (1925), pp. 355-7.
[3] Cic. *Ad Brut.* I, 4a, 2.

exert it are power, none the less real and legitimate for being undefined and not peremptory.[1]

The position of the Republican Senate rested entirely on its auctoritas, and even the advocates of senatorial supremacy never asked for more. No magistrate was obliged by law to subordinate his potestas to the auctoritas of the Senate, but by custom he was expected to do so. And the fact that a S.C. Ultimum could for all practical purposes suspend the indefeasible and inviolable civic rights of trial and appeal to the People, as well as the note of censure present in the phrase "contra senatus auctoritatem"[2] give an idea of what weight the auctoritas of the Senate carried.[3] And what the auctoritas of an individual might mean is well illustrated by the incident related by Cicero:

> Q. Metellus...cuius paucos pares haec civitas tulit...designatus consul, cum quidam tribunus plebis suo auxilio magistros ludos contra senatus consultum facere iussisset, privatus fieri vetuit; atque id, quod nondum potestate poterat, obtinuit auctoritate.[4]

But if by virtue of auctoritas so decisive an influence could be exerted on public affairs, Brutus's view that an unlimited auctoritas of an individual is impossible in a free State is not unreasonable; and this fact alone should warn us against hasty assumptions that the pre-eminent auctoritas of the Princeps was consistent with the traditional idea of republican freedom at Rome.

[1] E. Schönbauer, *op. cit.* pp. 290 f., describes auctoritas as follows: "Das Wesen der auctoritas im staatlichen Leben ist es gerade dass sie eine Macht darstellt, die nicht mit äusseren Mitteln eine Befolgung erzwingt, sondern die einen inneren Zwang schafft, der das Gefühl erzeugt, dass die Befolgung eine selbstgewählte freiwillig übernommene Pflicht darstelle."

[2] See Cic. *In Pis.* 8; *Phil.* II, 48; *De Senect.* 11; Hirt. *Bell. Gall.* VIII, 52, 3; Sallust, *Hist.* I, 77, 22 M.

[3] Mommsen, *op. cit.* III, 1033, says of the auctoritas senatus: "Die ebenso eminente wie unbestimmte und formell unfundirte Machtstellung des Senats wird in der späteren Republik regelmässig mit dem in entsprechender Weise verschwommenen und aller strenger Definition sich entziehenden Worte 'auctoritas' bezeichnet." Mutatis mutandis this is also true of the auctoritas of individuals in public affairs. Things may have been different in purely private matters. It is to be observed that Heinze's conclusions are largely based on an inference from private to public life.

[4] *In Pis.* 8. See also Tac. *Dial.* 36, 8: Hi ne privati quidem sine potestate erant, cum et populum et senatum consilio et auctoritate regerent.

It is of course true that there were in Republican times statesmen whose auctoritas was eminent and even pre-eminent; it is also true that outstanding statesmen were called, and even called themselves, principes,[1] and it was nothing unusual if one of them was at some time regarded as the princeps. It also may be, although it cannot be proved, that the Republican principes were so called on account of their auctoritas. Nevertheless there is all the difference between the position of the Republican principes, or even princeps, and the Princeps, and to overlook that difference is to miss the true nature of the Principate.

As has been seen, competition for power and dignitas was the mainspring of domestic politics in Republican, or at any rate Late Republican, Rome. As a result of incessant competition between individuals and unrelenting rivalry between factions the auctoritas of any individual statesman might grow or wane. For the auctoritas of an individual depended not only on one's personal qualities but also, and perhaps mainly, on one's position in public life in any particular state of affairs, as is abundantly illustrated by the vicissitudes of Cicero's auctoritas during the period between the First and Second Triumvirates.[2] There might be several statesmen of outstanding auctoritas at a time, and there was to some extent a free choice between various auctores. Things changed completely with the establishment of the Principate. The auctoritas of the Princeps was permanently pre-eminent, just as he was permanently supreme; it overshadowed and dwarfed all other auctoritates,[3] and, since it had no equal, the only course open to the Romans was to accept the auctoritas of the Princeps or defy it at their own risk. This state of affairs may have been of no appreciable consequence to those who themselves never had, nor were likely to have, an auctoritas, but it made all the difference in the world to those who did have, and who might have been striving for primacy were it not for the un-rivalled supremacy of the Princeps.[4] "Certare ingenio, contendere

[1] See Gelzer, *Nobilität*, pp. 35 ff. and Sprey, *op. cit.* pp. 198 ff., 208 ff.

[2] Compare, e.g., *Ad Q. Fr.* III, 5 and 6, 4 with *Ad Brut.* I, 4a, 2.

[3] Tac. *Ann.* XIV, 47, 1: Memmius Regulus, auctoritate constantia fama, in quantum praeumbrante imperatoris fastigio datur, clarus.

[4] Augustus is reported as having said to L. Cinna, who plotted against his life: "Cedo, si spes tuas (*sc.* ut ipse sis princeps) solus impedio, Paulusne te

nobilitate"[1] was a way of life of the Republican ruling class. It may therefore be doubted whether those who believed that their freedom was the right to obtain the government of others,[2] those who thought that a man's ideal was to become "princeps dignitate",[3] those who considered the desire for primacy to be evidence of "magnitudo animi",[4] those who could not bear Caesar's "principatus",[5] would have agreed that to live constantly under someone else's supremacy without being able to attain supremacy for oneself was full freedom in the old Republican sense.

There is also another thing to be observed about the relation between the Principate, even if it were based on auctoritas only, and Roman republicanism. "Princeps" originally is neither an official title nor a designation of a magistracy; it is a complimentary statement of fact.[6] In Republican times a princeps was only "primus inter pares", and in recent times the Princeps has often been described in the same way. But, although there is a measure of truth in it, the description as the first among equals does not apply to the Princeps in the same sense as it applies to the Republican principes. For if primacy remains always with one and the same "first one" the parity of the equals is impaired, because equality in this case exists only so long as any one of the equals may become the first among his peers. But whatever Augustus's efforts to appear unassuming in civil life,[7] his very name "Augustus" signified that he was in some way above ordinary human standards,[8] and the way in which he used in his *Res Gestae* the phrase "me principe"[9] shows that he, and doubtless everybody else, thought of his principate as an institution.[10] But an institutional principate is inconsistent with the Republican practice of equality, or at least pretended equality, between the nobles. In

Fabius Maximus et Cossi et Servilii ferent tantumque agmen nobilium non inania nomina praeferentium, sed eorum, qui imaginibus suis decori sint?" (Seneca, *De Clem.* I, 9, 10). Cf. also Tac. *Ann.* I, 13, 1–3.

[1] The phrase is from Lucretius II, 11 f. For the matter see above, pp. 88 f.
[2] See Scipio's dictum quoted above, p. 38.
[3] See Cic. *Phil.* I, 34.   [4] See Cic. *De Off.* I, 13 and 64.
[5] See, e.g., Brutus's letter, Cic. *Ad Brut.* I, 16; and also Cic. *De Off.* I, 26.
[6] Cf. F. E. Adcock, *C.A.H.* x, p. 588.
[7] See Suet. *Div. Aug.* 53–6. Cf. Seneca, *De Clem.* I, 15, 3.
[8] Dio Cass. LIII, 16, 8.   [9] *Res Gestae*, 13; 30; 32, 3.
[10] The fact that "Princeps" does not appear in official titulature shows only that it was not an official title.

Republican times nobles might voluntarily defer to the auctoritas of other nobles; now they were expected always to defer to the auctoritas of the Princeps.[1] From the standpoint of the Republican nobility Tacitus was right in saying: "Igitur verso civitatis statu nihil usquam prisci et integri moris: omnes exuta aequalitate iussa principis aspectare."[2]

The practical implications of supremacy by virtue of auctoritas are far-reaching. Unlike potestas, auctoritas is not defined, and therefore, whereas potestas is confined within certain limits, there is, in theory at least, no limit to the scope of auctoritas: it can be brought to bear on any matter. This fact may explain the peculiar character of the Augustan Principate. His auctoritas enabled Augustus to perform functions for which, strictly speaking, he had no legal warrant. A notable example is the cura legum et morum. Suetonius and Dio Cassius are at variance in this matter: the former asserts that Augustus was made supervisor of morals and laws for life,[3] whereas the latter tells of two quinquennial terms during which Augustus held that office.[4] Ovid and Horace allude to the fact that Augustus supervised the laws and morals, but their allusions do not necessarily imply that he held a specific office for that purpose.[5] Augustus himself says that he declined the office of supreme and sole superintendent of laws and morals which the Senate and People offered him, but he performed by virtue of his tribunician power those duties which the Senate wished at that time to entrust him with.[6] There is no compelling reason to doubt the truth of Augustus's statement. For although superintendence of laws and morals was beyond the scope of tribunician power, Augustus's auctoritas supplemented his potestas. If the mutilated text of Res Gestae, 8, 5 has been restored aright, Augustus himself says that his auctoritas exerted a decisive influence upon legislation: "Legibus novis m[e auctore

---

[1] Tac. *Ann.* III, 22, 6: adsentiendi necessitas. *Ann.* I, 74, 3–6: "Quo loco censebis, Caesar? Si primus, habebo quod sequar; si post omnes, vereor ne imprudens dissentiam." *Ann.* VI, 8, 7 (a remark put into the mouth of a knight): "Tibi (Caesar) summum rerum iudicium di dedere, nobis obsequii gloria relicta est." Cf. also *Hist.* IV, 8 and *Agric.* 42, 5.

[2] *Ann.* I, 4, 1.   [3] Suet. *Div. Aug.* 27, 5.

[4] Dio Cass. LIV, 10, 5; 30, 1.

[5] Ovid, *Metam.* XV, 832 ff.; Horace, *Ep.* II, 1, 1 ff.

[6] *Res Gestae*, 6.

l]atis m[ulta e]xempla maiorum exolescentia iam ex nostro [saecul]o red[uxi et ipse] multarum rer[um exe]mpla imitanda pos[teris tradidi]."[1]

There are some examples which illustrate the above statement of Augustus. "Sciendum itaque est," say the compilers of Justinian's Institutions, "omnia fideicommissa primis temporibus infirma esse (? fuisse)...Postea primus divus Augustus semel iterumque gratia personarum motus...iussit consulibus auctoritatem suam interponere." The result was that it gradually became established law (ideo divus Augustus ad necessitatem iuris ea detraxit).[2]

In view of the fact that the interpretation of law by jurists (responsa prudentium) was a potent factor in the administration of justice at Rome, great importance attaches to the following:

Ante tempora Augusti publice respondendi ius non a principibus dabatur, sed qui fiduciam studiorum suorum habebant consulentibus respondebant...Primus divus Augustus, ut maior iuris auctoritas haberetur, constituit, ut ex auctoritate eius responderent; et ex illo tempore peti hoc pro beneficio coepit.[3]

It may be that until the times of Hadrian the responsa ex auctoritate principis were in theory not binding on the judges,[4] but they carried all the weight that the auctoritas of the Princeps could lend them, and that was much.[5]

It appears from the above instances that by virtue of his auctoritas Augustus could intervene in matters which, if judged by strict legal rules and Republican practice, were beyond his tribunicia potestas and imperium proconsulare. But once his auctoritas was accepted there was no need to amplify his prerogative or grant him sweeping discretionary powers. He had in effect enjoyed all, or most of, the rights that were at a later time granted to Vespasian, and performed so many diverse functions as to amount in effect to a "cura et tutela

---

[1] Cf. Ovid. *Metam.* xv, 833: Legesque feret iustissimus auctor.

[2] *Inst.* II, 23, 1 and 12. Cf. *Inst.* II, 25 pr. about the effect of Augustus's auctoritas on the institution of codicilli.

[3] Pompon. *Dig.* I, 2, 2, 49.   [4] See *Gai Inst.* I, 7.

[5] The following passages from Tacitus, *Ann.* I, 77, 4, may also be relevant to the auctoritas of Augustus: Valuit tamen intercessio (against a proposal that the praetors should have the right to impose the penalty of flogging on actors) quia divus Augustus immunis verberum histriones quondam responderat, neque fas Tiberio infringere dicta eius.

rei publicae universa". Nevertheless, it seems unlikely that an enabling act of the kind of the S.C. de Imperio Vespasiani,[1] or an enactment which invested Augustus with discretionary powers as supreme guardian of the commonwealth,[2] was ever passed.[3] The fact that the S.C. de Imperio Vespasiani mentions every now and then the precedent of Augustus proves only that Augustus performed the functions mentioned in that Senatus Consultum, but it does not prove that those functions were delegated to him by special law. It was only when, with use, the Principate gradually hardened into a more rigid form of potestas, and when the auctoritas of certain Principes was not so obviously superior and their title to the Principate not so indisputable as were those of Augustus, that general enabling acts were passed.[4] There is no reason to doubt that Augustus's supremacy largely depended on his auctoritas. But at the same time it ought to be observed that supremacy by virtue of auctoritas may be, indeed, less offensive than supremacy by reason of extraordinary powers, but none the less real and efficacious, and perhaps not even less dangerous to freedom.

To complete the examination of the auctoritas Principis it is necessary to see in what manner it affected the auctoritas senatus and popular sovereignty.

---

[1] See Bruns, *Fontes*[7], p. 202, esp. ll. 17 ff.

[2] Dio Cass. LIII, 12, 1: τὴν μὲν φροντίδα τήν τε προστασίαν τῶν κοινῶν πᾶσαν ὡς καὶ ἐπιμελείας τινὸς δεομένων ὑπεδέξατο. Von Premerstein, *op. cit.* p. 117, maintains, mainly on the strength of Dio's statement, that Augustus was invested with a cura et tutela rei publicae universa, which carried with it discretionary powers. This contention, however, is inconsistent with Augustus's own account in his *Res Gestae*. And even if it were assumed that Augustus for some reason suppressed the truth, it would still be difficult to see why no Latin author seems to know anything about the delegation of the cura rei publicae to Augustus. The Greek authorities, and particularly Dio, may be very misleading in this matter. Incidentally, Dio's phrase need not necessarily mean that a definite grant of powers took place in 27 B.C. That phrase may just as well be a summary of the total effect of the Principate.

[3] For a similar interpretation of Augustus's powers see H. Last, *C.A.H.* XI, pp. 404 ff.; R. Syme, *op. cit.* p. 313 n. 1; D. McFayden, *op. cit.* pp. 183 ff.; E. Schönbauer, *op. cit.* pp. 288 ff., esp. 293.

[4] Speaking of the accession of Vitellius, Tacitus says (*Hist.* II, 55, 2): In senatu cuncta longis aliorum principatibus conposita statim decernuntur. Similarly, on the accession of Vespasian (*Hist.* IV, 3, 3): Senatus cuncta principibus solita Vespasiano decernit. The latter passage is clearly an allusion to the S.C. de Imperio Vespasiani.

As has been seen, the Optimates interpreted republicanism and libertas as meaning government by the Senate. Auctoritas senatus as a political slogan under the Late Republic expressed the doctrine of senatorial supremacy, in the sense that the Executive should submit to the direction and control of the Senate even if deference to the Senate involved the self-abnegation of magisterial potestas.[1] Under the Principate, however, the Senate was reduced to the role of an inferior partner to the Princeps. By virtue of his tribunicia potestas Augustus could veto any resolution of the Senate he did not approve of; on the other hand, he was de facto allowed to take any measure he deemed right and the Senate ratified his acts in anticipation.[2] It seems therefore that the activity of the Senate depended on the auctoritas of the Princeps rather than the activity of the Princeps on the auctoritas of the Senate.

"Liberum suffragium" was a plank in the platform of the Populares,[3] and was regarded as a manifestation of popular sovereignty. Time was when electoral and legislative Assemblies were essential organs of the Roman constitution. But when in A.D. 14 Tiberius, acting on Augustus's instructions, abolished popular elections,[4] he did away with what had become a sham. Augustus revived the elections,[5] but electoral freedom was severely curtailed by the commendatio of the Princeps[6] which was a virtual designation for appointment, very much in the same manner as it was under Caesar's dictatorship.[7] It is true that elections at Rome never were entirely free, but, whatever the amount of electoral freedom, the People considered it part and parcel of its political libertas, as is shown, for example, by the struggle for secret ballots. Commendation by virtue of the auctoritas of the Princeps[8] largely reduced the elections to a mere formality, and thereby eliminated the popular element from

---

[1] See Cic. Pro Sest. 137. Cf. above, pp. 40 ff.
[2] See S.C. de Imp. Vesp. ll. 17–19 and Dio Cass. LVI, 28, 3.
[3] Cf. above, p. 50.⁻   [4] See Vell. Pat. II, 124, 3.
[5] Suet. Div. Aug. 40, 2; 56, 1.
[6] Dio Cass. LIII, 21, 7. Cf. Mommsen, Staatsrecht II³, pp. 921 ff. On two occasions of disorderly elections Augustus appointed magistrates without a popular vote at all, see Dio Cass. LIV, 10, 2; LV, 34, 2.
[7] Suet. Div. Jul. 41, 2. Cf. Lucan V, 391 ff.
[8] Ovid, Ex Ponto IV, 9, 67 f.: Multiplicat tamen hunc gravitas auctoris honorem Et maiestatem res data dantis habet.

I

the Roman constitution. Judged by old Republican standards this was undoubtedly an encroachment upon the political freedom of the Roman People. Yet, principles apart, the change was of no great consequence. During the closing decades of the Republic electoral freedom at Rome became a kind of privilege of the urban populace in which the entire Populus Romanus had little cause to be interested. If Tacitus is right in saying that the abolition of popular elections called forth no other protest on the part of the People than "idle talk",[1] this would suggest that the Populus Romanus did not consider the innovation a severe loss of rights.

It appears from what has hitherto been said that the potestas and auctoritas of the Princeps, if judged by the old standards, went far beyond the Republican practice and made the very existence of a free commonwealth, in the old Republican sense, questionable. However, how many Romans were in a mood to judge the Principate by Republican standards, and to appraise it solely on its conformity to strict republicanism? There was the intransigent jurist Antistius Labeo who would not approve of anything that did not exist of old.[2] But was Labeo representative of his contemporaries? There is much truth in Tacitus's remark: "Iuniores post Actiacam victoriam, etiam senes plerique inter bella civium nati; quotus quisque reliquus, qui rem publicam vidisset?"[3] The second successive generation to endure civil war could hardly be disposed to regard constitutional propriety as the supreme criterion of the merits or demerits of a régime that offered peace. And once their desire for peace, security, and stability was satisfied, they may have been inclined to see freedom even where it did not exist. Nevertheless, it would not be right to assume on that account that all the talk about restoration of the res publica and libertas was merely make-believe.

[1] *Ann.* I, 15, 2.

[2] Ateius Capito (Labeo's contemporary and rival, see Tac. *Ann.* III, 75 and *Dig.* I, 2, 2, 47) ap. Gell. *N.A.* XIII, 12, 2: Agitabat hominem libertas quaedam nimia atque vecors usque eo, ut divo Augusto iam principe et rem publicam obtinente ratum tamen pensumque nihil haberet nisi quod iussum sanctumque esse in Romanis antiquitatibus legisset. Horace, *Sat.* I, 3, 81: Labeone insanior; and Porphyrio *ad loc. cit.*: (Labeo) memor libertatis in qua natus erat multa contumaciter adversus Caesarem dixisse et fecisse dicitur.

[3] *Ann.* I, 3, 7. Cf. *Hist.* I, 1, 1: inscitia rei publicae ut alienae. And also *Ann.* I, 2, 1.

The Republic became an "imago sine re" long before the establishment of the Principate, and many must have realized that just as
Cicero and Caesar had.[1] The contemporaries of Augustus knew the
Republic as a form without much substance, and that form was
largely preserved: "Non regno...neque dictatura, sed principis
nomine constitutam rem publicam."[2] The familiar magistracies
were retained ("eadem magistratuum vocabula"[3]), the Senate
deliberated and passed resolutions, the People cast votes in the
Assembly. If compared with the remote past, all this may have
seemed a sham. But every sensible person knew that the "vetus illa
et antiqua rei publicae forma" was irretrievably gone long before.
If people felt inclined to compare the Augustan Principate with the
past, it was with the immediate, not the remote, past that they
compared it, and the Principate doubtless compared more than
favourably with Caesar's dictatorship and the arbitrary régime of
the Second Triumvirate.

The Principate could also be rightly regarded as a restoration of
the res publica in another, and perhaps more important, respect.
Res publica signifies not only a form of government but also, and
primarily, a purpose of government. The quintessence of·a res
publica is that it is not simply a State, but a State which is a "common
wealth", that is to say, it consists of the interests of all citizens and
exists for all citizens.[4] A State in which the People have no political
rights is not a res publica at all.[5] The direct opposite to a res publica
is what the Romans called regnum, that is arbitrary despotism under
which the State is, as it were, a private property (res privata) of the
ruler, and the people are his rightless subjects. It seems that in order

[1] Cic. De Rep. v, 2; De Off. II, 29; Ad Att. IV, 18, 2; Suet. Div.
Jul. 77.
[2] Tac. Ann. I, 9, 6.
[3] Ib. I, 3, 7. Cf. Vell. Pat. II, 89, 3.
[4] R. Stark, Res Publica, seems to have entirely overlooked this aspect of
the Roman notion of res publica. The fact that the Romans continued to call
their State res publica under the Empire does not by itself prove that res
publica meant simply State, in the modern sense. Why the Romans applied the
term res publica to their State under the Empire can best be seen from the
following quotation: "Et in contione et in senatu saepe dixit (Hadrianus) ita se
rem publicam gesturum ut sciret populi rem esse non propriam", S.H.A.
Hadr. 8, 3.
[5] See Cic. De Rep. III, 43 ff. Cf. above, pp. 80 ff.

to understand the sentiments of the Romans under Augustus, the Principate must be compared, not with the bygone vetus res publica, but with arbitrary despotism which the Romans detested and feared so much.[1] Augustus was neither a despot (rex)[2] nor a dictator who wields unlimited power; his prerogative, as distinct from his auctoritas, was wide, but constitutional and limited. Under his rule no Roman had reason to feel like a rightless subject. All Romans continued to be free citizens of their own res publica which was directed by the Princeps, not for his own advantage, but for the well-being of all.[3] They lived again under a system of law and order which safeguarded their rights. The manner in which the State was directed changed, but its purpose remained the same. And this meant that the essentials of libertas remained. Libertas at Rome never meant anarchic negativism; it was founded on a positive doctrine which, put in a nutshell, was that "libertas in legibus consistit".[4] This means that the citizen holds his position in the community not in despite of the State but with the aid and by the guarantee of the State, because the State secures the rights which are the condition of his holding any position at all. Under Augustus the essential rights and liberties of Roman citizens remained untouched. It is true, the nobiles lost their de facto privilege of self-assertion in the conduct of public affairs. But, on the other hand, the formerly under-privileged classes, the potential homines novi, were given under the Principate a far better chance to make a public career than ever before.[5]

It appears therefore that there were valid reasons to consider Rome under the Augustan Principate a res publica (not the Res Publica) in which libertas existed. The real change was in the fundamental principle of government rather than in its form or

---

[1] See, e.g., Livy II, 15, 3.

[2] The Romans were conscious of the essential difference between principatus and regnum. See Ovid, *Fasti* II, 142: Tu (Romule) domini nomen, principis ille (Augustus) tenet. The same contrast is to be found, for example, in Suet. *Calig.* 22: Nec multum afuit quin statim diadema sumeret speciemque principatus in regni formam converteret. See also Pliny, *Paneg.* 45, 3; 55, 6 f.

[3] Cf. F. E. Adcock, *C.A.H.* x, p. 587.

[4] Cic. *De Lege Agr.* II, 102. Cf. above, pp. 7 ff.

[5] Cf. especially R. Syme, *The Roman Revolution*, ch. 25–33.

purpose; for whereas the salient feature of Republican government was distribution of power with a resultant system of checks and balances, the new régime rested on a somewhat veiled concentration of power in the hands of the Princeps. It was a profound change, but it did not immediately affect the lives of the people other than the old nobiles. Yet there were latent in it dangerous potentialities the actualization of which was bound to undermine the very foundations of libertas.

PRINCIPATUS ET LIBERTAS
RES OLIM DISSOCIABILES

Freedom of man under government is to have a standing rule
to live by, common to every one of that society and made by
the legislative power erected in it.

LOCKE, *Two Treatises on Civil Government*, ii, 4, 22.

Liberty alone demands for its realisation the limitation of the
public authority.

ACTON, 'Nationalism', in *The History of Freedom*, p. 288.

I. THE NATURE OF THE PROBLEM

Lucan, writing the later part of his epic in defiance of Nero's tyranny,[1]
observed that ever since the battle of Pharsalus there had been afoot
a conflict between liberty and Caesar, and Tacitus remarked that
prior to Nerva the Principate and freedom were incompatible.[2] It is
a well-known fact that the Julio-Claudian and Flavian emperors had
from time to time to face an opposition varying in form and intensity.
After Caligula's assassination Libertas was the watchword of those
who attempted to abolish the Principate;[3] some of Nero's victims
died with the name of Iuppiter Liberator on their lips;[4] and after
Nero's downfall Libertas Restituta became a popular slogan.[5] It
seems therefore that in some form or other freedom and the Principate clashed, and, in a way, Tacitus's historical writings, particularly
the *Annals*, were perhaps conceived and executed as the story of
that struggle.[6]

---

[1] See G. Boissier, *L' Opposition sous les Césars*[5] (1905), pp. 280 ff.

[2] Lucan VII, 691 ff. (ed. Housman). Housman's paraphrase of this somewhat obscure passage is: Ut Thapsi Mundae Alexandreae, sic post Pompei
fugam in proelio Pharsalico non favor in eum popularis aut bellandi studium,
quod utrumque iam sublatum est, in causa erit cur usque pugnaretur, sed
immortale libertatis cum Caesare certamen. Tac. *Agric.* 3, 1.

[3] See Josephus, *Ant.* XIX, 186.

[4] Tac. *Ann.* XV, 64, 4; XVI, 35, 2.

[5] See H. Mattingly and E. A. Sydenham, *op. cit.* I, pp. 210, 215, 225, 229, 230.

[6] Nos saeva iussa, continuas accusationes, fallaces amicitias, perniciem
innocentium et easdem exitu causas coniungimus, *Ann.* IV, 33, 3. Cf. *Hist.* I, 2, 3.

But while the conflict between the Principate and libertas under the emperors from Tiberius to Domitian appears to have been a fact, it is by no means clear what was the nature of that conflict. The real issue is somewhat obscured, for the modern student at least, by the ambiguity of the relevant political terms, above all libertas itself. Libertas means either personal and civic rights, or republicanism, or both, and, while under each of these heads fall several cognate but distinct notions, it is not always easy to ascertain exactly what libertas means in each particular instance. Similarly, principatus may mean either what the Principate actually became, but never ought to have become, or what it ought to be, but seldom was.

Nevertheless, the nature of the conflict between freedom and the Principate as well as the scope of libertas under the Early Empire (both of which are in fact only different aspects of the same problem) can be ascertained, if the available evidence is placed in due perspective and against its true background. In view of the variety of meanings that attach to libertas it is necessary, in order to avoid confusion when dealing with the question before us, to distinguish as clearly as possible between the seeming problems and the real ones. It may therefore be easier to show what the conflict between freedom and the Principate was, if we first eliminate from the discussion what it was not.

If a distinction is drawn between opposition to an emperor, or the Principate, and risings against, or dissatisfaction with, Roman rule, it will appear that, in so far as there existed opposition to the Julio-Claudian and Flavian emperors, it was not a widespread popular movement. The opposition was largely confined to the city of Rome, and even there it came principally from senators, nobles, and intellectuals. There was much truth in the observation which Tacitus put into the mouth of Cerialis: "Laudatorum principum usus ex aequo quamvis procul agentibus; saevi proximis ingruunt."[1]

As regards its motives, this chiefly senatorial opposition did not aim at abolishing the Principate and restoring the Republic. Tacitus says that immediately after the death of Augustus some people talked idly of the blessings of freedom.[2] There were rumours circulating about Drusus that he would restore the Republic if he came to power,[3] and the same was believed about Germanicus.[4]

---

[1] *Hist.* IV, 74, 2.   [2] *Ann.* I, 4, 2.   [3] *Ann.* I, 33, 3.   [4] *Ann.* II, 82, 3.

When Furius Camillus Scribonianus, the governor of Dalmatia, planned a revolt against Claudius in 42 he promised his soldiers to restore the Republic, but they would not listen to him.[1] The sincerity of his promise may well be doubted in view of the fact that after Caligula's death he was a potential candidate for the Principate.[2] All this shows that the ideas of libertas and res publica were not dead, but it shows nothing more.

The only known occasion on which the restoration of the Republic was seriously contemplated was the short interregnum between the assassination of Caligula and the accession of Claudius.[3] But even on that exceptional occasion the Senate did not arrive at a unanimous decision in favour of the Republic. The desire to restore the Republican form of government is easily understandable in view of the Senate's plight under Caligula's tyranny. Even so, the enthusiasm for the restoration of the Republic was not shared by all: some thought the Senate ought merely to appoint a new princeps. But whatever its opinions, the Senate soon realized that it was not the master of the situation; it had to sanction with a good grace the choice of the Praetorian Guard. It may be that the events of those two days drove home a lesson that the Senate never forgot. There were plots against the lives of nearly all the emperors from Augustus to Domitian, but the object of the conspirators was to remove the Princeps of the day, not to abolish the Principate. It is noteworthy that at the time of the Pisonian conspiracy against Nero it was believed at Rome that Piso did not admit the consul Vestinus to the secret "ne ad libertatem oreretur, vel delecto imperatore alio sui muneris rem publicam faceret".[4] Republicanism was no longer considered practical politics.

This view of the aims of the opposition is not inconsistent with the fact that there were under the Early Empire at Rome a number of distinguished persons who admired the Republic, some of whom even worshipped the memory of Cato, Brutus, and Cassius. On the face of it, this admiration of the Republic and this hero-worship seem to imply that there was a body of opinion strongly in favour of republicanism; this is, however, far from being so. It is no doubt

---

[1] Dio Cass. LX, 15, 3.   [2] See *C.A.H.* X, p. 667.
[3] See Josephus, *Ant.* XIX, 162 ff. and Suet. *Div. Claud.* 10, 3 ff.
[4] Tac. *Ann.* XV, 52, 4.

true that there were irreconcilable republicans under the Empire, as for example the jurist Labeo,[1] but admiration of the Republic and its heroes was not necessarily the concomitant of confirmed republicanism in politics.

It was part of the political genius of the Romans to see the unbroken continuity underlying all the new departures in their history. Under Augustus the form of government changed but this did not mean severing all the ties with the past. On the contrary, the Augustan Principate inspired a conscious effort to emphasize the links between past and present. The Republic was the glorious and heroic period of Roman history, and as such it could not fail to arouse the admiration of a Roman patriot. But sensible patriots knew only too well that, if Rome was to survive, the Principate had to continue,[2] and this is why their glorification of Rome's Republican history could be—and in many cases was—wedded to the support of the Principate.[3] Livy's and Virgil's Republican sympathies were in no way inconsistent with their allegiance to the Principate. Did not the Principate at its best aim at preserving Roman traditions?

Nor was the worship of Cato, Brutus, and Cassius necessarily inspired by allegiance to their lost cause. Titinius Capito, an imperial civil servant by profession and a thorough-going hero-worshipper by inclination, had his house filled with busts of Bruti, Cassii, and Catones.[4] The attitude of Seneca is no less revealing. Seneca combined boundless admiration for Cato with determined and outspoken support of monarchy. On reading what he has to say about Cato one can easily see that there was no inconsistency in Seneca's attitude: he admired in the Stoic Cato the courage and integrity of a man who remained true to himself in all circumstances,

[1] See above, p. 120 n. 2.

[2] See Seneca, *De Clem.* I, 4, 3; Tac. *Hist.* I, 1, 1; I, 16, 1; *Ann.* I, 9, 5; IV, 33, 2.

[3] "Ce serait donc une grande erreur de croire que tous ceux qui parlaient avec tant de respect des hommes et des choses de l'ancien temps regrettaient le gouvernement ancien et qu'on ne pouvait pas louer la république sans être républicain," Boissier, *op. cit.* pp. 92 f. For the attitude of Tacitus see below, pp. 160 ff.

[4] Pliny, *Ep.* I, 17, 3. See J. M. C. Toynbee, Dictators and Philosophers in the First Century A.D., *Greece and Rome* XIII (1944), pp. 43 f.

and defied Fortune in his life and by his death.¹ Cato is the paragon of Stoic virtues, he is a model above imitation.² But with the enthusiastic admiration of Cato's fortitude mingles criticism of his politics.

Quid tibi vis, Marce Cato? Iam non agitur de libertate; olim pessumdata est. Quaeritur, utrum Caesar an Pompeius possideat rem publicam; quid tibi cum ista contentione? Nullae partes tuae sunt; dominus eligitur. Quid tua uter vincat? Potest melior vincere, non potest non peior esse qui vicerit.³

Apparently Seneca thought that his hero failed rightly to appreciate the political situation of his own times. Similarly he criticized Brutus for having failed to see that, after the decay of the old morality, nothing could restore the old constitution.⁴

Seneca's example supplies a warning against a generalization that admiration of Republican heroes amounted to republicanism in politics. The cult of Republican personages may be a symbolical assertion of faith in republicanism,⁵ and it was represented by malevolent critics as savouring of revolution;⁶ but it may just as well indicate that republicanism had spent itself as a political force, and survived only in the form of romantic devotion to bygone times and a politically harmless hero-worship. It is noteworthy that, in spite of his *Philippics* and his proscription, Cicero did not figure among the venerated heroes and martyrs of the Republic.⁷ The reason seems to be that there was nothing in Cicero's character or his death to commend him to the admiration of posterity. Seneca knew what was Cato's title to fame: "Catoni gladium adsertorem

¹ Nemo mutatum Catonem totiens mutata in re publica vidit; and: Cato ...ostendit virum fortem posse invita fortuna vivere, invita mori, *Ep.* 104, 29 ff. Cf. also *Ep.* 24, 6 ff.; 95, 69 ff.; 98, 12.

² Catonem autem certius exemplar sapientis viri nobis deos immortales dedisse quam Ulixen et Herculem prioribus saeculis, etc.; *Dial.* II (*De Const. Sap.*), 2, 1. Cf. *Dial.* I (*De Provid.*), 3, 14. See also *Ep.* 70, 22 and *Dial.* II, 7, 1.

³ *Ep.* 14, 13.   ⁴ *De Benef.* II, 20, 2.

⁵ Whether this was really so in the case of Thrasea Paetus and Helvidius Priscus, who are known both as admirers of Cato, Brutus, and Cassius, and as martyrs of libertas under the Early Empire, will be discussed later.

⁶ See Tac. *Ann.* XIV, 57, 5; XVI, 22, 7 ff.

⁷ A restrained tribute is paid to him by Quintilian, a professed admirer of Ciceronian style, see *Inst.* XII, 1, 16.

libertatis extorque, magnam partem detraxeris gloriae."[1] Perhaps if republicanism mattered most, Cicero would have found an honourable place beside Cato and the Liberators. Anyhow, the worship of heroes whom death ennobled and tradition idealized does not prove adherence to their real politics.

There remains another thing to be observed. In his well-known study *L'Opposition sous les Césars*, Gaston Boissier denied to the opposition a political character. He asserted that while the opponents detested the vices of the emperors, they were not concerned to resent their power; the opposition was in principle moral, not political: it blamed in the emperor the man, not the sovereign.[2] Elsewhere in the same study[3] Boissier seems to have somewhat modified this view, perhaps unwittingly. In the main, however, his thesis is that the opposition was not political.[4]

It seems that Boissier denied the opposition a political character because, on the one hand, he saw quite rightly that it did not aim at restoring the Republic, and, on the other, implicitly assumed that a political conflict with the Principate could be nothing but a conflict between republicanism and monarchy.

The object of the following pages is to show that the conflict between libertas and principatus was a political issue, although not between republicanism and monarchy.

The Augustan Principate was not, and was not meant to be, an absolute monarchy in republican disguise. Augustus did not attempt or wish to do away with the Republic once for all; rather his aim was to preserve as much of it as was practically possible.[5] Two great political ideas survived the collapse of the Republic, and both of them were received as fundamental principles of the new régime: the one was the idea that law, the chief guarantor of all rights and liberties to which a Roman citizen was entitled, was above all power; the other, that the Roman State was the common concern of the Roman People. These clearly distinct ideas are in fact, as has been seen, only two different aspects of libertas. And it is precisely these two aspects of libertas that are uppermost in the conflict between freedom and the Principate.

---

[1] *Ep.* 13, 14. [2] Boissier, *op. cit.* pp. 102–3. [3] *Ib.* pp. 345 f.
[4] For a somewhat similar view see J. M. C. Toynbee, *op. cit.* p. 47.
[5] See F. E. Adcock, *C.A.H.* x, p. 587.

2. Princeps Supra Leges

Pliny, when he praised in his *Panegyric* Trajan's deference to law, declared among other things:

> Quod ego nunc primum audio, nunc primum disco, non est princeps supra leges, sed leges supra principem idemque Caesari consuli quod ceteris non licet.[1]

One would have thought that the laws were binding on the Princeps as a matter of course; seeing, however, that Pliny went on to praise Trajan on that score, it seems that this was neither obvious nor certain. How far Pliny's statement is true with regard to Trajan will be seen later; all we need consider here is whether what his words imply, namely that before Trajan the Princeps was above the law, is exaggerated or correct.

The Princeps, as Augustus conceived of him, was undoubtedly the first citizen, but a citizen, and as such subject to the laws of Rome and to the constitutional organs. From the standpoint of the constitutional theory of the Principate it is interesting that when Claudius hesitated whether he might contract a marriage with his niece Agrippina, Vitellius asked him whether he would yield to the command of the People and the authority of the Senate, to which the emperor replied "unum se civium et consensui imparem".[2] Nor did the first Princeps claim to be the master of the State: Augustus considered himself a soldier at a post;[3] Tiberius asserted that the Princeps ought to be the servant of the State;[4] and both of them eschewed the appellation "dominus".[5]

---

[1] *Paneg.* 65, 1.

[2] Tac. *Ann.* XII, 5. Cf. Suet. *Div. Claud.* 26, 3. See also *Ann.* IV, 6, 7: Ac si quando cum privatis disceptaret (Tiberius)—forum et ius.

[3] See Gellius, *N.A.* XV, 7, 3. Cf. Seneca, *De Clem.* I, 3, 3 (excubare). See also F. E. Adcock, *C.A.H.* X, 594. If the idea of statio principis goes at all beyond Roman military tradition, it may derive from Socrates no less than from Hellenistic kingship, see Plato, *Apology*, 28 D ff. Cf. Dio Chrys. III, 55: ὑπὸ τοῦ μεγίστου θεοῦ ταχθείς. For a detailed discussion see E. Köstermann, Statio Principis, *Philologus* LXXXVII (1932), pp. 358–68, 430–44; and J. Béranger, Pour une définition du principat, *Rev. Ét. Lat.* XXI–XXII (1943–4), pp. 144–54.

[4] Suet. *Tib.* 29. Cf. 24, 2; Tac. *Ann.* I, 11, 2. See also Dio Chrys. III, 75, where kingship is represented as δουλεία.

[5] Suet. *Div. Aug.* 53, 1; *Tib.* 27; Dio Cass. LVII, 8, 2.

But if this was so, why was it possible for Domitian to become "dominus et deus" without having changed the constitution? Why did it occur to Pliny to say that the Princeps was above the law? Why did a conflict between the Principate and libertas develop at all?

"Si le pouvoir de l'empereur n'était pas tout à fait illimité," says Boissier, "il était au moins mal limité: de là vint tout le mal."[1] It is only to be regretted that, having hit the nail on the head, he went on to explain that the power of the Princeps rested on his dignitas,[2] and that "cette autorité mal définie et incertaine, rendue plus puissante par son obscurité même, paralysait tout le reste".[3] This explanation is obviously inspired by Montesquieu's theory of Separation of Powers according to which the strict division of functions is the most effective check on power.[4] But there was never separation of powers at Rome, and, as the Republican constitution shows, the Romans, unlike Montesquieu and his many followers, were well aware of the essential difference between delimitation of functions and limitation of power. In the eyes of the Romans, under the Republic at any rate, limitation of power consists, not in a precise circumscription of functions, but rather in effective safeguards against the abuse of power within its statutory province. What made the power of the consul limited were the provisions whereby its duration was fixed, and its abuse could be prevented by par potestas or intercessio, or, failing this, punished later. The separation of the military and administrative functions of the consul from the juridical and judicial functions of the praetor was no more than a division of labour; nor did consuls cease to be judges or praetors cease to be generals. It was because of the threefold protection against the abuse of power—par potestas and intercessio, provocatio, potestas ad tempus—that the Republican constitution could rightly be described as "imperia legum potentiora quam hominum".[5] And so long as law was above power, freedom was secure.

---

[1] Boissier, op. cit. p. 63.

[2] This was at that time the accepted reading in the Res Gestae, 34, instead of the correct "auctoritate".

[3] Op. cit. p. 64.

[4] It will be noticed that Boissier uses "mal limité" and "mal définie et incertaine" as meaning the same thing.

[5] Livy II, 1, 1.

What was wrong in the Principate from the point of view of libertas was the absence of effective safeguards against the abuse of power by the emperor. Not that the Princeps was exempted from all existing checks; in theory some checks existed as before, but in practice they could not be applied against the Princeps simply because there was no adequate force behind them. What made those checks effective under the Republic was the distribution of power (not separation of Powers). Their effectiveness continued so long as distribution of power continued; but when a concentrated and permanently overwhelming power emerged, those checks were of little, if any, use. They were not abolished, but they became shams.

The jurist Gaius asserts that "nec umquam dubitatum est quin (constitutio principis) legis vicem optineat".[1] It is of course true that senior magistrates were always empowered to issue binding edicts, but there is a world of difference between a magisterial edict and an imperial constitutio: the former was legal and binding only in so far as it complied with the established law, whereas the latter supplanted the law. That is to say that, unlike the magistrate who governed in compliance with general rules, the Princeps was empowered to rule by direct command. But, even if beneficial, government by command which takes the place of law is incompatible with the fundamental idea of freedom as it was conceived of under the Republic. That idea, epitomized in Cicero's dictum "Legum idcirco omnes servi sumus ut liberi esse possimus",[2] postulates that the Roman People should be governed in accordance with the general rules laid down in the statutes which the People enacted and by so doing bound themselves to observe. Under such a government the Romans could feel they were their own masters, notwithstanding the fact that they were not really self-governing. The moment, however, an imperial decree, edict, or instruction[3]

---

[1] *Gai Inst.* I, 5. Cf. *Dig.* I, 4, I (Ulpian) = *Inst.* I, 2, 6. Ulpian's text in the *Digest* is obviously interpolated. F. Schulz, Bracton on Kingship, *Eng. Hist. Rev.* LX (1945), p. 154, reconstructs Ulpian's original phrasing: Quod principi placuit legis habet vicem, utpote cum lege quae de imperio eius lata est populus ei hanc potestatem conferat.

[2] Cic. *Pro Cluent.* 146.

[3] Constitutio principis est quod imperator decreto vel edicto vel epistula constituit, *Gai Inst.* I, 5. Cf. *Dig.* I, 4, I, I (Ulpian).

acquired the force of a lex, the Roman People was exposed to domination. It is true the Princeps was not yet exempted from all laws;[1] on the other hand, there were no effective means of coercing him to obey the laws. But a power which is de facto above the law is a grave menace to freedom; and the menace was all the graver for the technical legitimacy of that power. Gaius and Ulpian argue that the emperor's decrees and regulations are law because his power was conferred on him by an enactment of the People. Thus the Enabling Act becomes a legitimate title to virtual absolutism.[2] But legitimacy is not freedom, and "the dogma that absolute power may, by the hypothesis of a popular origin, be as legitimate as constitutional freedom, began...to darken the air".[3]

The Hellenistic philosophy of kingship, and especially the doctrine that the true king is Law Incarnate, νόμος ἔμψυχος,[4] was known in Rome and, by a kind of misinterpretation, may have stimulated absolutism under the Early Empire (the Late Empire is a different matter, but it cannot be dealt with here). In its true and original form, however, the doctrine of the king as Law Incarnate is concerned with a problem totally different from that which faced the Romans. This doctrine is not at all concerned with positive law.[5] The philosopher-king, by virtue of his wisdom, is capable of

[1] For a full discussion of the view here accepted see F. Schulz, *op. cit.* p. 158. See also S.C. de Imp. Vesp. ll. 22 ff.

[2] See *Gai Inst.* I, 5; Ulpian, *Dig.* I, 4, 1. Gradually the Lex de Imperio came to be looked upon as an exemption from law in general, see *Cod. Iust.* VI, 23, 3 (Severus Alexander, A.D. 232): Licet enim lex imperii sollemnibus iuris imperatorem solverit, nihil tamen tam proprium imperii est ut legibus vivere. Cf. *Inst.* II, 17, 8:...Divi quoque Severus et Antoninus saepissime rescripserunt: licet enim, inquiunt, legibus soluti sumus, attamen legibus vivimus.

[3] Lord Acton, *History of Freedom*, p. 78.

[4] For a discussion of this doctrine see Erwin R. Goodenough, The Political Philosophy of Hellenistic Kingship, *Yale Classical Studies*, I (1928), pp. 55–102; and *The Politics of Philo Judaeus* (1938), pp. 55, 107–10. It is hard to say whether Professor Goodenough noticed that his conclusions in the earlier work, pp. 99 ff., (which are not accepted here) are at variance with those of the later one.

[5] See Seneca, *De Clem.* I, 1, 4 and I, 1, 2; and especially Plutarch, *Ad Principem Ineruditum*, 3 (= *Moralia*, 780c): τίς οὖν ἄρξει τοῦ ἄρχοντος; ὁ νόμος...οὐκ ἐν βιβλίοις ἔξω γεγραμμένος οὐδέ τισι ξύλοις, ἀλλ᾽ ἔμψυχος ὢν ἐν αὐτῷ λόγος.

understanding the precepts of right reason[1] and he enjoins them on his subjects. He is God's vicegerent on earth,[2] and in exercising his power has to imitate the benignity of God.[3] The foundation of his rule, however, is obedience to the unwritten laws of right reason, in default of which he becomes a tyrant. The king is therefore an absolute ruler, in the sense that he is not responsible to his subjects, but he is subject to those divine, or natural, laws which he embodies on earth.

The problem that faced the Romans was the relation between the Princeps, whose power rested on an Act of the Senate and People of Rome, and the positive laws of the Romans. It is quite clear that, originally, the doctrine that the king is Law Incarnate and the principle "quod principi placuit legis habet vigorem" move on different planes. The Hellenistic doctrine could of course be adapted to the sphere of positive law (a procedure greatly facilitated by the ambiguity of the term νόμος) to reinforce an already existing absolutism. But it could also be used to mitigate absolutism, and this is perhaps what Seneca attempted to do in his De Clementia. It seems that Seneca, because he realized that the positive laws of Rome could not be enforced on the Princeps, tried to impress on Nero the idea that it was his duty as ruler spontaneously to accept the unwritten laws of morality.

Livy recorded the truly Roman view "neminem unum tantum eminere civem debere ut legibus interrogari non possit".[4] He lived to see this fundamental principle of Roman freedom giving way: the emperor, his family, and their friends began to arrogate a position "supra leges": the administration of justice proved almost ineffective against a friend of Livia Augusta.[5] Presently Claudius banished without a hearing two innocent Romans: the one because he strongly pleaded against him in court before he became emperor; the other because as aedile he fined the tenants of Claudius's estate for the breach of a certain administrative law and flogged his bailiff

[1] See Musonius, ed. Hense, p. 36, 23 ff.; Plutarch, loc. cit.; Dio Chrys. 1, 75: Νόμος, ὁ δὲ αὐτὸς καὶ Λόγος Ὀρθὸς κέκληται.
[2] Seneca, De Clem. 1, 1, 2; Pliny, Paneg. 80, 5.
[3] Musonius, loc. cit.; Dio Chrys. 1, 37 ff. Cf. Seneca, De Clem. 1, 14, 2.
[4] XXXVIII, 50, 8.
[5] Tac. Ann. 11, 34, 3–8. Cf. IV, 21, 1 and also II, 51, 3; III, 12, 10; XII, 60, 6.

when he remonstrated.[1] The laws, although not invalidated, proved
de facto powerless against the overwhelming power of the Princeps.
And if such power, and the consciousness of such power, happened
to be combined with depravity, the awareness that prohibitions were
ineffective might easily inspire the belief that everything was
permissible. "Remember that I am permitted to do anything to
anybody" was Caligula's reply to his grandmother when she once
admonished him.[2] And Nero, having perpetrated many crimes with
complete impunity, drew the conclusion that no Princeps had ever
realized what power he really possessed.[3] One would be tempted to
dismiss these assertions as the vagaries of men drunk with power,
were it not for the fact that thoughtful contemporaries realized and
admitted the omnipotence of the emperor. "Caesar...cui omnia
licent" and "qui omnia potest" says Seneca.[4] And Dio Chrysostom
asks, τίνι δὲ (δεῖ) ἀκριβεστέρας δικαιοσύνης ἢ τῷ μείζονι τῶν νόμων;
τίνι δὲ σωφροσύνης ἐγκρατεστέρας ἢ ὅτῳ πάντα ἔξεστι; [5]

This was by no means a true exposition of the constitutional
theory of the Principate; it was nevertheless a fact, and to a large
extent that fact found legal expression and sanction in the S.C. de
Imperio Vespasiani.[6]

The power of the Princeps became increasingly absolute, and,
being absolute, it might at any time become autocratic, despotic,
tyrannical. And if from the point of view of libertas the great problem
of the Late Republic was to prevent limited power from becoming
absolute, the great problem of the Early Empire was to prevent absolute power from becoming despotic. This was the crux, and this was
the ultimate cause of the conflict between libertas and principatus.

Before we describe in what manner the Romans sought to recon-
cile freedom and absolutism there is another thing to be observed.
The real sufferer under despotism was the senatorial class. Other
classes also suffered to some extent,[7] and in so far as they suffered

---

[1] Suet. *Div. Claud.* 38, 2.   [2] Suet. *Calig.* 29, 1. Cf. 32, 3.
[3] Suet. *Nero*, 37, 3. Cf. Nero's ironical remark: Sane legem Iuliam timeo,
ib. 33, 2.
[4] *Ad Polyb.* 7, 2; *De Clem.* I, 8, 5.
[5] *Or.* III, 10.   [6] Ll. 17 ff. Cf. above, p. 133 n. 2.
[7] As, for instance, from heavy taxes and predatory confiscations, see Suet.
Calig. 38; *Nero*, 32; Tac. *Ann.* xv, 45; or from spies and informers. For
Domitian's policy in this respect see M. P. Charlesworth, *C.A.H.* xi, pp. 41 f.

K

were discontented. But the suspicion and wrath of despots as well as their autocratic régime hit the Senate and nobility more than any one else. And this is why opposition to despotism was confined almost exclusively to the senatorial class.

3. LIBERTAS SENATUS

During the early decades of the Empire the Senate underwent a profound transformation. In Republican times, and especially since Sulla, it was indirectly elected by the People and therefore was to some extent representative of the People, although People and Senate as constitutional organs, or Plebs and Senate as social classes, were often opposed to each other. With the abolition of popular elections under Tiberius the Senate became a co-opting body; but, while its representative character was thereby diminished, it largely took the place of the Assembly,[1] and the voice of Senatus Populusque Romanus was henceforth heard through the mouth of the Senate alone. Thus, in so far as the res publica was expressed in terms of political institutions, it was now embodied in the first place by the Senate and the ordinary magistrates (as distinct from the imperial legates and procurators). But, tradition and constitutional convention apart, the Senate was not the representative of the Roman People, nor were the magistrates the People's delegates. In point of fact the Senate was a kind of co-opting corporation which provided the personnel for the administration, and acted as partner to the Princeps. And the character of this partnership determined the attitude of the Senate towards the Princeps of the day.

Had there really been, as Mommsen thought there was, a dyarchy of a sovereign Senate and the Princeps, the conflict between principatus and libertas might have never taken place. Indeed it seems that some kind of dyarchy was the ideal of certain senatorial die-hards. It was the absence of dyarchy, that is to say, the fact that the Senate was not an independent authority of equal status, if not power, in relation to the Princeps, that was a serious, though not the sole, cause of discontent.

---

[1] *Gai Inst.* I, 4; Mommsen, *Staatsrecht* III, pp. 1265 f.; F. Schulz, *Prinzipien des römischen Rechts*, p. 7.

It is no doubt a fact of no small consequence that what, in the eyes of our Latin authorities, reflects credit on an emperor is in the first place his respect for the Senate and magistrates.[1] And libertas, with regard to Roman domestic politics under the Empire, often means, explicitly or implicitly, libertas senatus.[2] Libertas senatus means that important matters of State shall be brought before the Senate, and that senators may freely express their opinions and vote without constraint. What the Senate sought was, not to reassert its lost supremacy, but to maintain an honourable position as the emperor's partner.[3] Since, however, the partnership between Senate and emperor was based on a division of labour without a corresponding division of power,[4] it was hardly possible for the Senate to hold its own. The Principate gradually absorbed the functions and prestige of the Senate and the ordinary magistrates,[5] not always with ill intentions. The Senate was not equal to its duties, and, while anxious to retain its prestige, was on occasions only too glad to leave the more arduous tasks to the Princeps.[6] With the expansion of the imperial administration the power of the procurators increased at the expense of the magistrates.[7] And it was certainly galling for senators and nobles to see the influence and wealth of the freedmen in charge of the emperor's secretariate.[8]

The awareness of impotence and dependence does not inspire self-respect. And if Tiberius was disgusted with the Senate's docility,[9] one can imagine the resentment and dejection of those adherents of senatorial traditions who witnessed the humiliation

[1] See Tac. *Ann.* IV, 6; 15, 3; XIII, 4, 3; *Hist.* II, 91, 2; Suet. *Tib.* 30 ff.; *Calig.* 16, 2; *Div. Claud.* 12, 1–2.

[2] Tac. *Agric.* 2, 2; *Ann.* XIII, 49; I, 74, 6; 77, 2–3; 81, 3; II, 35; III, 60, 1–6; *Hist.* IV, 44, 1; Suet. *Tib.* 30.

[3] See Tac. *Ann.* II, 35, 2: Piso...agendas censebat, ut absente principe senatum et equites posse sua munia sustinere decorum rei publicae foret. Cf. *Hist.* IV, 9. Dio Cass. LII, 32, 1, is also very interesting.

[4] See F. E. Adcock, *C.A.H.* X, p. 587.

[5] See *Ann.* I, 2, 1; III, 60, 1; XI, 5, 1.

[6] See *Ann.* II, 35; III, 35, 1; *Hist.* IV, 9.

[7] See *Ann.* XII, 60. Cf. Suet. *Div. Claud.* 12, 1 and also 24, 1.

[8] *Ann.* XII, 60, 6. Cf. XI, 33, 2; 35, 1; 37–8; XII, 1–2; 25, 1; 53, 5; XV, 72, 3–4; *Hist.* I, 7, 3; Suet. *Div. Claud.* 28 and 37; *Domit.* 7, 2. Seneca wreaked a literary vengeance on Claudius: in his *Apocolocyntosis Divi Claudii*, 15, 2, Claudius is declared a slave and made a freedman's secretary.

[9] See Tac. *Ann.* III, 65, 3.

of the Senate under Caligula or Nero or Domitian, when flattery, servility, and self-abasement were the price of a precarious existence.[1]

Yet although the Senate kissed the rod, Nero threatened that he would destroy it altogether.[2] It may be doubted whether the degradation of the Senate mattered much to the ordinary citizens, and whether its abolition would have appreciably affected their position. But by virtue of its tradition and by the strength of convention the Senate was regarded, by senators at any rate, as the constitutional embodiment of the res publica. Consequently, the rights and dignity of the Senate and the magistrates who sat in it were looked upon as a manifestation of the res publica.[3] And this is why in senatorial quarters under the Empire the assertion of the Senate's rights becomes libertas *tout court*, whereas the watchword of so staunch a champion of senatorial supremacy as Cicero was always auctoritas senatus et populi Romani libertas.

4. THRASEA PAETUS

The sorry plight of the Senate under Nero's despotism is the background against which the well-known but variously interpreted opposition of Thrasea Paetus appears in its true light.[4] Thrasea is usually cited as an example of what is known as the philosophic opposition under the Early Empire. But, as his recorded words and deeds show, he acted primarily as a courageous and upright Roman senator who held Stoic views, not as a Stoic philosopher who happened to be a senator at Rome. Our authorities tell enough about him to enable us to see where his motives sprang from. Thus Tacitus says:

Non referrem vulgarissimum senatus consultum quo civitati Syracusanorum egredi numerum edendis gladiatoribus finitum permittebatur, nisi

[1] See, e.g., Tac. *Ann.* XIV, 12; 14; 20; 61; XV, 23; XVI, 4, from among many examples of adulation and self-abasement.

[2] Suet. *Nero*, 37, 3. Cf. Tac. *Hist.* IV, 42, 4.

[3] Tac. *Ann.* XIII, 28; *Hist.* I, 84, 3: . . . Vitellius imaginem quandam exercitus habet, senatus nobiscum est. Sic fit ut hinc respublica, inde hostes rei publicae constiterint.

[4] For various interpretations of Thrasea's opposition see G. Boissier, *op. cit.* pp. 99 ff.; H. Furneaux, *The Annals of Tacitus*, II (1891), pp. 80 ff.; B. W. Henderson, *The Life and Principate of the Emperor Nero* (1905), pp. 294 ff.; D. R. Dudley, *A History of Cynicism* (1937), pp. 130 ff.; J. M. C. Toynbee, *op. cit.* pp. 49 ff.

Paetus Thrasea contra dixisset praebuissetque materiem obtrectatoribus arguendae sententiae. Cur enim, si rem publicam egere libertate senatoria crederet, tam levia consectaretur?...An solum emendatione dignum ne Syracusis spectacula largius ederentur; cetera per omnes imperii partes perinde egregia, quam si non Nero sed Thrasea regimen teneret? Quod si summa dissimulatione transmitterentur, quanto magis inanibus abstinendum? Thrasea contra, rationem poscentibus amicis, non praesentium ignarum respondebat eius modi consulta corrigere, sed patrum honori dare ut manifestum fieret magnarum rerum curam non dissimulaturos, qui animum etiam levissimis adverterent.[1]

Epigrammatic phrasing and arrangement apart, there is no reason to doubt the veracity of this account. It appears, therefore, that in Thrasea's opinion the State, in the year 58, suffered from the lack of senatorial freedom; by paying undue attention to a trivial subject he wished to show, for the sake of the Senate's honour, that the evasion of important matters was not due to negligence. It seems from the tenor of the passage that to "dissimulaturos" something like "si facultas data esset" should be supplied.

Whenever the Senate abased itself to flatter the emperor, Thrasea would be silent or would briefly give his assent. But when Nero's dispatch, which dealt with the execution of his own mother, was read in the Senate, and illustrious men vied with each other in moving honorific resolutions, Thrasea left the house without saying a word, for "he could not say what he would, and would not say what he could".[2]

In the year 62 a praetor, Antistius by name, was tried in the Senate for maiestas. A death sentence was proposed, but Thrasea disagreed: "Multo cum honore Caesaris et acerrime increpito Antistio, non quidquid nocens reus pati mereretur, id egregio sub principe et nulla necessitate obstricto senatui statuendum, disseruit." There were, he continued, penalties sanctioned by law (esse poenas legibus constitutas) and they must be adhered to if the judges are not to be cruel and the times infamous.[3]

In the same year an influential provincial from Crete was tried.[4] An utterance of his went so far as to be an insult to the Senate (una vox eius usque ad contumeliam senatus penetraverat), for he

---

[1] *Ann.* XIII, 49. [2] *Ann.* XIV, 12 and Dio Cass. LXI, 15, 2.
[3] *Ann.* XIV, 48. Cf. Dio Cass. LXII, 15, 7, 1a.
[4] See Tac. *Ann.* XV, 20 f.

said that it lay in his power to decide whether or not votes of thanks for the proconsular governors of Crete should be proposed. Thrasea seized upon the opportunity and moved that provincials should be prohibited from proposing votes of thanks for retiring governors. The tone of his speech, as reproduced by Tacitus, is that of a proud and narrow Italian nationalism, well in tune with Thrasea's senatorial rank and municipal extraction, but not at all with Stoic cosmopolitanism.[1] It is noteworthy that Thrasea's motion received Nero's sanction,[2] which shows that as late as 62 he was not yet out of favour with the emperor. It must also be remembered that he held the consulship in 56[3] and was an influential consular, as appears from the fact that his auctoritas prevailed in the condemnation of Capito Cossutianus—his future prosecutor—who was charged de repetundis in 58,[4] and in 62 secured a milder sentence for Antistius. It is clear therefore that Thrasea could not have been a persona non grata under Claudius or during the earlier part of Nero's reign.

This fact shows that Thrasea's "republican sympathies" were not necessarily political in character. He wrote a book on Cato,[5] and used to celebrate the birthdays of the Bruti and of Cassius.[6] But Cato and Brutus were not only champions of the republican form of government; they were great Romans (Cato certainly was) and model Stoics.

It appears from Tacitus that Thrasea's libertas was a courageous independence of opinion, not republicanism.[7] Far from being the leader of a movement aiming at the overthrow of the Empire, as his accuser alleged,[8] he discouraged some of his friends who wished to launch a vocal, ostentatious, and active opposition to Nero.[9] And this explains his conduct during his last years.

Some time about 63–4[10] Thrasea adopted a policy of out-and-out abstention from public life, especially from the Senate. Nero, in his

---

[1] *Ann.* XV. 21, 1–2.   [2] *Ib.* XV, 22, 1.
[3] H. Furneaux, *ad Ann.* XIII, 49, 1 (vol. II, p. 373 f.).
[4] *Ann.* XIII, 33, 3 and XVI, 21, 3.
[5] Plut. *Cato Min.* 37.   [6] Juvenal, v, 36–7.
[7] *Ann.* XIV, 12; 49; *Hist.* IV, 5, 2.
[8] *Ann.* XVI, 22, 7–8.
[9] *Ann.* XIII, 49, 2; XVI, 25, 2; 26, 6.
[10] "Triennio non introisse curiam", said his accuser in 66, see *Ann.* XVI, 22, 1.

message to the Senate, deliberately called it quietism and neglect of
duty.[1] But this was not the case. It was a considered[2] policy of
protest, all the more marked for being silent. "I miss," said Thrasea's
prosecutor, "the consular in the Senate, the priest at the sacrifices, the
citizen at the taking of the oath; unless by defying the established
way of life and form of worship Thrasea has openly assumed the
character of an enemy of his country. Let him come, he who was
wont to play the senator (senatorem agere) and protect the slanderers
of the emperor, let him come and state what he wants to be corrected
or changed. Facilius perlaturos singula increpantis vocem quam
nunc silentium perferrent omnia damnantis."[3] In so far as Thrasea's
motives are concerned his accuser was, in the main, right: Thrasea
was a discontented senator who expressed his disapproval of the
régime and asserted his integrity and freedom of judgement through
silence and non-participation.[4] Such a policy was not altogether
new. L. Piso, under Tiberius, declared that he would retire to
a remote village to mark his disapproval of the state of public
affairs, and his protest greatly impressed Tiberius.[5] Cicero, under
Caesar's dictatorship, adopted a similar course of silent inactivity,[6]
and Caesar rightly regarded Cicero's self-imposed retirement from
public life as a stricture on the régime, and tried to conciliate
him.

Perhaps opposition is not the right word for Thrasea's attitude;
it is a protest, a demonstration of disapproval, an attempt to dissociate
oneself from a régime which is condemned by that very dissociation.
Thrasea's abstention gained notoriety, because he was known as
a man devoted to his senatorial duties, and, since the man was
respected,[7] it must have carried weight. Abstention is the principal
count in his indictment, and from it derive several of the charges
brought against him. For, obviously, if for years he would not, as
a matter of principle, set foot in the Senate, he could not be there
when divine honours were decreed for the deceased empress (in the

---

[1] *Ann.* XVI, 27, 2 f.   [2] *Ib.* XVI, 26, 7–8.
[3] *Ann.* XVI, 28, 3 f.   Cf. Dio Cass. LXII, 26, 3.
[4] This point is rightly stressed by D. R. Dudley, *op. cit.* p. 131.
[5] Tac. *Ann.* II, 34, 1 f.
[6] See Cic. *Pro Marc.* 1; *Ad Fam.* IV, 9, 2; IX, 16, 3.
[7] Even Nero, shortly before he put him to death, praised Thrasea's justice,
see Plutarch, *Moralia*, 810a.

year 65), or when an oath "in acta" was taken.[1] Once his abstention was interpreted as treason, the prosecution dragged in anything, relevant or irrelevant, which would help to achieve its sole aim, condemnation, a thing that was not too difficult under Nero. The prosecutor had only to harp on things particularly offensive to Nero, as for instance contempt of his histrionic mania,[2] or the commonplace allegation that the stern bearing of the philosopher is intended as a stricture on the emperor's dissolute life.[3] And, as will be seen later, the allegation that Thrasea and his friends wished to destroy the State,[4] was also a commonplace frequently levelled against all philosophers, especially the Stoics.

But, if their political significance was overdone in his indictment, Thrasea's Stoicism and devotion to Republican heroes found full expression in the manner of his death, and it is perhaps from this that the meaning of his admiration of Cato can be seen. If the extant account of his last hours is true, it is quite obvious that Thrasea studiously modelled his death on the examples of Socrates and Cato.[5] He discussed the immortality of the soul with Demetrius the Cynic, and when his veins were cut he sprinkled his blood, saying to the quaestor who brought the Senate's decree: "Libamus Iovi Liberatori.[6] Specta iuvenis; et omen quidem di prohibeant, ceterum in ea tempora natus es, quibus firmare animum expediat constantibus exemplis." He no doubt believed that, like Cato, he gave an example of steadfastness which would be remembered,[7] and inspire others just as Cato's example inspired him. "It is better to die like a freeman than abase oneself to no purpose and then perish like a slave" said Thrasea, for he realized that, even at the price of self-degradation, one could not buy security of life under a tyrant.[8]

---

[1] *Ann.* XVI, 21, 2; 22, 1 and 5.

[2] *Ib.* XVI, 21, 1; 22, 1; Dio Cass. LXI, 20, 4; LXII, 26, 3 f.

[3] *Ann.* XVI, 22, 3: Rigidi et tristes quo tibi lasciviam exprobrent. Cf. Seneca, *Ep.* 123, 11 f.: Istos tristes et superciliosos alienae vitae censores, suae hostes, publicos paedagogos, assis ne feceris nec dubitaveris bonam vitam quam opinionem bonam malle. Hae voces non aliter fugiendae sunt, etc. Obviously Seneca is combating a widespread opinion, which appears also in Quintil. *Inst.* XII, 3, 12.   [4] *Ann.* XVI, 22, 7–8.

[5] *Ann.* XVI, 34–5. For Cato's last hours see Seneca, *Ep.* 24, 6 ff.

[6] Cf. Dio Cass. LXII, 26, 4. Seneca made a similar libation, see *Ann.* XV, 64, 4.

[7] Dio Cass. LXI, 15, 4.   [8] Id. LXI, 15, 3.

There is nothing to prove that Thrasea wished for the overthrow of the Empire and the restoration of the Republic; but to say that he and his like resented Nero's personal character only[1] is an understatement which misses the vital point. It is an essential characteristic of autocratic despotism that no line of demarcation can at all be drawn between the personal character of the despot and his power, because a despot's power is what the despot makes it. And certainly those who live under a perverse despot are incapable of considering separately the psycho-pathological and the constitutional aspect of their oppression. Nero's perversity made him a charioteer, an actor, a matricide; but it was his power that enabled him to be an emperor at the same time. And this is what mattered. Nero made the Principate a tyranny; his follies, which were applauded, and his crimes, which went unpunished, only emphasized the enormity of that tyranny. Thrasea was not the embodiment of Stoic virtue outraged by vice; he was in the first place a Roman senator who tried to assert his freedom and dignity in the face of the malignant despot of Rome. And this is probably the reason why his name evoked in Tacitus (*Hist.* II, 91, 3) associations of an "exemplar verae gloriae".

5. STOICISM AND LIBERTAS

Thrasea's prosecutor alleged that Stoicism was politically subversive. With regard to Thrasea this allegation may have been unfounded, but it voiced a widely-held view of Stoicism. Philosophy was frowned upon in influential quarters: it was believed that it nurtured arrogance and disobedience, and Seneca felt obliged to rebut the charge. "Errare mihi videntur," he says, "qui existimant philosophiae fideliter deditos contumaces esse ac refractarios, contemptores magistratuum aut regum eorumve, per quos publica administrantur."[2]

Dio Chrysostom in his younger days violently attacked philosophy in a lost speech κατὰ τῶν φιλοσόφων. He inveighed against Socrates and Zeno and declared that their followers should be driven from the face of the earth as being "the plague of cities and of

---

[1] G. Boissier, *op. cit.* pp. 102–3; J. M. C. Toynbee, *op. cit.* p. 49.
[2] *Ep.* 73, 1.

the constitution".[1] The conflict between sophistic or rhetoric and philosophy was age-old and it is not surprising that Dio the sophist, as he then was, should have assailed philosophy. But Dio's was an invective with a political sting in it, and it is possible that it was made at a time when persecution of philosophy was, in a measure, topical.[2]

In first-century Rome philosophy meant primarily Stoicism or Cynicism. It is noteworthy that the charge of arrogance and disobedience was levelled expressly against the Stoics.[3] And it is also a fact of some importance that Musonius Rufus, although at first exempted from the general expulsion of philosophers from Rome in 71, was subsequently banned and not recalled until the reign of Titus.[4]

Since not only philosophers but also Magi and Chaldaeans were expelled from Rome, the ban on philosophers does not by itself prove that all or most of them were politically suspect. The fact, however, that so tolerant an emperor as Vespasian banished all philosophers seems to imply that philosophy in general was considered to be worse than just a nuisance. It is no doubt true that disreputable pseudo-philosophers, especially the itinerant pseudo-Cynics, undermined the reputation of philosophy.[5] But it would be wrong to assume on that account that the relations between the government and genuine Stoicism were invariably happy. They were not. As has been seen, Stoicism was accused of fostering treason and anarchy; Stoics were conspicuous in the opposition; they were also conspicuous among the victims of oppression. To put it mildly, Stoicism, from the standpoint of the Roman government, was not above suspicion and reproach.

---

[1] See Synesius, *Dio*, Patrol. Gr. LXVI (1864), p. 1116D f.: Βάλλοντι Σωκράτην καὶ Ζήνωνα τοῖς ἐκ Διονυσίων σκώμμασι, καὶ τοὺς ἀπ' αὐτῶν ἀξιοῦντι πάσης ἐλαύνεσθαι γῆς καὶ θαλάττης ὡς ὄντας κῆρας πόλεων τε καὶ πολιτείας (1117C). Cf. H. von Arnim, *Leben und Werke des Dio von Prusa* (1898), pp. 150 ff.

[2] Cf. v. Arnim, *loc. cit.* He thinks that Dio's speeches against philosophy were composed at Rome in A.D. 71. At any rate, it is quite clear from Synesius that they belong to the period when Dio was a sophist, i.e. before his exile.

[3] Tac. *Ann.* XIV, 57, 5: Adsumpta etiam Stoicorum adrogantia sectaque, quae turbidos et negotiorum adpetentes faciat. See also Quintil. *Inst.* XII, 3, 12, where philosophy is called "pigritia arrogantior".

[4] Dio Cass. LXVI, 13, 2; Musonius, ed. Hense, p. XXXV; M. P. Charlesworth, *Five Men* (1936), p. 36.

[5] D. R. Dudley, *op. cit.* pp. 144 ff.; M. P. Charlesworth, *C.A.H.* XI, pp. 9 ff.

Stoic political theory is often called an official philosophy of monarchy. This is to some extent true, but at the same time it is an over-simplification which obscures some of the essential features of Stoicism. It is of course true that Late Stoicism had no objection to monarchy as such; moreover, it considered monarchy the obviously preferable form of government.[1] But it does not follow from this that it accepted monarchy without reservation. The theme that runs through Stoic political thought is the difference between kingship and tyranny: quid interest inter tyrannum et regem?[2] The distinction is not based on the legitimacy of power or on its delimitation; what decides whether the ruler is a king or a tyrant is the manner in which he uses his power.[3] Stoicism described monarchy as it should be.[4] A king worthy of the name ought to realize this ideal monarchy, and he would be judged according as he conformed to or deviated from it.[5]

In so far as Stoics were prepared to acknowledge the emperor of the day as the embodiment of their lofty ideal of kingship, Stoicism might be welcome and become a kind of semi-official philosophy;[6] Stoics, who despaired of improvement[7] and acquiesced in a quietist contemplation of their ideals, may have been unwelcome, but nevertheless harmless; if, however, Stoic tenets were wedded to the Roman tradition of political activity, if they were preached in earnest as something to be implemented in action, Stoic idealism might, in the eyes of the Roman government, become dangerous. Few emperors

[1] Seneca, De Benef. II, 20; Dio Chrys. III, 50; 64 f.; and often elsewhere.

[2] Seneca, De Clem. I, 11, 4. Cf. Dio Chrys. III, 25. See also Dio Chrysostom's myth about the Peak of Kingship and Peak of Tyranny, which from a distance appear as one undivided mountain, Or. I, 66 ff.

[3] Seneca, De Clem. I, 11, 4–12, 1; Dio Chrys. loc. cit.

[4] Dio Chrys. III, 25: ποιήσομαι τοὺς λόγους ὑπὲρ τοῦ χρηστοῦ βασιλέως, ὁποῖον εἶναι δεῖ καὶ τίς ἡ διαφορὰ τοῦ προσποιουμένου μὲν ἄρχοντος εἶναι, πλεῖστον δὲ ἀπέχοντος ἀρχῆς καὶ βασιλείας.

[5] See Dio Chrys. I, 15 and 36. Note also the double meaning of the closing words of the first speech On Kingship: ἕως ἂν τυγχάνῃς βασιλεύων.

[6] Notable examples are Seneca's De Clementia and Dio Chrysostom's speeches On Kingship. The facts that Dio lived in exile a κυνικὸς βίος and that there are Cynic elements in several of his discourses do not make him a consistent Cynic. Stoicism is undoubtedly the salient feature of his philosophy of kingship.

[7] Seneca, Dial. VIII (De Otio), 3, 3: Si res publica corruptior est quam ut adiuvari possit, si occupata est malis, non nitetur sapiens in supervacuum.

had so clear a conscience that they could let people inveigh freely against tyranny.[1] The juxtaposition of tyranny and kingship, the reminders of the king's duties and the warnings against their neglect, the denunciation of the abuse of power and violation of justice, might become dangerous to a princeps who was not above criticism. For on one thing genuine Stoics were not prepared to compromise: freedom. Seneca preached a doctrine of resignation—suicide as the only escape to freedom;[2] Thrasea Paetus derived from Stoicism the courage to disapprove of tyranny and servility alike; others may have derived from it the courage to resist.

The political problem with which Stoicism was concerned is very much the same as the central problem of Roman politics from the standpoint of libertas, namely how to secure freedom under absolutism. The solution offered by Stoicism is in certain respects similar to the course the Principate followed in the second century. But, as will be seen later, the political ideas with which the development of the Principate is associated—Optimus Princeps and Adoption—derived direct from Roman concepts and from Roman political experience. To say that Stoicism, or Stoicism and Cynicism, exerted a decisive formative influence on the Principate, is to say too much. It seems to be nearer the truth that Stoic theory took the Principate as it found it and expressed it in terms of its theory of kingship. In so doing, Stoicism influenced the formulation of the theoretical aspect of the Principate, not its formation.

But if it did not remodel the Principate, Stoicism left a mark on the concept of freedom. As has been seen,[3] the Romans conceived libertas as a civic right based on positive law. Seneca expounded the idea of the rights of man based on natural law. "Nemo non, cui alia desunt, hominis nomine apud me gratiosus est" declares the good king.[4] "Cum in servum omnia liceant, est aliquid quod in hominem licere commune ius animantium vetet."[5] Man is inviolable, "homo res sacra homini".[6] Such ideas eventually found their way into

[1] Domitian put to death the sophist (?) Maternus because in a practice speech he had said something against tyranny, see Dio Cass. LXVII, 12, 5. Cf. D. R. Dudley, *op. cit.* p. 140 n. 1.
[2] *Ep.* 70, 14; *De Ira*, III, 15, 4 ff.
[3] Cf. above, p. 3.
[4] *De Clem.* I, 1, 3.
[5] *Ib.* I, 18, 2.
[6] *Ep.* 95, 33.

Roman legal theory and probably contributed much to the evolution of a humaner legislation concerning slaves. But they appeared too late, or too early, to affect the constitution. The constitutional implications of the rights of man materialized only after many centuries.

6. HELVIDIUS PRISCUS

As has been seen, consistent Stoicism was not always favourably disposed towards the government. It must be added that by his very frame of mind a true Stoic tends towards intransigence. For since Late Stoicism was not a system of speculative metaphysics but in the first place a practical guide to life, since it taught rigid ethics and contempt of pain and death, a thoroughgoing Stoic is not likely to be an opportunist in matters that affect his ideals. And it may be that on account of their intransigent and fearless idealism, combined as it was with exhibitionist superiority towards the "unconverted", the Stoics appeared as arrogant and refractory.

An example of such an uncompromising and unruly Stoic is Helvidius Priscus, the son-in-law of Thrasea Paetus.[1]

Tacitus says that Helvidius followed Stoicism "quo firmior adversus fortuita rem publicam capesseret" and that "e moribus soceri nihil aeque ac libertatem hausit".[2] As the context shows Tacitus means "libertas" as it is realized in the conduct of a man, not in the constitution of a State. Helvidius fearlessly asserted his freedom of opinion and championed the rights and dignity of the Senate.[3]

It is not at all clear what was the reason of his opposition to Vespasian.[4] Tacitus regarded the day on which the Senate installed Vespasian as the beginning of the conflict. Most unfortunately a lacuna obscures what Helvidius said on that occasion. "Prompsit

---

[1] For a different view, namely that Helvidius "went Cynic" and that Cynics were invariably anarchists, see J. M. C. Toynbee, *op. cit.* pp. 51 ff.

[2] Tac. *Hist.* IV, 5. Cf. Dio Cass. LXVI, 12, 1.

[3] *Hist.* II, 91, 3; IV, 7; 9; 43, 2: "Imus Prisce et relinquimus tibi senatum tuum."

[4] M. Rostovtzeff, *A Social and Economic History of the Roman Empire*, p. 519 n. 14, assumed that Helvidius was opposed to hereditary monarchy. This assumption, although based on very slender circumstantial evidence, is in itself not altogether improbable; did not Pliny, *Paneg.* 7, strongly reject hereditary monarchy? But even if true, the theory that Helvidius was opposed to hereditary monarchy obviously falls short of fully explaining his conduct.

sententiam ut honorificam in novum (Halm; bonum Codd.) principem...falsa aberant, et studiis senatus attollebatur. Isque prae-
cipuus illi dies magnae offensae initium et magnae gloriae fuit."[1]
Shortly afterwards the Senate debated the restoration of the Capitol:
"Censuerat Helvidius, ut Capitolium publice restitueretur, adiuvaret
Vespasianus. Eam sententiam modestissimus quisque silentio, deinde
oblivio transmisit; *fuere qui* et meminissent."[2] It appears from
Tacitus that, whatever else may have been the causes, Helvidius's
frank speaking and insistence on the rights of the Senate was
a major and perhaps the prime cause of friction. The scholiast on
Juvenal, v, 36, says that Helvidius behaved as if he lived in a free
State.[3] And Suetonius says that he refused to acknowledge Vespasian
as an emperor and heckled him.[4] The picture of Helvidius which
emerges from the Latin authorities is not unlike that of the jurist
Antistius Labeo[5] under Augustus and Tiberius, namely of a senator
who uncompromisingly adheres to the ideals of a bygone age
while ignoring the present.

Dio Cassius, however, offers an entirely different view. He says
that Helvidius inveighed against βασιλεία and praised δημοκρατία,
was unruly and incited the mob to revolution.[6] This statement looks
as if Helvidius was a fanatical and very stupid republican, for no man
with any sense could have believed that the Roman mob would ever
rise to overthrow the Principate. But perhaps Dio's statement is not
to be taken to mean all this. If indeed Helvidius made speeches
about βασιλεία and δημοκρατία, it can fairly be assumed that the
Latin words he used were "regnum" and "res publica". Now
opposition to "regnum" and praise of "res publica" may mean
extremist republicanism of the old type, but it may as well suit
something of the kind of the Augustan Principate, which was not
a regnum and which was to some extent a res publica, under which
the Senate enjoyed many rights. Which of the two was Helvidius's
choice is uncertain and probably will remain so. As for his

[1] *Hist.* IV, 4, 3.
[2] *Ib.* IV, 9, 2. Cf. also: Eam curam (*sc.* aerarii) consul designatus ob
magnitudinem oneris et remedii difficultatem principi reservabat; Helvidius
arbitrio senatus agendum censuit, IV, 9, 1.
[3] Non aliter quam libero civitatis statu egit.
[4] Suet. *Div. Vesp.* 15.
[5] Cf. above, p. 120 n. 2.   [6] Dio Cass. LXVI, 12, 2.

subversive preaching, it seems that Dio is only repeating common-places against philosophy.[1] It may be that such things were alleged against Helvidius, but what warrants their veracity?

If we were to assume with Dio Cassius that Helvidius was an irresponsible demagogue who preached sedition and anarchy, it would be difficult to see why Tacitus spoke of him with much respect, and why Marcus Aurelius considered it an advantage "to have acquainted oneself with Thrasea, Helvidius, Cato, Dio, Brutus, and to have conceived the idea of a State based on equality, fairness and freedom of speech, and of kingship respecting above all else the liberty of the subjects".[2] It is not at all certain whether Helvidius was an out-and-out republican; but if he was, he could not be an anarchist at the same time. We cannot have it both ways. We have to choose between all the Latin authorities and Marcus Aurelius on one hand, and Dio Cassius on the other; and there can be little doubt which way the choice must fall. Dio misunderstood Helvidius just as he misunderstood the Augustan Principate. For him Helvidius was a senseless trouble-maker, which in his official view meant anarchist.

All that can be said with certainty about Helvidius is that he tried to bring to book the prosecutors of his father-in-law, that he spoke his mind freely, and that he wished to enhance the prestige of the Senate. Anything else is speculation.

It seems therefore to be nearer the truth to assume—with the support of Tacitus and Marcus Aurelius—that Helvidius was not a mob agitator for anarchy after the pseudo-Cynic fashion, but a champion of freedom in the manner of the Roman Stoics.

Helvidius was not the only intransigent. It seems that the suppression of freedom drove many to ostentatious and provocative intransigence. Tacitus in his *Agricola* condemned the irreconcilables as persons who lost their lives for no other purpose than notoriety, and he preached the ideal of patience and devotion to public service embodied in Agricola, who did not provoke his own ruin by seeking fame in a vain ostentation of freedom:

Sciant, quibus moris est illicita mirari, posse etiam sub malis principibus magnos viros esse, obsequiumque ac modestiam, si industria ac vigor

---

[1] Compare Dio Cass. LXVI, 12, 2 with Seneca, *Ep.* 73, 1; Tac. *Ann.* XIV, 57, 5; XVI, 22, 8; Synesius, 1117C (quoted above, p. 144 n. 1).

[2] *Ad Semet Ipsum*, I, 14, 2.

adsint, eo laudis procedere, quo plerique per abrupta, sed in nullum rei publicae usum ⟨enisi⟩ ambitiosa morte inclaruerunt.[1]

And in his *Annals* he pointed to the example of a great and wise man who steered a middle course between self-assertive intransigence and servile submission.[2]

But patience, moderation, and resignation do not appeal to all. It is interesting in this respect to read the passage in which Tacitus summarizes the views of those of Thrasea's friends who advised him to speak in his own trial:

Nihil dicturum nisi quo gloriam augeret; segnes et pavidos supremis suis secretum circumdare; aspiceret populus virum morti obvium, audiret senatus voces quasi ex aliquo numine supra humanas; posse ipso miraculo etiam Neronem permoveri. sin crudelitati insisteret, distingui certe apud posteros memoriam honesti exitus ab ignavia per silentium pereuntium.[3]

The consciousness of oppression bred servility in many; but it inspired some to seek desperate self-assertion in ostentatious death.

7. Clementia

The awareness that an overwhelmingly strong power in the hands of the Princeps was necessary for the preservation of domestic and external peace, but that by its very nature such power could be, and sometimes was, abused with impunity, lent an ever-increasing importance to the manner in which the Princeps exercised his authority. The manner in which power is employed and the character of the person who employs it always matter, but not always to the same extent. Under the Empire, when the effectiveness of the safeguards of freedom was greatly reduced and the possibility of abusing power greatly enhanced, the manner in which the emperor actually used his power made all the difference in the world: "Tyrannus a rege factis distat, non nomine."[4] And this is why such personal virtues

---

[1] *Agric.* 42, 4 f. Cf. Seneca, *Ep.* 113, 32: Qui virtutem suam publicari vult, non virtuti laborat, sed gloriae.

[2] *Ann.* IV, 20, 4 f.

[3] *Ann.* XVI, 25. Tacitus reminded his readers that he did not detest those who perished tamely: Neque aliam defensionem ab iis quibus ista noscentur exegerim, quam ne oderim tam segniter pereuntes, *Ann.* XVI, 16, 2. See also Furneaux, *ad loc.*

[4] Seneca, *De Clem.* I, 12, 1.

as clemency or moderation become political watchwords of great significance in respect of freedom.

Clementia first appeared in the political vocabulary at Rome in the aftermath of the Civil War. The Romans, impressed with Caesar's lenient treatment of his vanquished adversaries, dedicated a temple to his Clemency.[1] It is interesting that, while Clementia is a common legend on Imperial coins, only one pre-Imperial instance of it is known: a coin struck in 44 B.C. with the temple of Clemency and the legend CLEMENTIAE CAESARIS on the obverse.[2] The political significance of Caesar's clemency is well illustrated in Cicero's speeches *Pro Marcello* and *Pro Ligario*, both of which were delivered in the year 46 B.C. Cicero praised Caesar's clemency, fully aware that on it depended the life of everyone,[3] and on it he pinned his hopes for a better future.[4] At the same time it was more than a mere metaphor to speak of himself and Ligarius as "prostrate suppliants":[5] in fact the *Pro Ligario* was a humble entreaty for pardon, not a defence; and it was so because Cicero realized only too well that there was in fact no law to base a case on, everything depending on Caesar's will.

Cicero's *Pro Marcello* and *Pro Ligario* mark a turning-point in the history of libertas, namely the decline of the idea that the citizen's rights have one guarantee—the law. Law as a guardian of freedom lost its paramountcy. The very life of the citizen who fought on the losing side depended entirely on the clemency of the victor. A hundred years later Seneca addressed to Nero his treatise *De Clementia*. And if Cicero's *Pro Marcello* and *Pro Ligario* represent the initial decline of the idea that "libertas in legibus consistit", Seneca's *De Clementia* represents its final collapse.

Seneca defines clemency as "temperantia animi in potestate ulciscendi vel lenitas superioris adversus inferiorem in constituendis poenis".[6] As will presently be seen, the application of clemency is much wider than this definition suggests, but the definition itself is very significant. When law reigned at Rome inferiors demanded

---

[1] Dio Cass. XLVI, 6, 4; Appian, *Bell. Civ.* II, 106, 443. Cf. H. Dahlmann, Clementia Caesaris, *N. J. f. Wiss.* X (1934), pp. 17 ff.

[2] *BMC Rep.* I, p. 549, no. 4176.

[3] See especially *Pro Marc.* 22; *Pro Lig.* 15.

[4] *Pro Marc.* 2. Cf. *ib.* 18.

[5] *Pro Lig.* 13.

[6] *De Clem.* II, 3, 1.

of their superiors justice, which for the Roman was equivalent to lawfulness. Apart from a paterfamilias in respect of his familia and a commander in the field in respect of his troops, no authority could impose a penalty other than that prescribed by law (esse poenas legibus constitutas[1]). Justice, not clemency, was what the Romans expected from the rule of law. This, however, changed with the advent of the Principate. When Augustus said to Cinna, who plotted against his life, "Vitam tibi, Cinna, iterum do, prius hosti, nunc insidiatori ac parricidae",[2] he acted, strictly speaking, ultra vires; for he had the right neither to put a citizen to death without trial, nor to pardon. But whatever his formal right, he possessed the actual power to do so, and this is the reason why clementia became so vital.

The basis of Seneca's reasoning in the first book of his De Clementia is that the tyrant and the king possess exactly the same amount of absolute power, the difference between them being only the manner in which they exercise it.[3] Clemency moderates the employment of power, it is a self-imposed check.[4] It is no doubt a significant fact that, although he argues that even a slave, who is otherwise rightless, enjoys certain natural rights of man,[5] Seneca does not so much as mention the civic rights of a Roman. The impression that Seneca's treatise gives is that, in the case of a conflict between a citizen and the emperor, the former is entirely dependent on the clemency of the latter. It is true that political theory was not Seneca's strong point, nor did he write as a jurist. Nevertheless, in view of the fact that he dwelt to some extent on the duties of the emperor and the nature of Imperial power, the complete absence of any mention of civic rights and positive law seems to suggest that Seneca realized that rights and law without force behind them were a broken reed. "In fact," says M. P. Charlesworth, "Clementia had become too much a despotic quality; the mercy of a conqueror towards those whose life he holds in his hands, the gracious act of an absolute monarch towards his subjects."[6] Cicero in his De Re Publica

---

[1] Tac. Ann. XIV, 48, 6.   [2] See Seneca, De Clem. I, 9, 1–12.

[3] Ib. I, 11, 4–12, 1.

[4] Ib. I, 5, 4 and I, 11, 2 (hebetare aciem imperii sui).

[5] Ib. I, 18, 2.

[6] M. P. Charlesworth, The Virtues of a Roman Emperor, Proc. Brit. Acad. XXIII (1937), p. 113.

based the difference between good kings and bad tyrants on justice; Seneca based it on clemency. Iustitia presupposes the existence of ius in its twofold sense, namely right and law, whereas clementia is but a kindness of heart. The difference of approach results not only from the fact that Cicero was in the first place a statesman and a lawyer, whereas Seneca was a Stoic philosopher, but from Seneca's awareness that justice alone would not suffice when the foundation of right and law was shattered. And this may be the reason why iustitia, unlike clementia, rarely figures on imperial coinage.[1]

8. Optimus Princeps

The same motives which account for the prominence of a particular virtue, or a group of virtues,[2] prompted the use of the superlative Optimus with regard to the Princeps. There are in this respect two different usages: "Optimus Princeps" in which "optimus" is an adjective, the phrase meaning "the excellent Princeps";[3] and "Optimus", without the following "princeps", used substantively after the name of the emperor as a kind of cognomen, in which case it means "the Perfect".[4]

There is a certain similarity between the latter use of Optimus and the Platonic-Stoic ideal of kingship, but this similarity is superficial and does not prove that the idea of the Princeps as Optimus derived from Greek philosophy. Several things must be observed in this connection: first, the philosopher-king is, primarily, sapientissimus,[5] not optimus. Secondly, the Greeks regarded the wisdom of the philosopher-king as his innate title to power, whereas to the Romans the "goodness" of the Princeps is the moderator of the power

[1] M. P. Charlesworth, *loc. cit.*, observes: "Iustitia figures rarely on coinage, and the reason for that I do not know."

[2] As, for example, Clementia under Caesar and Nero; Moderatio under Tiberius (see Mattingly and Sydenham, *op. cit.* I, p. 108; Tac. *Ann.* II, 36, 2; III, 56, 1; Suet. *Tib.* 32, 2); the shield dedicated to the virtus, clementia, iustitia, and pietas of Augustus (*Res Gestae*, 34), for which see M. P. Charlesworth, Pietas and Victoria: the Emperor and the Citizen, *J. R. S.* XXXIII (1943), esp. p. 3.

[3] Optimus Princeps appears as early as the reign of Tiberius, see *C.I.L.* VI, 902, 904; Optimus ac iustissimus princeps, VI, 93. Also *C.I.L.* X, 444 (= Dessau, *I.L.S.* 3546): Optumi principis et domini (viz. Domitian).

[4] Pliny, *Paneg.* 2, 7. For examples see Mattingly and Sydenham, *op. cit.* II, pp. 534 ff.   [5] See Tac. *Dial.* 41.

conferred by the Senate and People of Rome.[1] And, finally, "Optimus", as a compliment, is nothing but a heightened "vir bonus". Vir bonus means that the man is possessed of those virtues which the Romans respected; Optimus with regard to the emperor means in fact little more, only that courtesy alone demands for the emperor the superlative.[2]

From the standpoint of libertas the perfectness of the emperor is the only guarantee that his unlimited potestas will not become an oppressive potentia. This moral safeguard is all the more important in view of the fact that high moral standards were necessary to withstand the temptations of power. Under the Early Empire the Romans saw enough and endured enough to know that "power always tends to corrupt", to use Lord Acton's phrase. Their own experience brought home to them the truth that "the possession of unlimited power corrodes the conscience, hardens the heart, and confounds the understanding of monarchs".[3] It also did not escape them that, just as power exercised a demoralizing influence on the ruler, so the presence of a vicious ruler exercised a demoralizing influence on the whole society.[4] To eliminate the absolute power was impossible; the only thing that could be hoped for was its mitigation by the virtues of the Princeps. And this hope is expressed in the compliment Optimus.

9. ADOPTIO

If the virtues of the Princeps are the only effective safeguard against the abuse of authority, and the only counterpoise to the demoralizing influence of power, the choice of the right man, rather than the right

---

[1] Infinitae potestatis domitor ac frenator animus, Pliny, *Paneg.* 55, 9.

[2] That "Optimus", as a compliment, does not mean much more than bonus can be seen from the use of "optimus quisque" in the sense of "quivis bonus", see Cic. *De Leg.* III, 39, where "optimus quisque" and "boni" are used to denote the same thing, and compare *Pro Sest.* 96 with 137. See also *Ad Fam.* X, 31, 3; *De Senect.* 43; *De Off.* I, 154. The acclamation "Felicior Augusto, Melior Traiano" (Eutrop. VIII, 5) may also show that the compliment Optimus was felt to be equivalent to bonus. The usage of "optimus" is well illustrated by Tac. *Dial.* 30, 10: Ita est enim, optimi viri, ita.

[3] Lord Acton, *Freedom in Antiquity*, p. 11. See Tac. *Ann.* VI, 48, 4; XIV, 1, 1; *Hist.* I, 50, 3 f.; IV, 42, 5; Seneca, *Ep.* 14, 13; Suet. *Domit.* 10, 1. See also G. Boissier, *Tacitus* (English trans.), p. 154.

[4] See Tac. *Hist.* I, 2, 3.

delimitation of his sphere of action, becomes a matter of supreme importance. Besides, if Rome were to avoid serious crises whenever a demise of power took place, the succession to the Principate ought to be settled in a way that would remove any uncertainty and preclude the possibility of a prolonged interregnum, both of which could only afford temptations to ambitious competitors.

Dynastic succession offered stability, but it had obvious disadvantages. It meant that the successors to the Principate would be persons brought up as crown princes, a feature hardly palatable to the Roman nobility.[1] Even so, the quality of a dynastic successor was a matter of hazard.[2] Dynastic succession brought to the Principate Caligula and Nero, who, each in his turn, apart from being inexperienced youths when they came to power, proved to be pervert and cruel. In the unsettled state of affairs that followed immediately on Caligula's assassination the Praetorian Guard made their own choice and presented the Senate with a *fait accompli*; after Nero's downfall Italy was visited with civil war. It did not require a speculative mind to see that what Rome needed was a system that would ensure an unquestioned succession and yet be free from the disadvantages of a strictly dynastic monarchy. The Romans thought themselves to have found a solution of that problem in the principle of succession by adoption, as distinct from succession by birthright.

Rostovtzeff has advanced the view that the doctrine of adoption derived from Stoic-Cynic philosophy, which opposed hereditary monarchy as a matter of principle and advocated the rule of the wisest man. He also thinks that by accepting this doctrine the Principate was reconciled to the philosophy of the day.[3] This theory, however, does not take sufficient account of two facts:

First, the Stoic-Cynic philosopher-king is a ruler in his own right. His title is his wisdom, by virtue of which he is the vicar of God on earth. Such a theory of kingship may be opposed to hereditary monarchy in so far as the latter only means succession by the sole right of royal blood,[4] but it does not, of itself, lead to the

---

[1] See the critical remark about Tiberius in Tac. *Ann.* I, 4, 4.
[2] Seneca, *De Clem.* I, 1, 7: Magnam adibat aleam populus Romanus, cum incertum esset quo se ⟨ista tua⟩ nobilis indoles daret.
[3] See M. Rostovtzeff, *op. cit.* pp. 110–16.
[4] See, e.g., Dio Chrys. IV, 62; Cic. *De Rep.* II, 24.

principle of adoption.[1] Moreover, while Stoicism conceives king-ship as rulership in the light of a theory that regards law (*nomos*) solely as an expression of right reason (*orthos logos*),[2] thus making both conduct and direction the result of knowledge alone, it is not at all concerned with kingship as an historical institution, nor with its legitimacy.[3] It is not, therefore, concerned to explain precisely how the king shall be appointed. Thus it seems that the Stoic theory of kingship and the Roman practice of adoption move on different planes.

Secondly, the true basis of the truce between the Principate and philosophy was the readiness of the philosophers to identify the Princeps of the day with their ideal of philosopher-king, not the acceptance by the Principate of the doctrine of adoption.

Nor does the doctrine of adoption imply elective monarchy.[4] It is true that, in the speech on adoption which he put into the mouth of Galba, Tacitus says "Loco libertatis erit quod eligi coepimus",[5] but obviously "eligere" here means to select, not to elect in a con-stitutional sense. Elsewhere he described Galba as having declared "adoptari a se Pisonem exemplo divi Augusti et more militari, quo vir virum legeret".[6] And Pliny clearly says: "Imperaturus omnibus eligi debet *ex* omnibus",[7] not *ab* omnibus. From a constitutional point of view, as distinct from a social one, the doctrine of adoption means only the substitution of an heir designate for an heir apparent, but the principle of heredity is not thereby abolished, because in Roman law an adopted son and a legitimate son had the same standing in the familia.

The considerations that went to make the doctrine of adoption are clearly set out by Tacitus and Pliny the Younger. One has only to read the relevant passages, not in the light of Dio Chrysostom's speeches *On Kingship*, but against the background of the dynastic policy of the Julio-Claudian emperors.

[1] It is noteworthy that in Dio Chrysostom's discourses *On Kingship* adoption is never mentioned.

[2] See above, pp. 133 f.

[3] Cf. J. Kaerst, *Studien zur Entwickelung und theoretischen Begründung der Monarchie im Altertum* (1898), pp. 24 ff.

[4] As Reitzenstein thought, *Gött. Nachr.* (1914), p. 238, and Tacitus und sein Werk, *Neue Wege zur Antike*, IV, p. 9.

[5] *Hist.* I, 16, 1.   [6] *Ib.* I, 18, 2.   [7] *Paneg.* 7, 6.

Adoption as a form of designating the successor to the Principate was as old as the Principate itself: Augustus was the first to introduce it.[1] And, in point of fact, even he made thereby no innovation: he secured his dynastic policy by the long-established method to which Romans, and especially heads of noble families, resorted in default of male issue. As regards the Principate, adoption, combined with joint tenure of the tribunician power, ensured an undisturbed and unquestioned succession.[2] This was undoubtedly good and worth preserving; but Augustus based succession on a dynastic principle,[3] and it was there that the disadvantages came in. If kinship alone decides who is to succeed, there is a chance of an unworthy person coming to power, "nam generari et nasci a principibus fortuitum", and Nero should serve as a warning ("sit ante oculos Nero").[4] Moreover, if one dynasty continuously rules, the State becomes very much like the inheritance of one family.[5] But the Romans considered themselves free citizens of their res publica, not slaves of the master's household.[6] And, finally, a dynastic monarchy which perpetuates the rule of one family deprives all the other noble families, not only of pre-eminent position and of present access to the seat of power, but even of the opportunity of ever attaining them. In a State in which equality of opportunity counted for nearly as much as freedom, this was hardly acceptable: "Imperaturus omnibus eligi debet ex omnibus."[7]

It appears therefore that the doctrine of adoption as foreshadowed by Galba and accepted by Nerva was an improvement upon the example of Augustus in that it sought the successor in the State, i.e. in the senatorial class, not in one family.[8] This improved form of succession by adoption met the need of the Roman State for an undisturbed continuity of the imperial power, and it marked

---

[1] Tac. *Hist.* I, 15, 1; 18, 2; *Ann.* III, 56; Vell. Pat. II, 103. Pliny's exclamation "O novum atque inauditum ad principatum iter" (*Paneg.* 7, 1) is clearly inaccurate, and probably due to the excessive fervour of the panegyrist.

[2] *Ann.* I, 3, 3; III, 56; *Hist.* I, 29, 2.

[3] Augustus in domo successorem quaesivit, *Hist.* I, 15, 2.

[4] *Ib.* I, 16, 2.

[5] Sub Tiberio et Gaio unius familiae quasi hereditas fuimus, *Ib.* I, 16, 1. Cf. Pliny, *Paneg.* 7, 5 f.

[6] Non enim servulis tuis dominum, ut possis esse contentus quasi necessario herede, sed principem civibus daturus es imperator, *Paneg.* 7, 6.

[7] Cf. H. Last, *C.A.H.* XI, p. 413.   [8] See *Hist.* I, 15, 2.

a victory, not of Stoic philosophy, but of the new imperial nobility which asserted its right to provide candidates for the Principate just as it provided candidates for the administration. But this was not all. Tacitus represents Galba as saying that in circumstances that make monarchy indispensable the principle of adoption, as distinct from dynastic heredity, is a substitute for libertas.[1] The context clearly shows that libertas means res publica. It seems therefore that in his opinion adoption preserves as much of the res publica as is possible under monarchy, because it underlines the fact that the State is not the inheritance of one family but the common possession of all. Res publica is still res populi, if populus means the community.

Adoption as a constitutional principle was formulated by the Romans under the impact of events at Rome, not under the influence of Greek theory. It was gradually developed by statesmen who grappled with hard facts, not ideas. But, once formulated and accepted, it proved of great value to those philosophers who wished to accommodate their ideals to reality. All one had to do was to postulate—and who would dare, or care, to deny it?—that the adoptive father was guided in his choice by the gods themselves.[2] On that assumption it was possible, without loss of face, to identify the adopted emperor with the ideal king, in fact with any ideal. Philosophers may have gladly accepted the doctrine of adoption, but there is nothing to prove, or even to suggest, that they invented it. It is a fact to be remembered that the only Stoic philosopher on the throne of the Caesars broke the principle of adoption to ensure the succession of his own son.

10. Libertas Publica and Securitas

Security of life and property, sanctity of hearth and home, inviolability of civic rights were the chief elements of Roman libertas. But for the upper classes under the Early Empire these were on occasions an ideal rather than a fact. They often lived in insecurity and in fear of their lives. "Timetur inopia," says Seneca, "timentur morbi, timentur quae per vim potentioris eveniunt. Ex his omnibus nihil nos magis concutit quam quod ex aliena potentia impendet."[3]

---

[1] *Hist.* I, 16, 1. Cf. Pliny, *Paneg.* 8, 1.
[2] See *Paneg.* 8, 2.
[3] Seneca, *Ep.* 14, 3–4.

The actio laesae maiestatis hung above everyone's head as a sword of Damocles.[1] Anything might prove fatal: "Nobilitas, opes, omissi gestique honores pro crimine."[2] It was even fatal to mourn a condemned son.[3] Informers were everywhere and would note down ambiguous jokes, and even unguarded utterances of a drunken man.[4] Nero was wont to assail passers-by at night, and self-defence might cost a man his life.[5] Property was not safe: Nero's motto was "hoc agamus ne quis quicquam habeat".[6] It was dangerous to publish books that would not please an emperor, or to pursue one's studies in freedom.[7]

People who lived under oppression in danger of their lives came gradually to conceive libertas as meaning, primarily, order, security, and confidence. To Tacitus, after Domitian's reign, the realization of freedom appeared as "securitas publica" and as the happy state of affairs (felicitas temporum) when one could think as he pleased and say what he thought.[8]

It is interesting that from Galba onwards LIBERTAS PUBLICA becomes a very common legend on imperial coins.[9] Libertas publica means freedom as it is enjoyed by the public, that is to say absence of oppression and lawlessness;[10] it signifies a state of affairs, not a form of government. Under the Empire it meant order, security, and confidence. It was in fact tantamount to securitas. "An parva pronaque sunt ad aemulandum quod nemo incolumitatem turpitudine rependit? Salva est omnibus vita et dignitas vitae, nec iam consideratus ac sapiens qui aetatem in tenebris agit."[11] These words of Pliny's show what securitas and libertas publica must have meant.

---

[1] *Ann.* I, 72 f.; II, 50; III, 38, 1 f.; Suet. *Domit.* 12, 1.

[2] Tac. *Hist.* I, 2, 3.

[3] *Ann.* VI, 10, 1. Cf. Suet. *Tib.* 61, 2.

[4] Seneca, *De Benef.* III, 26, 1; *De Clem.* I, 26, 2; Tac. *Ann.* IV, 69, 6; VI, 7, 4; 5, 2; XIV, 48, 1 f.

[5] Tac. *Ann.* XIII, 25.

[6] Suet. *Nero,* 32, 4. Cf. *Calig.* 38; *Domit.* 12.

[7] Tac. *Ann.* IV, 34 f.; *Agric.* 2; *Dial.* 2; Pliny, *Ep.* III, 5, 5.

[8] Tac. *Agric.* 3, 1 and *Hist.* I, 1, 4.

[9] See Mattingly and Sydenham, *op. cit.* II, pp. 65 and 70.

[10] Cic. *De Dom.* 112 and 131 seem to imply that the statue of Liberty which Clodius erected in Cicero's house was dedicated Libertati Publicae.

[11] Pliny, *Paneg.* 44, 5.

11. What Libertas meant to Tacitus

No small importance attaches to the question how Tacitus conceived libertas under the Principate. Since he is one of our foremost
literary authorities, it would be interesting to know the view which
may have coloured his account. Besides, and this is perhaps still
more important for the present purpose, his is the view of a receptive
and critical contemporary whose opinions were shaped less by
wisdom after the event than by personal experience. Tacitus himself
lived under absolutism, at times despotic, at others enlightened. His
own conception of libertas may therefore be to some extent indicative
of what libertas at that time meant to his class.

Perhaps the most striking feature of Tacitus's attitude to the
Principate and to liberty is the fact that his estimate of the former
and his idea of the latter are not determined solely, nor even
primarily, by constitutional considerations. Tacitus, needless to say,
is no republican. On occasions, it is true, he uses "libertas" to
describe the republican form of government.[1] But this traditional
usage does not by any means prove that he desired the restoration
of the Republic, or that his criticism of certain emperors was inspired
by Republican sympathies. Whatever he may have thought of
republicanism as such, he did not fail to see, nor did he hesitate to
state, that the Late Republic was a period of corruption and lawlessness, *non mos non ius*.[2] His attitude is perhaps nowhere better
illustrated than in his *Dialogus de Oratoribus*.[3] Granted that the
Dialogus is no more historical than, for instance, Cicero's *De Re
Publica*,[4] we may consider significant the fact that it did not strike
Tacitus as unduly inconsistent to put unsparing criticism of the
Republic and, at the same time, appreciative comments on the

---

[1] See, e.g., *Ann.* I, 1, 1; XIII, 50, 3; *Hist.* III, 72, 2.

[2] *Ann.* III, 28, 2. Cf. I, 2, 2; 9, 4.

[3] For a discussion of the authorship of the *Dialogus* see A. Gudeman,
Cornelii Taciti Dialogus de Oratoribus, 2nd (German) edition, 1914, pp. 1–29;
W. Peterson, *Cornelii Taciti Dialogus de Oratoribus*, Oxford, 1893, pp. ii–xxii;
Fr. Leo, *G.G.A.* 1898, pp. 167 ff.

[4] See Gudeman, *op. cit.* pp. 81–5; K. v. Fritz, Aufbau und Absicht des
Dialogus de Oratoribus, *Rhein. Mus.* 81 (1932), pp. 275–300; K. Barwick,
Zur Erklärung und Komposition des Rednerdialogs des Tacitus, in *Festschrift
Walther Judeich*, Weimar, 1929, pp. 90 f.

Principate into the mouth of Maternus (*Dial.* 40 f.), whom he represented as having only the day before recited in public his "Cato", the contents of which were received with displeasure in high quarters (*Ib.* 2). It would seem that Tacitus, like Maternus, admitted and appreciated what was great in the Republic but nevertheless thought that his own generation, since it could not have the advantage of Republican freedom and Imperial peace at the same time, should make the best of its own blessings, "bono saeculi sui quisque citra obtrectationem alterius utatur" (*Ib.* 41).

Nor is it true, as has sometimes been assumed, that a polemical attitude to the Principate as a form of government is the key to his historical works.[1] Tacitus, we are told, was in the earlier period of his literary career a convinced monarchist.[2] He believed the Principate was the ideal mixed form of government.[3] But as he gained better knowledge of imperial history disillusionment set in, followed by a renunciation of the official theory of the Principate. He realized that "the downfall of the State inevitably lies in the institution of the Principate".[4] Therefore in a mood of disconsolate sorrow and sullen gloom he decided to expose the Augustan Principate. Hence the *Annals*. This theory, which purports to trace and explain the development of the political views of Tacitus, assumes in the first place that the Principate was in the official view represented as a mixed form of government. It further assumes that the attitude of Tacitus to the Principate as a form of government suffered complete change. The whole theory is clearly based on these two assumptions; neither of them, however, will bear closer examination.

Speculations about its philosophic basis apart, there is no important positive evidence that the Principate was in official quarters conceived, or represented, as a mixed form of government. Aelius Aristides, it is true, in his panegyric on Rome (Εἰς 'Ρώμην) described the Roman constitution as a mixture of all forms of government

[1] See R. Reitzenstein, Bemerkungen zu den kleinen Schriften des Tacitus, *Gött. Nach.* 1914, pp. 235–52; Id. Tacitus und sein Werk, *Neue Wege zur Antike*, IV, pp. 8 f.

[2] *Gött. Nach.* 1914, pp. 239 ff.; *Neue Wege zur Ant.* IV, 8.

[3] *Gött. Nach.* 1914, p. 248; *Neue Wege zur Ant.* IV, 9.

[4] "In der Institution des Prinzipats liegt notwendig der Untergang des Staates", *Neue Wege zur Ant.* IV, 8.

(κρᾶσις ἁπασῶν τῶν πολιτειῶν), but the relevant passage
(§ 90, Keil), if read without preconceived views, proves only that
Aristides reiterated a commonplace of political theory and, above
all, that he knew his Polybius well.[1] If the Principate were officially
represented as a mixed form of government, one would have
expected Pliny the Younger to expatiate on this theory in his
Panegyric. Yet he does not so much as mention it, and Pliny's
silence in this matter far outweighs all the eloquence of Aristides.
Finally, it seems more probable that in his well-known utterance
about the mixed form of government (*Ann.* IV, 33) Tacitus criticized
Cicero's view of the Republican constitution,[2] and not the Principate
of his own day. For he went on to describe the Republic as a period
when at times the People was most influential, at others the Senate
gained ascendancy, whereas Cicero described the Republican constitution as an even balance between the rights of the People, the
authority of the Senate, and the power of the magistrates.

As for the other assumption, namely that his attitude changed
according as Tacitus realized that the Principate was actually
government by one man, two things are to be observed. First, it is
of course true that Tacitus praised Nerva and Trajan in his prefaces
to the *Agricola* (chap. 3) and *Histories* (I, 1, 4). But praise of the
reigning emperor and of his adoptive father cannot bear the weight
that has been put on it as if it were an enthusiastic declaration of
faith. Secondly, it is well to bear in mind that as early as the
Dialogus de Oratoribus, which was probably written about the turn
of the first century,[3] he declared that in Rome ruled "sapientissimus
et *unus*" (*Dial.* 41, 7), and later in the preface to his *Histories* (I, 1, 1)
he said that after the Battle of Actium "omnem potentiam ad *unum*

---

[1] What Aristides' description of the Roman constitution of his day (second
cent. A.D.) is worth can easily be seen from his assertion: ὥστε ὅταν μὲν εἰς
τὴν τοῦ δήμου τις ἰσχὺν βλέψῃ, καὶ ὡς ἁπάντων ὧν ἂν βουληθῇ τε καὶ
αἰτήσῃ ῥᾳδίως τυγχάνει, δημοκρατίαν νομιεῖ καὶ οὐδὲν ἐνδεῖν πλὴν ὧν
ἐξαμαρτάνει δῆμος. ὅταν δὲ εἰς τὴν γερουσίαν ἴδῃ τὴν βουλευομένην τε
καὶ τὰς ἀρχὰς ἔχουσαν, ἀριστοκρατίαν οὐκ εἶναι ταύτης ἀκριβεστέραν
νομιεῖ. Cf. Polyb. VI, 11, 12.

[2] Just as in his *Dialogus* he criticized Cicero's view of eloquence; cf. *Dial.*
40, 5 f. with Cic. *Brut.* 45.

[3] See A. Kappelmacher, Zur Abfassungszeit von Tacitus' Dialogus de
oratoribus, *Wiener Studien*, L (1932), pp. 121–9. And also Fr. Leo, *G.G.A.*
1898, pp. 174 f.

conferri pacis interfuit". It was therefore nothing new if he said in the *Annals* (IV, 33, 2) "converso statu neque alia re Romana quam si *unus* imperitet". And far from holding that the decline of Rome was inherent in the very institution of the Principate, he repeatedly declared that the Principate brought and secured peace and order.[1] Thus it appears that, in so far as we can gather the views of Tacitus from his writings, his attitude to the Principate as a form of government remained in the main unchanged. And if, nevertheless, in the name of libertas he criticized the servitus that he found under the Principate, we have to look for the reasons, not to his view of the constitution, but elsewhere.

In so far as libertas consists in political institutions, Tacitus seems to have regarded the freedom of the Senate as freedom *par excellence*.[2] Nevertheless, to him, unlike Cicero, political institutions are not the fullest expression of political life but only the framework in which political life is set. That constitutional framework matters a great deal but it does not matter most. What matters most is how people use their institutions, not what their institutions are. Tacitus knew that at its best the Republican constitution provided genuine political freedom,[3] but at the same time it did not escape him that the lack of the old freedom under the Principate was the price the Romans had to pay for the immense extension of their power.[4] There seems indeed to be in his view of the Principate an inner conflict between the recognition that absolutism is the inevitable prerequisite of the Pax Romana, on the one hand, and the awareness that, since the possession of power tends to corrupt, absolutism is apt to become despotism, on the other. And the clearer he sees the danger to freedom the less is he inclined to rest his hopes on constitutional formulae.[5] For he is only too well aware that, the power of the Princeps being in fact supra leges, law as the supreme

[1] *Dial.* 38, 7; *Hist.* I, 1, 1; *Ann.* I, 9, 5; III, 28, 3.
[2] See above, p. 137.
[3] See, e.g., *Ann.* III, 60, 6; *Agric.* 2, 3.
[4] Si immensum imperii corpus stare ac librari sine rectore posset, dignus eram a quo res publica inciperet, *Hist.* I, 16, 1 (Galba). See also *Hist.* II, 38.
[5] Reitzenstein, *Gött. Nach.* 1914, p. 238 n. 4, and *Neue Wege zur Ant.* IV, 9, attaches undue importance to the phrase (*Hist.* I, 16, 1) loco libertatis erit quod eligi coepimus. Adoption did not render the Principate elective, cf. above, p. 156.

guardian of the citizen's rights has lost its effectiveness. Accordingly, to him libertas and servitus issue in the first place, not from the form of government as expressed in terms of constitutional law, but from the manner in which the de facto absolute power of the Princeps is employed, and particularly from the manner in which people behave *vis-à-vis* the Princeps. For bad though despotism is, the willingness to obey the despot's whims is still worse.

Tacitus thought the wretched state in which under the Principate the Romans repeatedly found themselves was of their own doing no less than of the emperor's. The Romans themselves "rushed into slavery" (ruere in servitium, *Ann.* I, 7, 1); they abandoned their dignity and vied with each other in contemptible adulation and abject servility.[1] It seems that the intense gloom of the *Annals*, in so far as it is not due to the nature of the subject matter, is born of the realization that the moral degeneration of the Romans[2] is just as perilous as the worst despotism. Indeed, what makes despotism so dreadful is the fact that it can stimulate and release the worst potentialities of men whose moral standards are gone.[3] And because he is aware that autocracy renders all constitutional safeguards futile and at the same time corrodes the conscience of rulers and subjects alike, Tacitus attaches greater importance to character than to the constitution.[4] What is most significant of his view is that he conceives servitus and libertas not only as either external constraint or the lack of it, but above all as inner proneness to servility or, in the case of libertas, as courage to be free. Since the constitution can no longer effectively protect the citizen, libertas and servitus become modes of personal conduct rather than expressions of political rights or rightlessness.[5]

[1] See, e.g., *Ann.* II, 32, 2 f.; III, 57; 65; XIV, 12, 1.

[2] Tam saeva et infesta virtutibus tempora, *Agric.* 1, 4; corruptissimum saeculum, *Hist.* II, 37, 2; Ceterum tempora illa adeo infecta et adulatione sordida fuere, ut non modo primores civitatis, quibus claritudo sua obsequiis protegenda erat, sed omnes consulares, magna pars eorum qui praetura functi multique etiam pedarii senatores certatim exsurgerent foedaque et nimia censerent, *Ann.* III, 65, 2.

[3] See *Ann.* IV, 28, 1 and *Hist.* IV, 42, 2.

[4] For a similar interpretation of Tacitus see Ed. Fraenkel, Tacitus, *N. J. f. Wiss.* VIII (1932), p. 225.

[5] (Helvidius) e *moribus* soceri nihil aeque ac libertatem hausit, *Hist.* IV, 5, 2. See also *Ann.* XVI, 11, 2–3.

A few instances may illustrate the last point. Describing the effect of Thrasea's courageous intervention in the Senate during a trial for maiestas, Tacitus says: "Libertas Thraseae servitium aliorum rupit" (*Ann.* XIV, 49, 1). Obviously, neither libertas nor servitium here have anything to do with the constitution: libertas denotes Thrasea's undaunted spirit, and servitium the servile submissiveness of the other senators.[1] Similarly, Seneca is said to have declared "nec sibi promptum in adulationes ingenium. Idque nulli magis gnarum quam Neroni, qui saepius libertatem Senecae quam servitium expertus esset" (*Ib.* XV, 61, 3). Here, as in the previous instance, libertas is outspokenness, whereas servitium is fawning subservience.[2] What libertas means can also be gathered from the nouns with which Tacitus contrasts it: "Sed Labeo incorrupta libertate et ob id fama celebratior, Capitonis *obsequium* dominantibus magis probabatur" (*Ib.* III, 75, 3). "Scilicet etiam illum, qui libertatem publicam nollet, tam *proiectae* servientium *patientiae* taedebat" (*Ib.* III, 65, 4). "Unde angusta et lubrica oratio sub principe, qui libertatem metuebat, *adulationem* oderat" (*Ib.* II, 87).[3] Needless to say, outspokenness and self-respect are not the only meanings that Tacitus attaches to libertas.[4] But in order to understand him, it is necessary to distinguish in his usage between what is traditional and what is peculiar to him. And it is undoubtedly the most characteristic and significant feature of his idea of freedom under the Principate that he conceived libertas less as a constitutional right than as the individual will and courage to be free.

---

[1] Speaking of the occasion on which Thrasea marked his disapproval by leaving the Senate, Tacitus says: "Sibi causam periculi fecit, ceteris libertatis initium non praebuit" (*Ann.* XIV, 12, 2). It is unlikely that Tacitus meant to say that Thrasea's gesture did not prove to be a turning-point in the political situation. Rather he meant that Thrasea's example did not inspire other senators to take courage to express their true sentiments in some such way as Thrasea did. And for this reason it seems unlikely that Tacitus's remark contains a censure of Thrasea, as Furneaux *ad loc.* thought.

[2] For libertas in the sense of frankness see also *Dial.* 10 *ad fin.*; 27, 4; *Hist.* I, 1, 1; 85, 3; IV, 44, 1; *Ann.* I, 74, 6.

[3] Cf. also *Dial.* 13, 6.

[4] In regard to Britons or Germans libertas often means independence, see, e.g., *Agric.* 30; *Ann.* II, 15, 4; 45, 4; XII, 34, 2; XIV, 31, 4. And in regard to Rome it sometimes means republicanism, and more often the freedom of the Senate.

Yet it would be wrong to infer from his view of *libertas* and *servitus* that Tacitus regarded defiant intransigence or outspoken opposition as a short road to freedom. The irreconcilables who admired forbidden ideals and sought glory in martyrdom seemed to him useless exhibitionists. He believed ostentatious assertion of freedom, even if it brought fame to an individual, did not serve the commonwealth.[1] And therefore while Helvidius Priscus won from him a partial respect, the unstinted praise and admiration of Tacitus is reserved for men of a different cast of mind: M'. Lepidus, L. Piso, and above all Agricola. What he praises in them throws much light on his own conception of freedom and may for this reason be here quoted at length:

Hunc ego Lepidum temporibus illis gravem et sapientem virum fuisse comperior: nam pleraque ab saevis adulationibus aliorum in melius flexit. Neque tamen temperamenti egebat, cum aequabili auctoritate et gratia apud Tiberium viguerit. Unde dubitare cogor, fato et sorte nascendi, ut cetera, ita principum inclinatio in hos, offensio in illos, an sit aliquid in nostris consiliis liceatque inter abruptam contumaciam et deforme obsequium pergere iter ambitione ac periculis vacuum (*Ann.* IV, 20, 4–5).

Per idem tempus L. Piso pontifex, rarum in tanta claritudine, fato obiit, nullius servilis sententiae sponte auctor, et quotiens necessitas ingrueret, sapienter moderans:...sed praecipua ex eo gloria quod praefectus urbi recens continuam potestatem et insolentia parendi graviorem mire temperavit (*Ann.* VI, 10, 3–5).

Domitiani vero natura praeceps in iram...moderatione tamen prudentiaque Agricolae leniebatur, quia non contumacia neque inani iactatione libertatis famam fatumque provocabat (*Agric.* 42, 4).

It is unwisdom to be refractory and provocative. But while he bows to the inevitable the true Roman will yet be mindful of his own dignity. Thus the scope of *libertas*, in so far as it is not personal freedom expressed in terms of civil law, shrinks beyond recognition. It appears that by *libertas* Tacitus understands, not the freedom of the citizen to determine his own destiny and the destiny of his country, nor the constitutional safeguards of the citizen's rights, but merely the courage to preserve one's self-respect in the face of despotism and amidst adulation. And, narrow as it is, this *libertas* is sustained by a consciousness, not of what one is entitled to, but of what one owes to one's own dignity. Unlike Seneca who was

See *Agric.* 42, 5.

concerned about human dignity above all else, Tacitus is concerned in the first place about dignity as it is realized in the Senate and the service of the commonwealth. But, whereas to Republican nobles libertas was the right to assert and enhance their dignitas, to Tacitus libertas is merely the courage to keep one's dignitas alive.

12. FREEDOM UNDER TUTELAGE

Libertas and the Principate are said to have been reconciled towards the end of the first century A.D.,[1] and, in so far as there was such a reconciliation, Pliny's *Panegyric*, delivered in the year 100, is certainly its outstanding literary monument. For the purpose of this study "the doubtful light of a panegyric" is unusually illuminating in that it reveals the mind of the panegyrist. The topics that Pliny chose to speak about, as well as the manner in which he presented them, give a very clear idea of what the reconciliation between freedom and the Principate really was. It is therefore necessary to review briefly what Pliny apparently considered to be praiseworthy in Trajan's Principate.[2]

The emperor was not imposed by the army (9, 2), nor did he seize power in the tumult of civil war (5, 1). He was adopted by the late emperor (7, 1 f.) and the Senate and People of Rome concurred (10, 2). He was chosen from the Senate (2, 4; 7, 6). The Senate regained its dignity, it no longer deliberates about trifles (54); there is amicable concord between the Princeps and the Senate (62, 3 f.); senators can speak their mind freely (76, 2); the terror of maiestas and of the informers does not exist (36, 2; 42, 1). Senators have easy access to the Princeps (48, 1 f.). The magistrates regained their prestige (58, 3 f.; 63, 1 f.; 64, 1 f.; 93, 1). Nobility is no longer fatal (69, 5). The road to an honourable career is open to all (70, 8). Property is safe (50, 1 f.). The emperor's freedmen do not domineer (88, 1 f.). The Princeps is a veritable vicar of God on earth (80, 4 f.). But he is a princeps, not a despot. "Scis, ut sunt diversa natura dominatio et principatus, ita non aliis esse principem gratiorem, quam

[1] Tac. *Agric.* 3, 1. Dessau, *I.L.S.* 274: Libertati ab imp. Nerva Ca(es)ar(e) Aug. anno ab urbe condita DCCC XXXXIIX. XIIII (k). Oc(t). restitu(tae) s.p.q.R. The year corresponds to A.D. 96.

[2] The chapters and paragraphs of the *Panegyric* (ed. Schuster, Teubner, 1933) are given in brackets.

qui dominum graventur" (45, 3). "Visuntur eadem e materia Caesaris statuae qua Brutorum, qua Camillorum. Nec discrepat causa: illi enim reges hostemque victorem moenibus depulerunt; hic regnum ipsum, quaeque alia captivitas gignit, arcet et summovet, sedemque obtinet principis, ne sit domino locus" (55, 6 f.).

It may be well to consider why the Princeps is not a despot. The answer seems to be: "Regimur quidem a te et subiecti tibi, sed quemadmodum legibus sumus" (24, 4). And similarly: "Quod ego nunc primum audio, nunc primum disco, non est princeps supra leges, sed leges supra principem, idemque Caesari consuli quod ceteris non licet" (65, 1). But was it true that the sovereignty of law was re-established? The truth was different. "In rostris...ipse te legibus subiecisti, legibus, Caesar, quas nemo principi scripsit" (65, 1). That is to say that the emperor's subjection to the law is voluntary, not compulsory, and it is of course in his power to change his mind. The power of the Princeps is unlimited; it is checked, not by law, but by his character, "infinitae potestatis domitor ac frenator animus" (55, 9). And if that was the case, it is quite obvious that all the blessings that Pliny counted, even if they were true, owed their existence, not to a constitutional reform, but solely to the fact that the emperor happened to be a kind and generous master. Hence the interminable praise of the Optimus Princeps, of his moderation (54, 5), clemency (35, 1), benignity (50, 7), justice, humanity, and patience (59, 3).

Pliny speaks of restoration of freedom (libertas reddita, 58, 3; libertas recuperata, 78, 3). But what kind of freedom is it? He inadvertently admits that it is a very precarious freedom. "Iubes esse liberos, erimus; iubes quae sentimus promere in medium, proferemus" (66, 4). And, "Tenebit ergo semper quid suaserit, scietque nos, quotiens libertatem quam dedit experiemur, sibi parere" (67, 2). How very different is this concept of freedom—if indeed it is freedom which is enjoyed at an emperor's bidding— from that which Livy had in mind when he wrote that libertas "suis stat viribus nec ex alieno arbitrio pendet"! This is freedom born of right, Pliny's is freedom on sufferance.

What is it that common people expect from the Princeps? "Magnum quidem est educandi incitamentum tollere liberos in spem alimentorum, in spem congiariorum; maius tamen, in spem

libertatis, in spem securitatis" (27, 1). What can a senator expect? The answer is given in one of Pliny's letters (III, 20, 12): "Sunt quidem cuncta sub unius arbitrio, qui pro utilitate communi solus omnium curas laboresque suscepit; quidam tamen salubri tempera-mento ad nos quoque velut rivi ex illo benignissimo fonte decurrunt." It was not a slip of the tongue nor an undue exaggeration when Pliny said in the *Panegyric* (7, 5): "An senatum populumque Romanum, exercitus, provincias, socios transmissurus uni, successorem e sinu uxoris accipias summaeque potestatis heredem tantum intra domum tuam quaeras?" For although in theory the Princeps was the delegate of the Senate and People of Rome, he was, for all practical purposes, their master.

It appears, therefore, that there was no real reconciliation between libertas and the Principate based on mutual concessions, but a con-ciliation of libertas to the Principate based on resignation and abdication. The power of the Princeps remained as absolute as it was before; the wilful abuse of that power disappeared, but no objective safeguards against the recurrence of such abuse were instituted. Libertas, however, if compared with what it had been before, underwent a complete change. The original idea, which Augustus tried to preserve to some extent, was that the Romans were ultimately their own masters. In the last resort their freedom depended on the laws which they enacted or the customs which they evolved. Now they were subjects whose welfare depended on the care of an absolute autocrat who ruled them by direct command. In the last resort their freedom depended on whether their ruler was kind and enlightened. All that remained of the idea of the res publica was government for the people.

It was not only the political institutions that changed. Under a régime of tutelage, even if enlightened, libertas lost much that was most precious in it: the independence and self-reliance of the individual, or, as Livy would have said, suis stare viribus nec ex alieno arbitrio pendere. All care and all responsibility now gradually devolved on the Princeps, with the inevitable result that his super-vision became so close and his intervention so frequent that even in municipal affairs little was left to the initiative and responsibility of the citizens; imperial legati and procuratores, acting under precise orders and in constant consultation with the imperial headquarters,

had the last word in everything.[1] The people may have enjoyed a considerable amount of freedom, but freedom without responsibility and self-reliance is, at best, very much like the freedom children enjoy under the parental care of a benign father. Indeed, the emperor becomes Pater, but imperial paternalism and political liberty go ill together. What had been libertas populi Romani Quiritium turned out to be libertas Augusti,[2] the freedom that the emperor accords to his people or, in the phrase of Marcus Aurelius, ἐλευθερία τῶν ἀρχομένων.[3] Libertas now means respect for the person and property of the citizen, security and welfare; but under tutelage it hardly means independence, and under absolutism it is not a political right at all.

Having said all this, it would be wrong to belittle the achievement of the Roman enlightened despotism. If one looks beyond Rome to the Empire as a whole, there is truth in what Lord Acton said of the emperors: "Their power was arbitrary even when it was most wisely employed, and yet the Roman Empire rendered greater services to the cause of liberty than the Roman Republic."[4] During the second century, the Romans themselves were not oppressed, and from an administrative point of view gained much: they were ably and humanely governed. But from the point of view of libertas there is one fundamental thing to be observed: good government is no substitute for limited government. Freedom is of necessity precarious under absolutism, because an unlimited power can cause just as much harm as good. The great thing about the system of sovereignty of law and limitation of all powers was that under it a bad government could do least harm:

Ubi regium imperium, quod initio conservandae libertatis atque augendae rei publicae fuerat, in superbiam dominationemque se convortit,

---

[1] Pliny's correspondence with Trajan sheds much light on this state of affairs.

[2] Mattingly and Sydenham, op. cit. I, p. 228 and II, p. 68.

[3] Ad Semet Ipsum, I, 14, 2.

[4] Freedom in Antiquity, The History of Freedom, p. 15. See also Aelius Aristides, Εἰς Ῥώμην (ed. Keil), 31 f.; 36: μόνοι γὰρ τῶν πώποτε ἐλευθέρων ἄρχετε; 51:...ὅτι οὔπω πρὸ ὑμῶν ἦν τὸ ἄρχειν εἰδέναι; 59 ff. With due allowance for the art of the panegyrist, Aristides' remarks are to some extent indicative of the attitude of an educated Greek to the Pax Romana.

inmutato more annua imperia binosque imperatores sibi fecere: eo modo minume posse putabant per licentiam insolescere animum humanum.[1]

It was different under absolutism: according as the autocrat was benevolent or malevolent, the same power might do most good or infinite harm.

Libertas which was reconciled with the Principate was personal freedom without constitutional safeguards, or, to be precise, with illusory constitutional safeguards. It would take more than Pliny's rhetoric to conceal the fact that his *Panegyric* marked the surrender of constitutional freedom. The defeat of the old idea of freedom was inevitable: autocracy seemed an absolute necessity, but autocracy and constitutional freedom are incompatible.

What this study has sought to trace is the nature and effectiveness of an idea in the sphere of Roman politics. Owing to the diversity of its elements and the partial vagueness of its meaning, libertas easily assumed new shapes, and while at times it inspired political movements, at others it was used for political ends, until at length it came to express political hopes rather than claims. The Romans of the Republic conceived libertas as freedom of the citizen in a free State, in which law was the guarantee of indefeasible personal rights. Those personal rights sought expression in political rights, and safeguards in political institutions. But, in the aristocratic State which the Republic never truly ceased to be, egalitarianism was not at home: the strong impulse towards the assertion of dignitas which nerved the Roman aristocracy of birth and office was incompatible with an advance towards full democracy. The Late Republic developed towards the conflicts of dignitas rather than the fortification of libertas, until the conflicts issued in the Principate. Under the Principate the ruling law which had been the basis of libertas was in fact replaced by the will of the Princeps. Within the Roman community itself, the possession of libertas became a gift rather than a right and, ceasing to be a right, lost what had been its essential quality.

[1] Sallust, *Cat.* 6, 7.

BIBLIOGRAPHY

I. TEXTS AND COMMENTARIES

The following texts and commentaries have been used for the citation of fragments or documents or for the interpretation of particular points.

BRUNS, C. G. *Fontes Iuris Romani Antiqui, septimum edidit O. Gradenwitz.* Tübingen, 1909.

DESSAU, H. *Inscriptiones Latinae Selectae.* Berlin, 1892–1916.

FURNEAUX, H. *The Annals of Tacitus.* Oxford, vol. I, 1896; vol. II, 1891; 2nd ed. revised by H. F. Pelham and C. D. Fisher, 1907.

GAGÉ, J. *Res Gestae Divi Augusti, ex monumentis Ancyrano et Antiocheno Latinis et Ancyrano et Apolloniensi Graecis. Texte établi et commenté.* Paris, 1935.

HARDY, E. G. *The Monumentum Ancyranum.* Oxford, 1923.

MOMMSEN, TH. *Res Gestae Divi Augusti ex monumentis Ancyrano et Apolloniensi,* 2nd ed. Berlin, 1883.

GUDEMAN, A. *P. Cornelii Taciti Dialogus de Oratoribus mit Prolegomena ...und kritischem Kommentar,* 2nd ed. Leipzig–Berlin, 1914.

PETERSON, W. *Cornelii Taciti Dialogus de Oratoribus.* Oxford, 1893.

MALCOVATI, H. *Oratorum Romanorum Fragmenta,* vols. I–III. Turin, 1930.

MAURENBRECHER, B. *C. Sallusti Crispi Historiarum Reliquiae.* Leipzig, Fasc. I. Prolegomena, 1891; Fasc. II. Fragmenta, 1893.

TYRRELL, R. Y. & PURSER, L. C. *The Correspondence of M. Tullius Cicero.* Dublin–London, vol. I (3rd ed.), 1904; II (2nd ed.), 1906; III (2nd ed.), 1914; IV (2nd ed.), 1918; V (2nd ed.), 1915; VI, 1899; VII (indices), 1901.

II. BOOKS AND ARTICLES REFERRED TO

ACTON, J. E. E., 1st Baron. *The History of Freedom and other Essays.* London, 1907.

ADCOCK, F. E. In *C.A.H.* vol. IX, chap. XV–XVII; vol. X, chap. XVIII.

ARNIM, H. von, *Leben und Werke des Dio von Prusa.* Berlin, 1898.

BARWICK, K. "Zur Erklärung und Komposition des Rednerdialogs des Tacitus", in *Festschrift Walther Judeich,* pp. 90 ff. Weimar, 1929.

BÉRANGER, J. "Pour une définition du principat: Auguste dans Aulu-Gelle, XV, 7, 3." *Rev. Ét. Lat.* XXI–XXII (1943–4), pp. 144–54.

BOISSIER, G. *L'Opposition sous les Césars,* 5th ed. Paris, 1905.

BOISSIER, G. *Tacitus and other Roman Studies,* Eng. trans. London, 1906.

BOTSFORD, G. W. *The Roman Assemblies from their Origin to the end of the Republic.* New York, 1909.

BRECHT, C. *s.v.* Occentatio in PW, XVII, 1752 ff.

BUCKLAND, W. W. *The Roman Law of Slavery.* Cambridge, 1908.

—— *A Textbook of Roman Law.* Cambridge, 1921.

Cambridge Ancient History (C.A.H.) vols. VII–XI.

CAUER, F. *Ciceros politisches Denken.* Berlin, 1903.

CHARLESWORTH, M. P. In *C.A.H.* vol. X, chap. XIX–XX; vol. XI, chap. I.

—— *Five Men.* Harvard Univ. Press, 1936.

—— "The Virtues of a Roman Emperor: Propaganda and the Creation of Belief", the British Academy Raleigh lecture. Oxford, 1937.

—— "Pietas and Victoria: the Emperor and the Citizen." *J.R.S.* XXXIII (1943), pp. 1 ff.

DAHLMANN, H. "Clementia Caesaris", *Neue Jahrb. für Wiss. und Jugendbildung,* X (1934), pp. 17–26.

DAUBE, D. "Two Early Patterns of Manumission", *J.R.S.* XXXVI (1946), pp. 57 ff.

DESSAU, H. *Geschichte der römischen Kaiserzeit,* vol. I. Berlin, 1924.

DOMASZEWSKI, A. von, "Die philosophische Grundlage des Augusteischen Principats", in *Bilder und Studien aus drei Jahrtausenden, Gothein-Festgabe,* pp. 63–71. Leipzig, 1923.

DUDLEY, D. R. *A History of Cynicism from Diogenes to the 6th century* A.D. London, 1937.

—— "Blossius of Cumae", *J.R.S.* XXXI (1941), pp. 95 ff.

EHRENBERG, V. "Monumentum Antiochenum", *Klio,* XIX (1925), pp. 189 ff.

ENSSLIN, W. "Die Demokratie und Rom", *Phil.* LXXXII (1927), pp. 313 ff.

FERRERO, G. *The Greatness and Decline of Rome,* trans. by H. J. Chaytor, vol. IV. London, 1908.

FRAENKEL, ED. "Tacitus", *Neue Jahrb. für Wiss. und Jugendbildung,* VIII (1932), pp. 218–33.

—— in *Gnomon,* I (1925), pp. 187 ff.

FRANK, T. In *C.A.H.* vol. VII, chap. XXV; vol. VIII, chap. XII.

—— "Naevius and Free Speech", *Amer. Journ. Phil.* XLVIII (1927), pp. 105 ff.

FRITZ, K. von, "Aufbau und Absicht des Dialogus de oratoribus", *Rhein. Mus.* N.F. 81 (1932), pp. 275–300.

FUCHS, H. *Augustin und der antike Friedensgedanke, Neue Philologische Untersuchungen,* 3. Heft. Berlin, 1926.

GELZER, M. *Die Nobilität der römischen Republik.* Leipzig–Berlin, 1912.

—— "Die römische Gesellschaft zur Zeit Ciceros", *Neue Jahrb. f. klass. Alt.* XLV (1920), pp. 1 ff.

GOODENOUGH, E. R. "The Political Philosophy of Hellenistic King-ship", *Yale Class. Stud.* I (1928), pp. 55 ff.

—— *The Politics of Philo Judaeus, Practice and Theory.* Yale Univ. Press, 1938.

GRANT, M. *From* Imperium *to* Auctoritas, *A Historical Study of Aes Coinage in the Roman Empire,* 49 B.C.–A.D. 14. Cambridge, 1946.

GRUEBER, H. A. *Coins of the Roman Republic in the British Museum,* 3 vols. London, 1910.

HAMMOND, M. *The Augustan Principate in Theory and Practice during the Julio–Claudian Period.* Harvard Univ. Press, 1933.

HANELL, K. "Bemerkungen zu der politischen Terminologie des Sallustius", *Eranos,* XLIII (1945), pp. 263–76.

HARDY, E. G. *Some Problems in Roman History.* Oxford, 1924.

HEINZE, R. "Ciceros politische Anfänge", *Abh. Sächs. Gesell. d. Wiss.* XXVII (1909), pp. 947 ff.

—— *Von den Ursachen der Grösse Roms.* Leipzig, 1921.

—— "Auctoritas", *Hermes,* LX (1925), pp. 348–66.

HENDERSON, B. W. *The Life and Principate of the Emperor Nero.* London, 1905.

HIRZEL, R. *Themis, Dike und Verwandtes: ein Beitrag zur Geschichte der Rechtsidee bei den Griechen.* Leipzig, 1907.

HOW, H. W. "Cicero's Ideal in his De Republica", *J.R.S.* XX (1930), pp. 24 ff.

IHERING, R. von, *Geist des römischen Rechts auf den verschiedenen Stufen seiner Entwicklung,* Teil. II, 1, 3rd ed. Leipzig, 1874.

JONES, A. H. M. "Civitates Liberae et Immunes in the East", *Anatolian Studies presented to W. H. Buckler,* pp. 103 ff. Manchester Univ. Press, 1939.

KAERST, J. *Studien zur Entwickelung und theoretischen Begründung der Monarchie im Altertum.* Munich–Leipzig, 1898.

—— "Scipio Aemilianus, die Stoa und der Prinzipat", *Neue Jahrb. für Wiss. und Jugendbildung,* V (1929), pp. 653–75.

KAPPELMACHER, A. "Zur Abfassungszeit von Tacitus' Dialogus de oratoribus", *Wien. Stud.* L (1932), pp. 121–9.

KEYES, C. W. "Original Elements in Cicero's Ideal Constitution", *Amer. Journ. Phil.* XLII (1921), pp. 309–23.

KLOESEL, H. *Libertas.* Breslau Dissertation, 1935.

KÖSTERMANN, E. "Statio Principis", *Phil.* LXXXVII (1932), pp. 358–68 and 430–44.

KOLBE, W. "Von der Republik zur Monarchie", in Aus Roms Zeitwende, *Das Erbe der Alten,* Heft 20 (1931), pp. 39–65.

KROLL, W. *Die Kultur der ciceronischen Zeit.* Leipzig, 1933.

LAST, H. In *C.A.H.* vol. IX, chap. I–IV, VI, VII; vol. X, chap. XIV; vol. XI, chap. X–XI.

LAST, H. "Imperium Maius: a Note." *J.R.S.* XXXVII (1947), pp. 157 ff.

LEO, FR. *Gött Gel. Anzeigen*, 1898, pp. 167–188.

McFAYDEN, D. "The Rise of the Princeps' Jurisdiction within the City of Rome", *Washington University Studies, Humanistic Series*, vol. X (1923), no. 2, pp. 181 ff.

MARSH, F. B. *The Founding of the Roman Empire*, 2nd ed. Oxford, 1927.

MATTINGLY, H. *Coins of the Roman Empire in the British Museum*, vol. I. London, 1923.

MATTINGLY, H. and SYDENHAM, E. A. *The Roman Imperial Coinage*. London, vol. I, 1923; vol. II, 1926.

MEYER, ED. *Caesars Monarchie und das Principat des Pompejus*, 3rd ed. Stuttgart–Berlin, 1922.

—— "Der Ursprung des Tribunats und die Gemeinde der vier Tribus", *Hermes*, XXX (1895), pp. 1 ff. = *Kl. Schr.* I², pp. 335 ff.

—— "Kaiser Augustus", *Kl. Schr.* I², pp. 425 ff.

MOMIGLIANO, A. In *J.R.S.* XXXI (1941), pp. 151 ff., and XXXII (1942), pp. 120 ff.

MOMMSEN, TH. "Bürgerlicher und peregrinischer Freiheitsschutz", *Juristische Abhandlungen, Festgabe fuer Georg Beseler*, pp. 255–72. Berlin, 1885.

—— *De Collegiis et Sodaliciis Romanorum*. Kiel, 1843.

—— *Römisches Staatsrecht*, vol. I (3rd ed.), 1887; vol. II (3rd ed.), 1887; vol. III, 1, 1887; vol. III, 2, 1888. Leipzig.

MÜNZER, F. *Römische Adelsparteien und Adelsfamilien*. Stuttgart, 1920.

PAULY-WISSOWA-KROLL. Real-Encyclopaedie der classischen Altertumswissenschaft (PW.).

PELHAM, H. F. "The Early Roman Emperors (Caesar–Nero)", *Essays*, collected and edited by F. Haverfield, pp. 21 ff. Oxford, 1911.

PLAUMANN, G. "Das sogenannte senatus consultum ultimum, die Quasidiktatur der späteren römischen Republik", *Klio*, XIII (1913), pp. 321–86.

PÖSCHL, V. Römischer Staat und griechisches Staatsdenken bei Cicero, Untersuchungen zu Ciceros Schrift de republica, *Neue Deutsche Forschungen, Band* 5 (104). Berlin, 1934.

POHLENZ, M. "Antikes Führertum, Cicero De Officiis und das Lebensideal des Panaitios", *Neue Wege zur Antike, zweite Reihe, Heft* 3, 1934.

—— "Cicero De Re Publica als Kunstwerk", in *Festschrift Richard Reitzenstein*, pp. 70–105. Leipzig–Berlin, 1931.

PREMERSTEIN, A. von, Vom Werden und Wesen des Prinzipats, *Abh. der bayer. Akad. phil.-hist. Abt. N.F.* 15, 1937.

REITZENSTEIN, R. "Die Idee des Prinzipats bei Cicero und Augustus", *Gött. Nach.* 1917, pp. 399 ff., 436 ff.

REITZENSTEIN, R. "Bemerkungen zu den kleinen Schriften des Tacitus", *Gött. Nach.* 1914, pp. 173–276.

—— "Tacitus und sein Werk", *Neue Wege zur Antike*, IV (1929).

REMY, E. "Dignitas cum otio", *Musée Belge*, XXXII (1928), pp. 113 ff.

RICE HOLMES, T. *The Roman Republic and the Founder of the Empire.* Oxford, 1923.

—— *The Architect of the Roman Empire.* Oxford, vol. I, 1928; vol. II, 1931.

ROBINSON, L. *Freedom of Speech in the Roman Republic*, Johns Hopkins University Dissertation. Baltimore, 1940.

ROSTOVTZEFF, M. *The Social and Economic History of the Roman Empire.* Oxford, 1928.

SCHÖNBAUER, E. "Untersuchungen zum römischen Staats- und Wirtschaftsrecht, Wesen und Ursprung des Prinzipats", *Z. d. Sav.-Stift. Rom. Abt.* XLVII (1927), pp. 264–318.

—— "Studien zum Personalitätsprinzip im antiken Rechte", *Z. d. Sav.-Stift. Rom. Abt.* XLIX (1929), pp. 345–403.

SCHULZ, F. *Prinzipien des römischen Rechts.* Munich, 1924.

—— "Bracton on Kingship", *Eng. Hist. Rev.* LX (1945), pp. 136 ff.

SCHUR, W. "Homo novus", *Bonner Jahrbücher*, CXXXIV (1929), pp. 54–66.

SHERWIN-WHITE, A. N. *The Roman Citizenship.* Oxford, 1939.

SPREY, K. *De M. Tullii Ciceronis Politica Doctrina*, Amsterdam Dissertation. Zutphen, 1928.

STARK, R. *Res Publica.* Göttingen Dissertation, 1937.

STRASBURGER, H. *Concordia Ordinum, eine Untersuchung zur Politik Ciceros.* Frankfurt Dissertation, 1931.

—— *s.v.* Nobiles in PW, XVII, 785 ff.

—— *s.v.* Novus homo in PW, XVII, 1223 ff.

—— *s.v.* Optimates in PW, XVIII, 773 ff.

SYME, R. *The Roman Revolution.* Oxford, 1939.

TAEGER, F. *Untersuchungen zur römischen Geschichte und Quellenkunde: Tiberius Gracchus.* Stuttgart, 1928.

TOYNBEE, J. M. C. "Dictators and Philosophers in the First Century A.D.", *Greece and Rome*, XIII (1944), pp. 43 ff.

VANČURA, J. *s.v.* Leges agrariae in PW, XII, 1150 ff.

VOGT, J. *Homo novus. Ein Typus der römischen Republik.* Stuttgart, 1926.

WARDE FOWLER, W. "On a passage in the Rhetorica ad Herennium" *Journ. Phil.* X (1882), pp. 197 ff.

WEBER, W. *Princeps, Studien zur Geschichte des Prinzipats*, vol. I Stuttgart-Berlin, 1936.

WEGEHAUPT, H. *Die Bedeutung und Anwendung von dignitas in den Schriften der republikanischen Zeit.* Breslau Dissertation, 1932.

WISTRAND, E. "Gratus, grates, gratia, gratiosus." *Eranos*, XXXIX (1941), pp. 17–26.

INDEX

Romans are entered under the most familiar part of their name, and, where necessary for purposes of identification, dates of their offices have been added. Laws are entered under the heading Lex, leges.

Absolutism, theory of its legitimacy, 133; mitigated by the virtues of the Princeps, 154; incompatible with libertas, 169 f.

Actio laesae maiestatis, 159

Actium, battle of, 97, 98, 100, 105, 106

Adoptio, 154–8

Aelius Aristides, 161 f.

Aequae leges, notion explained, 10 f.; with regard to homines novi, 55

Aequitas, 10; compared with *isotes*, 13; in the propaganda of the Gracchi, 46

Aequum ius, identified with libertas, 11 f.; compared with *isonomia*, 13 f.; and homines novi, 55

Agricola, Cn. Iulius, 149, 166

Alieni iuris, 1

Allies (socii), their aims in the Social War, 66 f.; enrolment in Roman tribes, 69 f.

Appellatio, 26–7

Appius Claudius, xvir, 10

Aristotle, 14, 85

Army, influence on politics, 73 f.

Antistius Sosianus, tried for maiestas, 139

Antonius, M. (cos. 44 B.C.), 104, 105, 106

Antonius, M., orator, 15; defence of Norbanus, 49

Antonius, M., Creticus, 63

Assemblies of the People, functions and competence, 18 f., 20; a subversive factor in the Late Republic, 71 f.; popular elections abolished, 119

Auctoritas, nature of, 34 f., 112–13; and libertas, 35, 112; and dignitas, 36; of Augustus, 112–19; of the Senate, 113, 119; of Republican principes, 114

Augustus, *Res Gestae*, 100–4, 106; liberation of the State, 100 ff.; constitutional settlement, 107 ff.; potestas, 109–12; auctoritas, 112–19; the title Augustus, 115; cura legum et morum, 116; character of the Augustan Principate, 129; clementia, 152

Axia, 13, 14

Bibulus, M. Calpurnius, 76

Blossius of Cumae, 45 n.

Brutus, M. Iunius, attitude to autocracy, 90 f.; view of auctoritas, 112–13; memory worshipped, 126–9, 140

Caesar, C. Iulius, 37; and the Lex Domitia de Sacerdotiis, 49; attitude to the S.C. Ultimum, 56 f., 60; dictatorship, 56 n., 87–91: "regnum", 64; First Triumvirate, 76 f.; struggle for dignitas, 77–8; honoured as liberator, 104 n.; clementia, 151

Caligula, 126, 135, 138, 155

Capitis Deminutio Media, 3 n., 4

Capito Cossutianus, Thrasea's prosecutor, 140

Carbo, C. Papirius (cos. 120 B.C.), defence of Opimius, 58 f.

Cassius, C., Longinus (cos. 171 B.C.), 33

Cassius, C., Longinus, Caesar's murderer, attitude to Caesar, 90; memory worshipped, 126–9, 140

Cassius, L., Longinus (tr. pl. 137 B.C.), 40 n.

Cassius, L., Longinus (tr. pl. 104 B.C.), 49

Cato, C., 76 n.

Cato, M., Porcius, Maior, 15, 33 n., 38, 62

Cato, M., Porcius, Uticensis, opposed extraordinary powers, 63 f.; and the First Triumvirate, 76; laudations of, 89, 161; memory worshipped, 126–9, 140, 142

Catulus, Q. Lutatius, opposed Pompey's commands, 63

Censors, censorship, 27 f.

Cicero, rule of law, 7; view of egalitarianism, 12; view of sanctity of the home, 29; considered freedom and citizenship indefeasible rights, 30; *Pro Sestio*, 40 f., 93 f.; *De Re Publica*, 42 f., 79–83, 86 f., 152 f.; *De Legibus*,

D1559666